Internet Marketing Intelligence

Research Tools, Techniques, and Resources

McGraw-Hill/Irwin Series in Marketing

Arens
Contemporary Advertising
Eighth Edition

Arnould, Price & Zinkhan
Consumers
First Edition

Bearden, Ingram & LaForge
Marketing: Principles & Perspectives
Third Edition

Belch & Belch
Advertising & Promotion: An Integrated Marketing Communications Approach
Fifth Edition

Bingham & Gomes
Business Marketing Management
Second Edition

Boyd, Walker, Mullins & Larréché
Marketing Management: A Strategic Decision-Making Approach
Fourth Edition

Cateora & Graham
International Marketing
Eleventh Edition

Cole & Mishler
Consumer and Business Credit Management
Eleventh Edition

Cravens & Piercy
Strategic Marketing
Seventh Edition

Cravens, Lamb & Crittenden
Strategic Marketing Management Cases
Seventh Edition

Crawford & Di Benedetto
New Products Management
Seventh Edition

Dolan
Marketing Management: Text and Cases
First Edition

Duncan
IMC: Using Advertising and Promotion to Build Brands
First Edition

Dwyer & Tanner
Business Marketing
Second Edition

Eisenmann
Internet Business Models: Text and Cases
First Edition

Etzel, Walker & Stanton
Marketing
Twelfth Edition

Futrell
ABC's of Relationship Selling
Seventh Edition

Futrell
Fundamentals of Selling
Seventh Edition

Hair, Bush & Ortinau
Marketing Research
Second Edition

Hawkins, Best & Coney
Consumer Behavior
Eighth Edition

Johansson
Global Marketing
Third Edition

Johnston & Marshall
Churchill/Ford/Walker's Sales Force Management
Seventh Edition

Kerin, Berkowitz, Hartley & Rudelius
Marketing
Seventh Edition

Lehmann & Winer
Analysis for Marketing Planning
Fifth Edition

Lehmann & Winer
Product Management
Third Edition

Levy & Weitz
Retailing Management
Fourth Edition

Mason & Perreault
The Marketing Game!
Third Edition

McDonald
Direct Marketing: An Integrated Approach
First Edition

Mohammed, Fisher, Jaworski & Cahill
Internet Marketing: Building Advantage in a Networked Economy
First Edition

Monroe
Pricing
Third Edition

Pelton, Strutton & Lumpkin
Marketing Channels: A Relationship Management Approach
Second Edition

Perreault & McCarthy
Basic Marketing: A Global Managerial Approach
Fourteenth Edition

Perreault & McCarthy
Essentials of Marketing: A Global Managerial Approach
Eighth Edition

Peter & Donnelly
A Preface to Marketing Management
Ninth Edition

Peter & Donnelly
Marketing Management: Knowledge and Skills
Sixth Edition

Peter & Olson
Consumer Behavior
Sixth Edition

Rayport & Jaworski
Introduction to e-Commerce
First Edition

Rayport & Jaworski
e-Commerce
First Edition

Rayport & Jaworski
Cases in e-Commerce
First Edition

Richardson
Internet Marketing
First Edition

Roberts
Internet Marketing: Integrating Online and Offline Strategies
First Edition

Spiro, Stanton, Rich
Management of a Sales Force
Eleventh Edition

Stock & Lambert
Strategic Logistics Management
Fourth Edition

Ulrich & Eppinger
Product Design and Development
Second Edition

Walker, Boyd, Mullins & Larréché
Marketing Strategy: A Decision-Focused Approach
Fourth Edition

Weitz, Castleberry & Tanner
Selling: Building Partnerships
Fourth Edition

Zeithaml & Bitner
Services Marketing
Third Edition

Internet Marketing Intelligence

Research Tools, Techniques, and Resources

Edward Forrest

University of Alaska—Anchorage

Boston   Burr Ridge, IL   Dubuque, IA   Madison, WI   New York   San Francisco   St. Louis
Bangkok   Bogotá   Caracas   Kuala Lumpur   Lisbon   London   Madrid   Mexico City
Milan   Montreal   New Delhi   Santiago   Seoul   Singapore   Sydney   Taipei   Toronto

McGraw-Hill Higher Education
A Division of The McGraw-Hill Companies

INTERNET MARKETING INTELLIGENCE: RESEARCH TOOLS, TECHNIQUES, AND RESOURCES
Published by McGraw-Hill/Irwin, a business unit of The McGraw-Hill Companies, Inc., 1221 Avenue of the Americas, New York, NY, 10020. Copyright © 2003 by The McGraw-Hill Companies, Inc. All rights reserved.
No part of this publication may be reproduced or distributed in any form or by any means, or stored in a database or retrieval system, without the prior written consent of The McGraw-Hill Companies, Inc., including, but not limited to, in any network or other electronic storage or transmission, or broadcast for distance learning. Some ancillaries, including electronic and print components, may not be available to customers outside the United States.

This book is printed on acid-free paper.

1 2 3 4 5 6 7 8 9 0 QPD/QPD 0 9 8 7 6 5 4 3 2

ISBN 0-07-282111-6

Publisher: *John E. Biernat*
Executive editor: *Linda Schreiber*
Editorial coordinator: *Sarah Crago*
Marketing manager: *Kim Kanakes*
Media producer: *Craig Atkins*
Project manager: *Laura Griffin*
Senior production supervisor: *Michael R. McCormick*
Designer: *Adam Rooke*
Supplement producer: *Matthew Perry*
Senior digital content specialist: *Brian Nacik*
Cover design: *Srdjan Savanovic*
Typeface: *10/12 Times New Roman*
Compositor: *GAC Indianapolis*
Printer: *Quebecor World Dubuque Inc.*

Library of Congress Cataloging-in-Publication Data
Forrest, Edward.
    Internet marketing intelligence : research tools, techniques, and resources / Edward Forrest.
        p. cm.—(McGraw-Hill/Irwin series in marketing)
    Includes bibliographical references and index.
    ISBN 0-07-282111-6 (alk. paper)
    1. Marketing research—Data processing. 2. Marketing research—Computer network
    resources. 3. Internet. I. Title. II. Series.
    HF5415.2 .F67 2003
    658.8'3'02854678--dc21

                                                                    2002026484

www.mhhe.com

This book is dedicated to:
Pooky, LoLo, Brown-Eyes, Bad-Boy, Big-Sis,
Stan, Magas, and Lug-Nuts.

About the Author

Edward Forrest

University of Alaska—Anchorage

Edward Forrest is professor and associate dean of the College of Business and Public Policy at the University of Alaska (Anchorage), where he joined the faculty in 2000. He received his PhD degree from the University of Wisconsin in 1981, and from 1977 to 1987 he directed the advertising curriculum in the College of Communication at Florida State University. During his directorship Florida State won nine national advertising competitions sponsored by such companies as Philip Morris, Datsun, and MacCaffrey-McCall.

In 1989, he developed and directed one of the country's first graduate degree curriculums in interactive communication at Florida State. He moved to Griffith University (Queensland, Australia) in 1996, where he introduced that country's first courses in interactive marketing and Internet marketing research. He was also appointed head of the School of Marketing and made a Fellow of the Australian Marketing Institute.

Edward Forrest has authored numerous papers and articles on interactive communication and Internet marketing that have appeared in *The Journal of Advertising Research, Journal of Broadcasting and Electronic Media, Human Communication Research, Cornell Quarterly, Asia–Australia Marketing Journal,* and *The New York Times—CyberTimes.* In addition, he has authored and edited a CD-ROM entitled *Marketing: Your Desktop Companion*, as well as a number of books including *Interactive Marketing: The Future Present, Cybermarketing: Your Interactive Consultant, Internet Marketing Research: Resources and Techniques,* and *The New York Times: Guide to Marketing.*

Preface

At an old campus of mine, inscribed above the doorway to the library were the words: "The half of knowledge is knowing where to find knowledge." Indeed, with the advent of the Internet, this adage never rang truer. The Internet is now the largest repository of human knowledge. Therefore, how and where to find the information is an essential skill for every information worker and, in particular, the market researcher.

The market researcher is charged with the responsibility of providing timely and accurate information for decision making. Accordingly, the market researcher must devise a comprehensive research program that will provide a continuous flow of relevant data for every variable that can or does impact sales in the marketplace. It was within the twentieth century that the vocation of marketing research was established. To date, it has evolved into a profession that uses the most sophisticated data-gathering and analysis tools available. The twenty-first century will challenge market researchers to continue to upgrade their research skills and information-processing expertise. A thorough understanding of the structure and substance of the Internet will be a certain prerequisite for the complete market researcher. This book illustrates when, where, and how the Internet can assist the market researcher in monitoring the marketplace.

With respect to research tasks, the book documents how the Internet can be used for:

- Personal, environmental, consumer, and competitive intelligence.

- Survey, focus group, product, and copy testing.

With respect to research tools, this book overviews the nature and application of:

- E-mail, newsgroups, and discussion lists.

- Search and metasearch engines, metadexes, searchbots, knowbots, and agents.

- Cookies, server log files, and analyzers.

Also addressed are the critical concerns of every market researcher regarding:

- Data source and website reliability and validity.

- The issues and legalities of user privacy, consumer protection, data security, intellectual property, fair use, trademarking, and copyright.

Today, the Internet exists as an important supplement to the marketer's traditional array of information resources and research tools. Yet the Internet is only in its infancy. In 2004 it will be only 15 years since Tim Berners-Lee introduced his Wide Web to the world, only 10 years since Mark Andressen translated Mosaic to Netscape. In the interim, tens of millions of people around the world have come to use the Internet as their primary information and communication vehicle.

With a new user logging on every two seconds, the predominance of the Internet is inevitable. For the marketer, knowledge of the Internet's resources and research techniques will be indispensable.

Acknowledgments

Internet Marketing Intelligence: Resources and Techniques is an amalgamation of the contributions of my colleagues at the University of Alaska (Anchorage), Griffith University (Queensland, Australia), McGraw-Hill (Australia), and McGraw-Hill/Irwin (United States). Without their acumen and dedication, this book would not have been as comprehensive or as complete.

Accordingly, for their contributions as well as their editorial assistance in the drafting and crafting of the chapters for this book, I would like to thank Terrence Tam and Marc Peterson for their contributions throughout the book and specifically Chapter 7, Internet Surveys, Chapter 8, An Introduction to Internet Newsgroups, and Chapter 9, Applied Research Methods for Newsgroups and Discussion Groups; Mark Brown, for his original contributions to Chapter 3, Personal Intelligence, and Chapter 10, Online Focus Groups; Jay Weerawardena, for his contributions to Chapter 1, Marketing Research: Established Traditions and Emerging Trends, and Chapter 12, Ethical Concerns and Legalities; Tino Fenech, for his original development of and contributions to Chapter 2, Internet Search and Research; Sharon Tan and Jeffery Lim, for their original research contributions to Chapter 4, Environmental Intelligence, and Chapter 5, Consumer Intelligence; and Victoria Hodgson, for her original contribution to Chapter 6, Competitive Intelligence, and Chapter 11, Websites, Sources, and Data—Reliability and Validity. Special thanks also go to Chris Gunn for his expert help in the construction of Chapter 9, Applied Research Methods for Newsgroups and Discussion Groups.

For their thoughtful comments and suggestions during the development process I would like to thank the following reviewers: Jamie Murphy (University of Western Australia); Jeancy Yip, Jeffrey Lim, and Timothy Bock (University of Sydney); Petra Bouvain (University of Canberra); Mike Shaw (Monash University); and Michael Gardiner (University of Southern Queensland).

No book can be successfully developed and published without supportive and motivating executive editors. Herein, I wish to acknowledge the efforts of two of the best in the business: Jane Clayton of McGraw-Hill (Australia) and Linda Schrieber of McGraw-Hill/Irwin (United States). I would be remiss not to thank Leanne Peters, my production editor at McGraw-Hill (Australia), who edited the manuscript for clarity, accuracy, and readability, and also double-checked every website to see if it was up and running. Thank you, Leanne. Your efforts significantly enhanced the value of this book. In addition, I would like to thank Sarah Crago, Anna Chan, Laura Griffin, Rebecca Nordbrock, and Kim Kanakes of McGraw-Hill Higher Education for their efforts in support of this book.

Table of Contents

Preface   viii

Chapter 1

Marketing Research: Established Traditions and Emerging Trends   1

Marketing Research Defined   2
Types of Marketing Research   3
The Marketing Research Process   3
   1. *Define the Research Question or Problem*   3
   2. *Create the Research Design or Master Plan*   4
   3. *Select the Research Method*   4
   4. *Select the Appropriate Sample*   4
   5. *Collect and Input the Data*   5
   6. *Interpret and Draw Conclusions about the Data*   5
   7. *Prepare a Report*   5
   8. *Follow Up the Research*   5
Evolution of Marketing Research   5
  Late 1800s to 1905: Application of Research to Marketing Problems   5
  1905 to 1918: Organized Approaches to Market Information   6
  1919 to 1930: Structuring the Marketing Research Discipline   6
  1930 to 1950: Solidification and Refinement of Marketing Research   6
  1950 to 1975: Restructuring and the Modern Era of Marketing Research   6
  1975 to 1995: Computerization and Globalization   6
  1995 to Present: The Emergence and Growing Impact of the Internet   6
Why the Internet Is Causing a Revolution in Market Research   8
Hurdles Faced in Internet Marketing Research   8
  Information Overload   8
  Sorting Out the Trash   9
  Speed of the Internet   9
  Hesitance to Divulge Information over the Internet   9
  Lack of Access to the Internet   9
The Future of Marketing Research and the Internet   9

  Emerging Functions of Marketing Research   9
  Moving from Market Research to Market-Focused Learning   10
The Internet's Marketing Research Applications   11
  Personal Intelligence   11
  Environmental Intelligence   11
  Consumer Intelligence   12
  Competitive Intelligence   12
Marketing Research on the Internet   12
  Internet Surveys   13
  Newsgroups   13
  Online Focus Groups and Product and Copy Testing   13
  Other Critical Concerns   13
Summary   14
Discussion Questions   14
Internet Project   15
Further Reading   15
References   16

Chapter 2

Internet Search and Research   17

Researching "Searching"   18
  The Evolution of Search Engines—A Truncated History   18
  Search Engines Today   18
Which Tool Is Best?   20
  For a Scholarly Topic   20
  For General Scholarly Information   21
  For a Reasonably Simple Topic   22
  For General Facts and Figures   23
Search Techniques   24
  Boolean Operators   24
  Word Stems and Wildcards   26
  Stoplist   26
  Consider the Spelling   26
Improving Your Search Skills   26
Outsourcing a Search   27
Summary   28
Discussion Questions   28
Internet Project   29
Further Reading   29
References   29

Chapter 3
Personal Intelligence   31

What Is Personal Intelligence?   31
Achieving Personal Intelligence: Finding,
    Downloading, Filtering, Displaying, and Managing
    Information   32
    Finding Information   32
    Exchanging Information   33
    Filtering Information   35
    Displaying Information   35
    Managing Information   35
    Bookmark Management   36
    Personalizing and Customizing
        Browsers   37
Research Tools   38
Gathering News and Information   41
    Portals   41
    Personalized Retrieval Services   42
    E-Zines   43
    E-Business   43
    E-Marketing   44
Marketing Research Information and
    Resources   45
Summary   48
Discussion Questions   49
Internet Project   49
Further Reading   49
References   49

Chapter 4
Environmental Intelligence   51

What Is Environmental Intelligence?   51
Defining Environmental Scanning   52
Environmental Scanning on the Internet   53
Macro-Environmental Websites   54
    Integrated/Global Information Resource
        Websites   54
    The Politico-Legal Environment   57
    The Economic Environment   58
    The Sociocultural Environment   61
    The Technological Environment   65
    The Physical Environment   67
Summary   68
Discussion Questions   69
Internet Project   69
Further Reading   69
References   69

Chapter 5
Consumer Intelligence   71

What Is Consumer Intelligence?   71
Consumer Intelligence and the Internet   72
Internet Resources Related to the Cornerstones of
    Consumer Research   72
    Occupations—What Constitutes the Markets?   73
    Objectives—Why Does the Market Buy?   79
    Objects, Occasions, Outlets—What, When, and Where
        Does the Market Buy?   81
Online/Off-Line Consumer Media Attitudes and Use
    Patterns   85
Online Media Attitudes and Use Patterns   86
Summary   88
Discussion Questions   89
Internet Project   89
References   89

Chapter 6
Competitive Intelligence   91

What Is Competitive Intelligence?   92
The Practicalities of an Effective Competitive
    Intelligence System   92
The Impact of the Internet on Competitive
    Intelligence   94
Twelve Steps for Conducting Competitive Intelligence
    on the Internet   94
    1. Check Key Competitive Intelligence Research
        Sources   95
    2. Search for Company Information   96
    3. Search the Websites and Personal Pages of
        Competitors   98
    4. Search for Trade Associations and
        Conferences   99
    5. Peruse Job and Career Websites   99
    6. Survey Competitors' Customers Online   100
    7. Utilize Comparative-Shopping Services   100
    8. Search Newsgroups and Read Mailing
        Lists   100
    9. Find News That Can Be Used   101
    10. Personalize Information Searches   102
    11. Outsource the Competitive Intelligence
        Function   102
    12. Start Your Search Engines   105
Professional and Educational Sources—Lifelong
    Learning about Competitive Intelligence   106
Join a Discussion Group   107

Summary   108
Discussion Questions   108
Internet Project   108
Further Reading   108
References   109

Chapter 7
Internet Surveys 111

Comparative Advantages of Internet Surveys   112
    Design   112
    Distribution   113
    Completion   113
    Return   115
Internet Survey Shortfalls   115
    Demography of Users   116
    Psychology of Users   116
Designing Internet Surveys   117
    Aesthetic Considerations   117
    Psychological Considerations   118
Sampling Methodologies for Internet Surveys   120
Internet Survey Distribution Options   121
    E-Mail Surveys   123
    On-Site Intercept Surveys   123
    Newsgroups and Discussion/Mailing Lists   123
In-House or Outsource? Internet Survey Research
    Firms and Services   124
    Online Directories of Internet Survey Research Firms
      and Services   125
    Internet Survey Firm Selection Criteria   125
Do-It-Yourself Internet Surveys: Just Add
    Questions   126
Online Surveying Software and Support   127
Summary   131
Discussion Questions   131
Internet Project   132
Further Reading   132
References   132

Chapter 8
An Introduction to Internet Newsgroups 135

Introduction   135
Newsgroup Applications in Marketing Research   136
Organization of the Hierarchy of Newsgroups   137
    The Big Ten   137
    Other Major Hierarchies   138
    Regional Categories   139
Finding the Right Newsgroup/s   139

Netiquette and Basic Guidelines for Using
    Newsgroups   139
    Basic Netiquette   139
Maintain the Quality of Newsgroup
    Messages   141
Commercial Postings and Announcements   141
Copyright Issues   142
Signatures   142
Spamming   143
Posting Messages   143
    Be Polite and Nonintrusive   143
    Asking Questions in Newsgroups   143
    Use Short Subject Topic Lines   144
    Deleting Posted Messages   144
    Cross-Pointing   144
    New Postings and Follow-Ups   144
The Twenty-Four Rules on Writing Proper Articles in
    Newsgroups   144
Conducting Surveys in Newsgroups   146
Other Useful Websites and Links   146
Summary   148
Discussion Questions   148
Internet Project   148
Further Reading   148
References   148

Chapter 9
Applied Research Methods for Newsgroups
and Discussion Groups 151

Introduction   151
    Three Main Methods of Researching
      Newsgroups   152
Step-by-Step Guide to Conducting Research in
    Newsgroups and Discussion Groups   152
    Step One: Read Introductory Postings   152
    Step Two: Perform an Advanced Search for Relevant
      Newsgroups   152
    Step Three: Read the FAQs   152
    Step Four: Read Postings in Relevant
      Newsgroups   153
    Step Five: E-Mail an Expert   153
    Step Six: Do a Posting   153
    Step Seven: Conduct a Survey   153
    Step Eight: Create a New Newsgroup   153
    Method A: Advanced Search Methods   153
    Method B: Posting to a Newsgroup   154
    Method C: Create a New Newsgroup   161

Summary   166
Internet Project   166
References   166

Chapter 10
Online Focus Groups   167

Focus Groups   167
Online Focus Groups   168
   Advantages of Online Focus Groups   170
   Disadvantages of Online Focus Groups   170
   When Are Online Groups Appropriate?   172
Conducting an Online Focus Group   173
Participating in Online Focus Groups   174
Some Organizations That Conduct Focus Groups   176
Metadexes of Market Research Firms   178
Other Online Focus Group Resources   179
Summary   180
Discussion Questions   180
Internet Project   181
Further Reading   181
References   181

Chapter 11
Websites, Sources, and Data—Reliability and Validity   183

Information on the Internet   184
   Who (Credibility/Authority)?   184
   Where (Comparability/Connectivity/Copyright/
    Citation/Accuracy)?   185
   What (Content/Objectivity)?   186
   When (Continuity/Currency)?   187
   Why (Context/Critical Thinking/Coverage)?   187

Websites about Websites   187
Meta-Information   188
   Evaluative Meta-Information   188
   Summary Meta-Information   190
Summary   190
Discussion Questions   191
Internet Project   191
Further Reading   191
References   191

Chapter 12
Ethical Concerns and Legalities   193

Introduction   194
Security   194
Consumer Protection   196
   Other Websites Relevant to Consumer Fraud and
    Protection   197
Intellectual Property and Copyright Law   197
Trademarks   202
Defamation   204
Obscenity   205
Privacy   207
Summary   209
Discussion Questions   210
Internet Project   210
Further Reading   210
References   210

Glossary   212
Index   218

Internet Marketing Intelligence

Research Tools, Techniques, and Resources

Chapter 1

Marketing Research: Established Traditions and Emerging Trends

Knowledge is power—Nam et ipsa scientia potestas est.

Francis Bacon (1561–1626), Meditationes Sacræ. De Hæresibus

The Internet has evolved from a highly restricted United States defense and academic research support network into the world's largest free and open repository of human knowledge. Experts predicted that the Web would contain "over half of all man's knowledge by the year 2001" (Murphy & Lacher, 1996). Since the mid-1990s the number of **websites** has grown by an annual factor of 10 and as of this writing, the number of pages on the Internet is past the billion-page mark (Waller, 2001). This ever expanding reservoir of data, in combination with over 420 million people globally who have access to the Internet (CyberAtlas, 2001), represents an unprecedented source of primary and secondary data. For market researchers, it is not a question of if they should use the Internet, but how. Thus arises the impetus and purpose of this text: to document the resources, delineate the tools, and demonstrate the techniques that one can utilize when conducting marketing research on and through the Internet.

Businesses need the right information about the right consumers at the right time to make the right decisions. Marketing research plays a critical role in facilitating an understanding of consumers, competitors, and market forces that impact one's business. Marketing research is used to answer a myriad of critical questions, such as:

- What kinds of people buy our products and/or our competitors' products?

- What are their demographic and psychographic profiles?

- What are their media use patterns?

- Are the markets for our products increasing or decreasing?

- What price should we charge for our products?

- Where, and by whom, should our products be sold?

- What is our market share?

- Are the customers satisfied with our products?

- What is our record for service?

In order to answer these and other relevant marketing questions, market researchers need access to an ongoing stream of relevant and timely data. With the emergence of the Internet, researchers have easy and instant access to an overwhelming amount and variety of marketing data. The Internet is a new and wholly unique research tool that not only enables access to an unprecedented amount of existing market information but also serves as a medium through which the user can gather new/primary marketing data.

Chapter objectives

This chapter aims to:

- Provide an understanding of the need and use of marketing research in an organization.

- Analyze the types of marketing research and their objectives.

- Provide an understanding of the marketing research process.

- Look at various stages of the evolution of marketing research.

- Define the traditional and emerging functions of marketing research.

- Examine the future of marketing research and the growing importance of the Internet.

Marketing Research Defined

The fundamental task of marketing research is to help specify and supply accurate information to reduce the uncertainty of decision making. Traditionally, marketing research has been viewed as a separate and distinct activity, performed on an ad hoc basis to solve one particular problem at one particular point in time. Accordingly, the American Marketing Association defined marketing research as:

> . . . the function that links the consumer, customer and the public to the marketer through information—information used to identify and define marketing opportunities and problems; generate, refine, and evaluate marketing actions; monitor marketing performance; and improve understanding of marketing as a process. (Bennett, 1988)

Today, business decision makers are faced with a multifaceted and ever changing environment. Increasing competition, shifting consumer tastes, regulatory changes, technological advances, and a variety of other factors blend together to shape a very complex marketplace. Add to the mix the fact that approximately 90 percent of all new products remain on the market for less than three years and it is easy to see why managers need to conduct research so as to avoid costly mistakes. Indeed, marketing managers need a fully integrated marketing information system that they can draw on when faced with any decision relating to the marketing of goods and services. The Internet's vast reservoir of information can and should be a central component of this system.

Types of Marketing Research

Marketing research is typically categorized as descriptive, diagnostic, or predictive. Table 1.1 lists objectives and examples for each type.

Descriptive research gathers and presents statements of facts. Managers often rely on descriptive research as a starting point in the research process to help them define their research problem. For example, the research objective could be to identify customer profiles in terms of demographic and attitudinal characteristics of early adopters/customers predisposed to the product concept.

Diagnostic research attempts to explain actions in the marketplace that provide managers with an understanding of the problem or situation. For example, what happened to product sales in the Sydney test market when the monthly advertising budget was increased from $25,000 to $40,000?

Predictive or causal research blends both descriptive and diagnostic research to project possible consequences of planned marketing actions. Based on the Sydney experience, what would happen to overall product sales across Australia if the advertising expenditures were increased by 60 percent? Managers often start with descriptive research and later follow with diagnostic and predictive research.

The Marketing Research Process

Regardless of whether information is gathered with pencil and paper questionnaires, telephone surveys, or computer-aided techniques, market researchers follow the same systematic process.

1. Define the Research Question or Problem

Researchers begin by defining the research question or problem and identifying specifically what they plan to research. The precise problem definition guides the investigation and helps ensure that the research yields pertinent information. Researchers must take care to define the problem rather than its symptoms. Three questions answered by the researchers can set the process moving in the correct direction.

- Why is the information sought?

- Does the information already exist?

- Can the research question really be answered?

TABLE 1.1
Types of Marketing Research and Their Objectives

Research Type	Objective	Example
Descriptive	To describe phenomena and to answer questions regarding who, how, when, why, how much, or where	What characteristics best describe the typical consumers of this product?
Diagnostic	To develop an understanding of the phenomena	What do consumers like and dislike about this product?
Predictive	To examine phenomena and determine cause and effect relationships	Does radio advertising increase product sales and, if so, by how much?

The initial time spent understanding and clarifying the problem is usually considerably less than the time (and money) wasted correcting the research later.

2. Create the Research Design or Master Plan

The research design, or master plan, is then created. This is the general framework used by the researcher to solve the specific problem identified in the first step of the process. It will detail the most suitable methods of investigation, the nature of the research instruments, the sampling plan, and the types of data, that is, quantitative or qualitative (or both).

3. Select the Research Method

Next, the marketer selects one of the three basic research methods to be used in the study: survey research, experimental research, and observational research (Kotler et al., 1998).

Observational research involves the gathering of primary data by observing relevant people, actions, and situations. Mechanical, electronic, and human observers can be employed to gather information. For example, traffic count hoses stretched across a road (mechanical), household purchases scanned at the checkout register (electronic), and the monitoring of a chat on the Internet (human) can provide marketers with valuable insights regarding how people actually behave outside controlled research conditions.

Survey research involves the gathering of primary data by asking people about their knowledge, attitudes, preferences, and buying behavior (Kotler et al., 1998). It is the approach best suited to gathering descriptive information and is also the most widely used method for primary data collection. Marketers use survey research to obtain facts, attitudes, and opinions from respondents by using a variety of techniques including face-to-face or telephone interviews and traditional mail or e-mail questionnaires.

Experimental research involves the gathering of primary data by selecting matched groups of subjects, giving them different treatments, controlling related factors, and checking for differences in group responses (Kotler et al., 1998). Experimental research tries to explain cause and effect relationships.

4. Select the Appropriate Sample

In most situations, researchers are unable to ask for feedback from everyone who uses a product or service, is exposed to an advertisement, or makes a buying decision. Instead, marketers must rely on the responses from a smaller group of the larger population. This population subset is called a **sample**. In the next step of the research process, the marketer establishes the procedure for selecting the appropriate sample. The researcher must identify the target population to sample, determine the number of people or size of the sample to yield reliable information, and decide on a method of picking participants. These basic decisions can take the form of three questions:

- Who should be sampled?

- How big should the sample be?

- How should the sample be selected?

Obviously, to maximize the significance and usefulness of the research, the sample group selected should resemble as closely as possible the key characteristics of the intended target market. Many excellent textbooks review the statistical procedures used to determine reliable sample size. Some of these are listed in the Further Reading section at the end of this chapter.

Marketers can choose between **probability** and **nonprobability sample** procedures. Every person in the target population has a known and equal chance to be selected to participate in a probability sample. This random selection procedure enables researchers to statistically estimate the sampling error that occurs in the study. Sometimes researchers make little or no attempt to ensure a random cross section of the target market. They trade off the ability to measure sampling error derived from using a probability sample for the convenience achieved by assembling the nonprobability sample. For example, researchers may survey shoppers at one mall or students in one large lecture hall because the procedure is easier than gathering a true cross section of all shoppers in a community or all students at the university.

5. Collect and Input the Data

Next, the data are collected, edited, coded, and input for analysis. Maximum accuracy and precision are ensured by reviewing responses for completeness, clarity, and legibility. In the editing phase, researchers may decide to exclude questionnaires containing unanswered key sections, those completed by someone who should not have participated in the study, or those that for any other reason may result in the data producing misleading results. All responses are assigned numerical values (codes) that facilitate statistical analysis when the data are entered into computers (input).

6. Interpret and Draw Conclusions about the Data

Researchers now interpret and draw conclusions about the data they have collected using a variety of qualitative (word-based) or quantitative (statistics-based) approaches ranging from simple frequency analyses to complex multivariate techniques. Their analysis should provide management with information that reduces some of the uncertainties of business decisions.

7. Prepare a Report

After the analysis is completed, researchers prepare a formal report of their findings. In order to effectively communicate the results of the study to management, the report should concisely, yet thoroughly, explain the results and draw appropriate conclusions. An executive summary can "bullet" the key points of the study and focus attention on important decision-making information.

8. Follow Up the Research

Finally, researchers should follow up their work. Time and money have been invested in the research project, and its findings should be utilized by the company. Researchers should evaluate whether their recommendations were followed. In cases where recommendations were not followed, prudent researchers should attempt to determine why the information was not used. This knowledge can contribute to more efficient research in the future.

Evolution of Marketing Research

Beginning at the outset of the last century, the nature and scope of market research have evolved through at least seven stages.

Late 1800s to 1905: Application of Research to Marketing Problems

The earliest recorded application of marketing research is generally agreed to have occurred during this period. By modern standards surveys conducted during this period were rudimentary but proved important in opening up new approaches to marketing problems.

1905 to 1918: Organized Approaches to Market Information

During this period, marketing research assumed a more significant role in business activities. In 1911, the Curtis Publishing Company created what is considered to be the first marketing research department; and R. O. Eastman, advertising manager for the Kellogg Company, is reported to have undertaken what was probably the first systematic readership survey. Another important development was the establishment of the Bureau of Business Research at the Harvard Graduate School of Business. During this period of growth, marketing research techniques were gradually being systematized, while in management literature the role of marketing research began to be noted.

1919 to 1930: Structuring the Marketing Research Discipline

In 1919, Dr. D. S. Duncan published the first book on commercial research. It was during this period that marketing research became more rigorous and disciplined in practice. George Gallup conducted the first recorded newspaper public opinion poll in 1928. Another important development during this period was the founding of the American Market Research Council in 1926. Also, a 1927 study into the methods of wholesale and retail distribution conducted by the U.S. Department of Commerce gave strong impetus to the adoption of business surveys and systematic sampling techniques.

1930 to 1950: Solidification and Refinement of Marketing Research

This period witnessed an extension and strong entrenchment of marketing research practices. The findings of a committee on marketing research techniques appointed by the American Marketing Association (AMA) played a key role in this context. The emergence of the British professional body, the Market Research Society, in 1947 also contributed significantly to raising the standards of survey practice.

1950 to 1975: Restructuring and the Modern Era of Marketing Research

This era is typified as a period of restructuring, refinement of techniques, and "interdisciplinary convergence." Sampling theory and research design were significantly improved; the testing of hypotheses and **multivariate analysis** received growing attention. **Nonparametric statistics** and a wide array of other statistical techniques were introduced. Psychological concepts and techniques were increasingly being borrowed in order to study consumer behavior. New attitudinal measuring techniques became popular in marketing research. These included Guttman's scaling, Osgood's semantic differential procedures, and Kelly's personal construct theory. Concepts such as opinion leadership, social class, family structure, group behavior, lifestyle, and cultural values added complexity to research designs.

1975 to 1995: Computerization and Globalization

The discipline of marketing research evolved from relatively crude and elementary investigative procedures to advanced statistical and computer-based methods of collecting, processing, and analyzing data. Indeed, the introduction of the personal computer was the most significant development during this period. In addition, marketing research exists as a distinct industry in its own right. It is a global multi-million-dollar business, employing thousands of people who continuously churn out thousands of reports, syndicated studies, and databases.

1995 to Present: The Emergence and Growing Impact of the Internet

The introduction of the World Wide Web and html in 1990 to 1991, Web browsers in 1993, and commercialization in 1994 set the stage for unprecedented growth. By 1996 market researchers were making extensive use of the Internet for a multitude of purposes. According to a Marketing Tool/Lexis-Nexis survey (*American Demographics,* 1996) by the mid-1990s market researchers were using the Internet for:

- Competitive intelligence (82 percent of the time).

- Conducting research (81 percent of the time).

- Broad overall market trends (72 percent of the time).

- Production and technology data (46 percent of the time).

- Information about international markets (36 percent of the time).

The 1996 survey also indicated that around 80 percent of all professional market researchers relied on the Internet and other online services for at least some of their research efforts. About 80 percent of researchers spent less than US$25,000 a year for online data and information; 10 percent of the respondents spent more than US$50,000 annually for online research.

By the mid-1990s observers and practitioners of market research were cognizant of a variety of areas wherein the Internet was registering an impact. The European Society for Opinion and Marketing Research delineated five major trends within which the Internet was an integral factor (Anselmi, 1997).

1. *Research techniques are in stronger demand:* Internet/online research, automated data collection, database management, market modeling, modeling of consumption behavior, market simulation, statistical analysis of decision process, qualitative research, and creative/interactive advertising tests.

2. *Major changes are affecting qualitative research:* major international projects, new customized design, growth in qualitative business-to-business research, more large-scale multistage qualitative research, wider use of videophone conferencing, interactive Internet group discussions, more branded qualitative research, multicountry qualitative networks, more integration with quantitative research, and growth of qualitative research by phone.

3. *Major changes are affecting quantitative research:* combination of surveys with databases, demand for more information and less data, more sophisticated methods of analysis, new technology to collect and handle data, direct data transmission to clients, interactive data collection, declining response rates, single source data, increasing costs, and concentration of the research profession.

4. *Certain types of research will grow strongest:* database-linked research, international studies, Internet surveys, predictive techniques, analysis of customer choice process, customer satisfaction research, early warning systems, business-to-business research, new product development, and new product/service testing.

5. *More companies will be going global:* fiercer competition among companies, increasing use of interactive communication technologies and databases, and better integration in the decision process.

Obviously, the use of the Internet for marketing research purposes has grown tremendously in the past few years and will, no doubt, continue to do so. Indeed, it has been projected that online research will make up 50 percent (over US$3 billion) of all marketing revenue by 2005 (McDaniel & Gates, 2002).

The Internet represents a revolution in the way market researchers gather data. It has significantly enhanced the marketing research process. By the end of the twentieth century almost every major marketing research firm had established an online presence and many were conducting at least part of their research efforts via the Internet.

Why the Internet Is Causing a Revolution in Market Research

The Internet is revolutionizing market research for a number of reasons. First, the Internet has *the ability to reach large numbers of people internationally while remaining economically feasible*. Prior to the Internet, when a researcher conducted a survey involving respondents from several countries, the researcher would accrue considerable added costs and time outlays. With the Internet, the market researcher can implement an international survey in considerably less time and with substantially less cost.

Second, the Internet has made *customers increasingly proactive*. The days when companies have to go out and ask customers what they think and want are coming to an end. The Internet allows customers to act on their own initiative and provide a company with relevant feedback, leading to consumers who are proactive rather than reactive. Accordingly, corporations need to be prepared to respond to a steady stream of customer input. Mass customization and one-on-one customer service should readily reciprocate the information that customers provide.

Third, the Internet has changed market research by providing *access to real-time information*. Decision makers should no longer have to wait several days for their data to be processed. The Internet allows the digitized data to be immediately processed into useful information for the decision maker.

Fourth, more and more researchers are using the Internet for *competitive intelligence* as increasing numbers of companies place greater amounts of information on the Internet. The amount and value of competitive intelligence that can be gleaned from the Web have mirrored the growth of e-commerce.

Fifth, the Internet makes *soliciting advice* easier. The advice and opinions of experts around the world can be solicited using newsgroups and discussion lists. Experts who would normally be unreachable or charge for consultation often have their own websites wherein the user can find samples and/or examples of their expertise—such as working papers, articles, and speeches. General searches on the Internet can also provide such examples of an expert's "expertise."

Hurdles Faced in Internet Marketing Research

Beyond its inherent benefits, the adoption of the Internet as a marketing research tool has been hindered by a number of shortcomings: information overload, having to sort out the trash, the speed of the Internet, hesitancy to divulge information, and the general lack of access to the Internet. However, efforts are being made to overcome these barriers.

Information Overload

Many corporations are already suffering from information overload. With the distinction as the world's largest storehouse of human knowledge also comes the distinction as the world's largest info-maze. In the Eighth Graphic, Visualization, and Usability (GVU) Center's World Wide Web User Survey, it was discovered that only 49 percent of users found what they were looking for on the Internet. Even among expert users, only 16 percent *always* found what they were looking for.

To overcome this dilemma MIS software is being developed to process data into more precise information that is useful for decision makers. The development of more powerful and intelligent search tools has also been helpful.

Sorting Out the Trash

A keyword search on a search engine typically yields thousands of hits, much of it irrelevant information. However, smart intelligent agent software that "learns" people's likes and dislikes is becoming more powerful and increasingly available.

Speed of the Internet

Initially, the speed of the Internet would often hinder the efforts of researchers. The World Wide Web was even dubbed by some as the "World Wide Wait." However, continuous advances in broadband technologies have rapidly improved the speed of Internet access, including the development of the New Generation Internet (for everyone) and Internet2 (specifically for universities and researchers).

Hesitance to Divulge Information over the Internet

Because of security and privacy concerns, lack of trust, and technological apathy, some users are hesitant to give personal information over the Internet. If researchers are to overcome this hurdle, they need to be more explicit than ever in their guarantees of anonymity and reasons for data gathering. Improvements in online security transactions have also helped to mitigate this problem. A privacy policy can be made available for all surveys conducted, encouraging greater openness and accountability.

Lack of Access to the Internet

Only 420 million of the more than 6 billion people in the world are Internet users. This produces a biased sample for researchers gathering data. In addition, the "pull" nature of websites means that people who respond to surveys often have stronger opinions on the subject, which further contributes to the self-selection problem. From another perspective, however, using the Internet as a primary research tool is no more problematic than relying on other tools.

Generally, governments worldwide support the "access to all" ideology, granting access in schools, universities, and hospitals. In the household sector, the opportunity costs of not getting Internet access will eventually be too great to forgo. Corporations are also finding ways of producing technologies that allow cheaper access.

Internet use will become more widespread as there is greater media convergence (e.g., Web TV) along with the great push by many corporations (e.g., Microsoft) to introduce cheaper means of Internet access, which will eventually make it as commonplace as telephone access.

The Future of Marketing Research and the Internet

Emerging Functions of Marketing Research

The functions of marketing research can be divided into three major domains: scanning, risk assessment, and monitoring. Marketing theorists believe that in the future the ratio of these activities will shift in favor of scanning and monitoring, with risk assessment losing ground. Scanning (and thus the use of the Internet for scanning purposes) will gain prominence because of increasing demands on early detection of change patterns, and monitoring will demand more attention as the provider of feedback, particularly in the area of customer satisfaction. Risk assessment will diminish because of lack of time and because a great deal of its content will be supplied by a better-organized scanning mechanism (Sggev, 1995).

Scanning

Effective marketing organizations recognize that they do not operate in a vacuum. The more familiar they are with the environment, the better prepared they will be for the future by detecting opportunities and threats as early as possible. Marketing research is used to scan the environment that affects marketing decisions, either directly or indirectly. And, as this book will demonstrate, when it comes to environmental scanning, the Internet may well be the market researcher's most potent tool.

Risk Assessment

Marketing strategy formulation involves the evaluation of strategic options. Each strategic option involves risk, and marketing research facilitates the assessment of the likelihood of success. Marketing research plays a critical role in linking strategy to tactics, making it a highly valued management tool. It replaces a manager's personal judgment and subjective opinions with objective results based on customers' reactions under simulated conditions.

Monitoring

Monitoring involves evaluating the effectiveness of the current action. In principle, sales and profit figures should suffice. But in marketing, that is rarely the case, because sales effects generally lag marketing inputs, and marketing effects are typically cumulative over time and not always reflected. The monitoring function is primarily diagnostic. Marketing research is used to diagnose problems; however, if properly conducted, it should also point to ways of fixing them. Research departments can cross the line between "diagnostic" and "curative," and venture into the realm of the latter, making their expertise available for instituting change if the corporate culture encourages and rewards it.

Moving from Market Research to Market-Focused Learning

The rapidly changing business environment requires marketing research to play an active role in the strategy formation process. The pace of technological, social, political, and cultural change is accelerating so fast that only those organizations that monitor and adapt to this incessant change will survive, let alone prosper. Proponents of this school of thought suggest that the ability to learn from market changes is critical for organizational growth in that it results in superior outcomes, such as greater new-product success, superior customer retention, higher customer-defined quality, and, ultimately, superior growth and/or profitability.

Some researchers (De Geus, 1988) argue that in today's dynamic and turbulent markets, the ability to learn faster than competitors may be the only source of sustainable competitive advantage. In this context, traditional roles of marketing research—namely, scanning and monitoring—would not be sufficient. Marketers must move beyond these activities and develop a market-focused learning capability that involves not only acquisition of knowledge on market changes but also dissemination of such knowledge across all layers of the organization. Such knowledge should then be used for competitive strategies such as innovation. Here again, today's market researcher can benefit enormously with an understanding of how the Internet can assist in knowledge acquisition and the **Intranet** can assist in interorganizational knowledge dissemination.

In terms of gathering **primary data**, there will be more representative populations to draw from, resulting in Internet surveys that are more valid and able to be generalized. The scope for international market research will increase as more people worldwide gain access to the Internet. Multimedia convergence will allow researchers to conduct more in-depth and accurate surveys than ever before with more interactive abilities, visual and audio capabilities, and advanced digitized data processing systems. Finding **secondary data**—used for competitive intelligence and environmental scanning—will become effortless with improvements in agent technology and the compilation of ever more comprehensive meta-indexes (metadexes). Further media convergence will create a new set of applications and uses for the Internet. Web TV and Internet telephony are just two of the initial convergence technologies that have already been introduced. With people's lives increasingly intertwined with the Internet, more and more data will become available to market researchers.

The market research industry will need to adjust to changes brought about by the Internet such as the globalization of companies and information overload. In order to deal with these problems, market research companies will form international networks, and we will continue to see an increasing demand for Internet survey research and automated data collection on a global scale.

The Internet's Marketing Research Applications

It is the intention of this book to document and demonstrate the increasing importance of the Internet to marketing researchers. Researchers can use the Internet to gather primary data by posting online Internet surveys in **newsgroups**, getting customers to answer a survey on a website, conducting **online focus groups**, and soliciting the advice of experts from online discussion lists. Marketing researchers can also use the Internet to access and analyze the world's greatest conglomeration of secondary data by utilizing a wide array of **search engines.** (Chapter 2 outlines a number of search engines and techniques to enhance search efforts and results.) Secondary data can also be gathered on the Internet by searching through Internet **metadexes** (indexes that have extended links on a specific topic), newsgroups, Web pages, online databases, and online journals and newspapers using the various tools and methods described.

Personal Intelligence

There is something *for* everyone—and it seems *from* everyone, as well—on the Internet. With the largest set of databases ever assembled and made accessible, researchers are faced with the problem of sifting and winnowing information of value and relevance. **Personal intelligence** refers to that information which is most relevant to your personal and/or professional well-being. It involves gathering information that is of most importance to a person and applying that knowledge to their personal and/or professional advantage. With personal intelligence tools, researchers are able to select the subjects of interest and let electronic **agents** or **knowbots** search for sources of information on any subject. Some of these personal intelligence agents are programmed to "learn" your preferences over time. You can also have electronic Web-based newspapers personalized to suit your news preferences. All this information can be accessed with a little time spent in finding the right websites, intelligence agents, newsgroups, and/or discussion/mailing lists. Chapter 3 outlines the many useful research utilities and reference tools available to simplify searches and maximize a user's efficiency and effectiveness in finding, downloading, filtering, displaying, and managing personal intelligence.

Environmental Intelligence

The environment plays an integral part in formulating the marketing mix. This is especially true given the rapid changes we now experience, making **environmental scanning** more important than ever before. With the Internet, companies have a powerful tool to acquire information about events, trends, and relationships that can assist marketers in decision making. The Internet makes the organization better connected to its environment, thus increasing its **environmental intelligence**. The Internet can help researchers in conducting environmental scanning tasks on the political/legal, economic, technological, and social/cultural environments. Chapter 4 provides a list of websites to conduct these environmental scanning tasks and discusses each area in detail.

Consumer Intelligence

The Internet is a medium that can be used for direct and continuous interaction between consumers and companies. Hence information about the consumer, or **consumer intelligence**, will be critical for any company wanting to gain a competitive edge. The Internet can provide profiling data on consumers from government, census, and consumer survey websites. Chapter 5 lists various websites and procedures for obtaining information on the following areas of consumer intelligence:

The General Structure and Characteristics of the Consumer Market

Consumer information can help marketers in generating a situational analysis of their target market and can assist them in designing strategies according to the characteristics of the consumer market.

Product and Media Consumption

Information on product and media consumption will help marketers determine consumption trends in the market. Such information can also assist marketers in making strategic marketing decisions, such as what type of product to launch and which media vehicle to use for advertising.

Market Trends

Trends in the marketplace can be assessed with the information provided through the Internet. Trends in **cyberspace** are also increasingly important as the world advances into a more digitally based era.

Competitive Intelligence

Competitive intelligence is a systematic way of identifying and then gathering timely, relevant information about a company's existing and potential competitors. After information is gathered from all relevant sources, it is analyzed in order to discern an understanding of competitors' strategies and future direction. Currently, competitive intelligence is one of the principal activities conducted by marketing researchers on the Internet. The Internet is an amalgamation of information-laden databases from which market researchers can monitor their competitors' every movement and assess competitors' strengths, weaknesses, and promotional and positioning strategies. The Internet proffers the ways and means to a more robust and efficient competitive intelligence system. Competitive intelligence can be obtained by using search engines, keeping a tab on competitors' websites, searching online trade associations, searching news archives, or even interacting with customers and competitors in newsgroups and mailing lists. Chapter 6 provides a stepwise program for gathering competitive intelligence using the Internet.

Marketing Research on the Internet

While the Internet may be a dream come true for some market researchers, it can, at the same time, be highly problematic, especially when it comes to finding the best and most relevant data among billions of pages of information. Chapter 7 introduces researchers to the various tools on the Internet that can help them cull the information they need. The chapter denotes the practical techniques and strategies for users when conducting research on or through the Internet.

Internet Surveys

The Internet represents a powerful new tool for researchers to gather primary data. This is due largely to the interactive nature of the Internet, which allows feedback from customers and interaction between the researchers and respondents. Albeit, there are many hurdles that Internet survey research has to overcome. Primarily, the problems of self-selection, respondent identification, and lack of representation need to be addressed. However, the advantages of the Internet as a survey medium when compared with existing methods are many, especially in terms of cost, speed of distribution, and the ability of researchers to gain access to real-time information on the survey. Internet surveys have become an increasingly powerful tool as the Internet has gained widespread adoption. At the same time, other traditional methods such as telephone surveys, mail surveys, and personal interviews have become increasingly ineffective, costly to researchers, and annoying to consumers. Chapter 7 provides guidelines on how to conduct proper surveys on the Internet and offers some suggestions on how to minimize or eliminate some of the inherent problems with Internet surveying.

Newsgroups

Newsgroups are electronic bulletin boards that record ongoing discussions among a multitude of individuals on thousands of topics. Usenet newsgroups allow people to regularly interact with each other, ask each other questions, discuss issues, and help each other with problems. Newsgroups essentially create **virtual communities** of users who are divided according to their areas of interest, with many experts in a field participating in them. Discussion-type mailing lists operate similar to newsgroups, the only difference being that instead of visiting the bulletin board, the messages posted are sent directly to a user's **e-mail** address. Chapters 8 and 9 provide the practical information needed to properly and effectively conduct research through newsgroups. Researchers can use newsgroups for soliciting advice and expert opinions and for finding information from newsgroup archives. Newsgroups are also useful for researchers in getting directions to websites containing useful information and in finding respondents for the purpose of conducting survey research. Newsgroups can also play a major role in keeping track of Internet users' sentiments on the industry and/or any given company.

Online Focus Groups and Product and Copy Testing

The use of the Internet for online focus groups is increasing, due largely to the savings in cost and time. In addition, different age, social, cultural, religious, and distance barriers can be mitigated using the Internet. The Web also represents a good medium for testing new products, concepts, and other marketing devices such as advertising, packaging, and, of course, websites. Graphics, video, audio, and text-based materials can be presented to respondents for reaction and response. Chapter 10 will assist researchers in understanding the benefits and limitations of conducting online focus groups.

Other Critical Concerns

Critical concerns about the Internet are based on the idea of *rights*.

- *Is the information right?* That is, is the information that one retrieves from the Internet accurate, reliable, and valid?

- *Is it right to use the information?* That is, is it morally and ethically appropriate—is it proper **netiquette**?

- *Do I have the right to use the information?* That is, is it legal?

As more individuals gain quicker access to a wider variety of information through the Internet, people will make more informed and (hopefully) better decisions. The disadvantage is that all this information makes it difficult for users to find what they want and to evaluate the quality of what they are finding. The open and freewheeling nature of the Internet has meant that no review procedures or information-filtering mechanisms are enforced. Moreover, the information is constantly changing and can easily be deleted. All of these factors reduce the validity of information on the Internet. Researchers will need to deal with these problems by developing skills to filter the information and determine what is relevant. Chapter 11 introduces evaluation criteria by which information on the Internet can be assessed.

Anyone and everyone who uses the Internet should have some awareness and understanding of the myriad of ethical, legal, and moral concerns it has raised. Market researchers in particular have an obligation to be sensitive to and cognizant of such issues as data security, user privacy, consumer protection, intellectual property, fair use, trademarking, and copyrights. Attention to and appreciation for these concepts and practices not only is proper netiquette but can be a legal obligation. The final chapter of the book (Chapter 12) addresses the legal and ethical issues of concern to the Internet researcher.

Summary

Timely and accurate information is essential for marketing decision making. A comprehensive research program should provide a continuous flow of relevant data that will increase one's knowledge of the marketplace and simultaneously reduce the chance of committing costly mistakes. Wily marketers have long recognized the value of research in running a successful business. Ancient Greek and Roman merchants calculated sales trends by monitoring daily sales in public markets. Today's market researcher continues to monitor the market for any and every variable that can or does impact sales. Throughout the twentieth century marketing research evolved into a professional field of endeavor that uses the most sophisticated data gathering and analysis tools available. The twenty-first century will further challenge marketers to continually upgrade their research skills and information processing expertise. A thorough understanding of the structure and substance of the Internet will be a certain prerequisite for the complete researcher.

 Your online learning center has a case study on *Established Traditions and Emerging Trends* available now at www.mhhe.com/forrest.

Discussion Questions

1. Define marketing research.
2. Name and describe the three types of marketing research.
3. Describe the eight stages of the marketing research process.
4. Name and describe the three basic research methods.
5. Provide an overview of the evolution of marketing research in the twentieth century.
6. What are the traditional and emerging functions of marketing research?
7. What are the key factors and directions of marketing research for the next five years?

8. Of the various activities that market researchers are able to undertake on the Internet, which activity/function do you believe to be the most important (there may be more than one)?

9. There are a couple of major obstacles impeding market research on the Internet. Which do you believe to be the most obstructive? Why?

Internet Project

For those who are involved in, or have any interest in, the marketing research field, go to @ResearchInfo.com (http://www.researchinfo.com/), which has an extensive array of valuable information resources on the market research industry. Specifically, search for additional information on:

• The history of market research.

• Instructions for creating online survey content.

• The role of marketing research in managerial decision making.

Further Reading

Burns, Alvin C., & Bush, Ronald F. (2000). *Marketing Research,* 3rd ed. New Jersey: Prentice Hall.
Hair, Joseph F., Jr., Bush, Robert P., & Ortinau, David J. (2000). *Marketing Research: A Practical Approach for the New Millennium.* New York: Irwin/McGraw-Hill.
McDaniel, Carl, & Gates, Roger (2002). *Marketing Research: The Impact of the Internet.* Ohio: South-Western Publishing.
McQuarrie, Edward F. (1996). *The Market Research Toolbox: A Concise Guide for Beginners.* California: Sage Publications.

References

American Demographics (1996). "Researching Researchers," September, pp. 34–6.
Anselmi, P. (1997). "Market Research in the Future." *ESCOMAR Newsbrief*, October, Vol. 5, No. 9, p. 5.
Bennett, Peter D. (Ed.) (1988). *Dictionary of Marketing Terms.* Chicago: American Marketing Association, pp. 117–18.
CyberAtlas (2001). "The World's Online Populations" (http://cyberatlas.internet.com/big_picture/geographics/article/0,13235911_151151,00.htm).
De Geus, A. P. (1988). "Planning as Learning." *Harvard Business Review*, March–April, Vol. 66, pp. 70–4.
De Ville, Barry (1995). "Internet for Marketing Researchers." *Marketing Research: A Magazine of Management and Applications*, Summer, Vol. 7, No. 3. pp. 36–38.
Duncan, D. S. (1919). *Commercial Research: An Outline of Working Principles.* U.K.: Macmillan.
Kotler, P., Armstrong, G., Brown, L., & Adam, S. (1998). *Marketing.* Sydney: Prentice Hall.
Lazer, W. (1974). "Marketing Research: Past Accomplishments and Potential Future Developments." *International Journal of Market Research* (formerly *Journal of the Market Research Society*), Vol. 16, No. 3.
McDaniel, Carl, & Gates, Roger (2002). *Marketing Research: The Impact of the Internet.* Ohio: South-Western Publishing, Chapter 6, pp. 182–93.
Murphy, Jamie, & Lacher, C. (1996). "1-Mississippi, 2-Mississippi: How to Measure the Web." *New York Times on the Web*, August 10–11.
Sggev, E. (1995). "A Role in Flux." *Marketing Management*, Winter, Vol. 4, No. 3, pp. 34–45.
Waller, Richard (2001). "How Big Is the Internet." July 10 (http://www.waller.co.uk/web.htm).

Chapter 2

Internet Search and Research

With 33 million domains and well over 1 billion pages, it is no wonder that Internet users spend a considerable amount of time and effort searching for particular websites and pertinent information. In fact, fully 33 per cent of Internet user sessions involve searching at engines and portals.

Sullivan, 2001

For the great majority of persons using the Internet—for personal and professional purposes alike—the use of a favorite search engine is often the one and only step ever taken when exploring the Internet. What search tool and technique the user employs will have a significant impact on the alacrity and accuracy of any and every search conducted. Search engines vary greatly in how they search and what and how much they return for any given query. Accordingly, it is in every Internet user's best interest to learn the variety and variations in search tools and techniques. For those engaged in marketing research, knowing the intricacies of Internet searching should be regarded as a professional prerequisite.

Chapter Objectives

This chapter aims to:

- Introduce some of the most comprehensive websites, enabling access to virtually any of the tens of thousands of search utilities on the Internet.

- Provide information about the operations and applications of search utilities.

- Give an overview of the steps and search utilities available to conduct various types of research.

- Provide methods and resources available to teach and improve users' Internet search and research techniques.

Researching "Searching"

Before the Web, file transfer protocol (FTP) was the main means of **downloading** files onto a computer's hard drive. Files can be exchanged across TCP/IP networks, of which FTP is a standard protocol, between client systems and servers in a way similar to peer-to-peer computing (Locke, 2001).

The Evolution of Search Engines—A Truncated History

The following brief history of the evolution of search engines is based on Sonnenreich (1997):

- The grandfather of all search engines was Archie, developed between 1989 and 1990 by Alan Emtage, a student at McGill University in Montreal. Archie combed FTP websites and indexed all the files it found, achieving what at the time was the best and most popular repository of Internet files.

- In 1993, the University of Nevada System Computing Services group developed Veronica (the grandmother of search engines).

- Matthew Gray's World Wide Web Wanderer captured URLs, creating the Wandex, the first Web database. This was developed in the early 1990s.

- In response to the Wanderer, Martijn Koster created Archie-like indexing of the Web, or ALIWEB, in October 1993.

- By December 1993, the Web had a case of the creepy crawlies. Three search engines powered by **robots** had made their debut: JumpStation, the World Wide Web Worm, and the Repository-Based Software Engineering (RBSE) spider.

- Unfortunately, these spiders all lacked the intelligence to understand what it was they were indexing. Therefore, if a user did not specifically know what they were looking for, it was unlikely that they would find it. This deficiency prompted the creation of EINet Galaxy, the oldest browseable/searchable Web, which went online in January 1994.

- In April 1994, two Stanford University PhD candidates, David Filo and Jerry Yang, created a comprehensive collection of Web pages called Yahoo!.

Search Engines Today

Since the advent of Galaxy and Yahoo!, there has been a truly mind-boggling profusion of search tools and utilities. Today, people can choose from thousands of engines, directories, portals, indexes, and meta-indexes. Thus, the first tasks are for a user to learn what choices are available and then to select those search tools and utilities that best serve their purpose. When it comes to searching for search tools and utilities, you would be hard-pressed to find a more inclusive and instructive website than searchability.com.

SearchAbility provides one of the most complete and comprehensive overviews of the search engines available on the Internet. SearchAbility lists search engines by size, collection quality, and subject/s covered. The website has links to:

- Guides A–Z.
- Giant Guides.
- Guides to Search Engines Focusing on Popular Topics.
- Guides to Academic Search Engines.

FIGURE 2.1
SearchAbility

Source:
http://www.searchability.com/

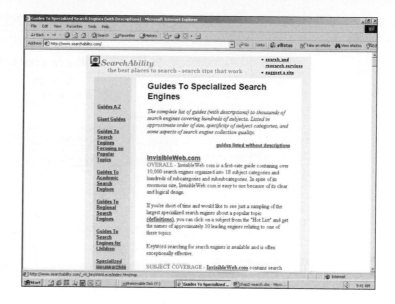

- Guides to Regional Search Engines.

- Guides to Search Engines for Children.

- Specialized Metasearches.

- About Specialized Search Engines.

- Boolean Operators.

  An abbreviated sample of the listings you will find at SearchAbility includes:

- InvisibleWeb (http://www.invisibleweb.com/), which contains over 10,000 search engines. These are organized into 18 subject categories with hundreds of further subcategories and sub-subcategories.

- Internets (http://www.internets.com/) is one of the most comprehensive guides due to the sheer number of search engines included and the specificity of its subject categories. Its drop-down menu lists 43 subjects.

- Search Engines Worldwide (http://www.twics.com/~takakuwa/search/search.html/) specializes in search engines from different regions, listing over 1,000 search engines from 174 countries.

In addition to SearchAbility, there is one other invaluable website that provides essentially anything and everything a user would want or need to know about the past, present, or future of search engines. Search Engine Watch (http://www.searchenginewatch.com/) provides "tips and information about searching the Web, analysis of the search engine industry, and help to website owners trying to improve their ability to be found by search engines."

This website makes available both general (free) and specific (paying-member) information. The free information includes topics such as Web searching tips, search engine listings, and reviews, ratings, and tests. It also lists upcoming search engine–related conferences and links to search engine news. A free e-newsletter is also available. Fee-based membership allows access to more detailed information of interest to Web-masters and marketers. Web-master information shows, for example, how various search engines

FIGURE 2.2
Search Engine Watch

Source:
http://www.searchenginewatch/com/

work. Marketer topics include search engine demographics and search engine advertising. Search Engine Watch's reviews, ratings, and tests report search engines' ratings and popularity, reviews and statistics, and comparative performance tests.

Which Tool Is Best?

Selecting the best search tool from among the thousands available can be a very daunting task. In the final analysis, which tool is best depends on the information required. As Dugas (1997) observed, "Knowing what you want to find will help you figure out how to find it." Accordingly, Dugas delineated the following search procedures to follow when researching simple versus scholarly topics.

For a Scholarly Topic

For a general topic, use a subject catalog (sometimes called directories). Subject catalogs provide links to resources arranged in subject hierarchies. Some examples are:

- Yahoo! (http://www.yahoo.com.au/).

- Librarians' Index to the Internet (http://lii.org/).

- Infomine (http://infomine.ucr.edu/).

An annotated subject catalog allows the use of preselected links. For example, WebCrawler (http://www.webcrawler.com/) provides concise summaries of linked pages, which should help indicate what the user will find when they click on a link (remember, however, that this involves relying on someone else's judgment).

Quality websites can be found quickly by using a subject guide. The work of a subject specialist often results in the most carefully selected and annotated links. This leads to the best websites in the quickest way, but you may miss out on some very important work. Examples of these types of websites are:

- Argus (http://www.clearinghouse.net/).

- WWW Virtual Library (http://www.vlib.org/).

FIGURE 2.3
Yahoo! Australia and
New Zealand

Source:
http://www.yahoo.com.au/

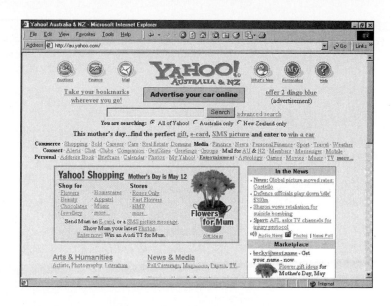

FIGURE 2.4
WWW Virtual
Library

Source: http://www.vlib.org/

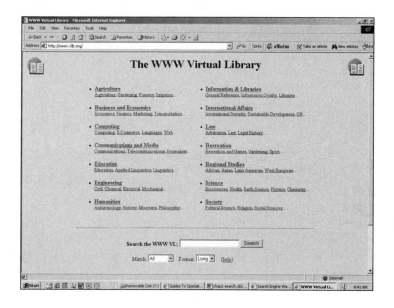

Avoid the omission of anything important by using a searchable index. Searchable indexes (sometimes called search engines) scan databases of millions and millions of pages with automated robots and allow for broad and often overwhelming searches.

Greg Notess has evaluated the comparative size of search engines in "Search Engines Statistics: Relative Size Showdown" (http://www.searchengineshowdown.com/stats/size.shtml/), the top five of which are listed in Table 2.1.

For General Scholarly Information

The search technique for general scholarly information is the same as just discussed. Using catalogs and guides first will yield the best (most reliable) information first. Then follow up with a searchable index for those unmined gems.

TABLE 2.1
Top Five Web Search
Engines

Rank	Engine	URL
1	Google	http://www.google.com/
2	Fast Search	http://www.alltheweb.com/
3	MSN Search	http://search.msn.com/
4	AltaVista	http://www.altavista.com/
5	Northern Light	http://www.northernlight.com/

TABLE 2.2
Popular MetaSearch
Engines

Engine	URL	Attributes
Ixquick Metasearch	http://www.ixquick.com/	Claims to be "the world's most powerful metasearch engine"; allows natural language or complex Boolean searches.
CNET: Search.com	http://www.search.com/	Can search over 800 search engines at a time including directories, storefronts, news sources, and reference websites.
Vivìsimo	http://www.vivisimo.com/	Vivìsimo features search result presentations with "document clustering." Herein the user will find a listing of categories related to the keyword, as well as a listing of individual websites.
InfoZoid	http://www.infozoid.com/	InfoZoid allows the user to concurrently search a variety of engines, select the number of results reported per page, and select the language in which the results are reported.
Query Server	http://www.queryserver.com/	This website currently provides the following types of search pages: Web, news, health, money, and government.

For a Reasonably Simple Topic

For a reasonably simple topic, or to obtain a lot of quick results, start with a searchable index. Use a single index to develop a workable search strategy, using the advanced features of that engine and Boolean logic (the latter is covered on pages 24–26). Then use a **meta-index** to search **multiple indexes** (sometimes called **metadex**). Some of the more popular metasearch engines are described in Table 2.2.

It is also possible to download free software that provides users with their own metasearch utility. One such software package is FerretSoft's WebFerret (http://www.ferretsoft.com/ or http://www.zdnet.com/ferret/index.html). WebFerret will search up to 20 search engines, based on user preference. From one search string entry, a user can select the search engines utilized. WebFerret's results can be ranked according to relevance and can be displayed in a Web browser. The user can dictate which sections of a website are searched for a match to the search string entry and can select the search string entry format. The user can also dictate how the search handles duplicate URLs, titles, and hosts.

For General Facts and Figures

A reference room is useful for finding general factual information, fulfilling the same function as a traditional library reference room. Examples of these are:

• The Internet Public Library (http://www.ipl.org/).

• Galaxy (http://www.galaxy.com/).

FIGURE 2.5
WebFerret

Source:
http://www.ferretsoft.com/

FIGURE 2.6
The Internet Public Library

Source: http://www.ipl.org/

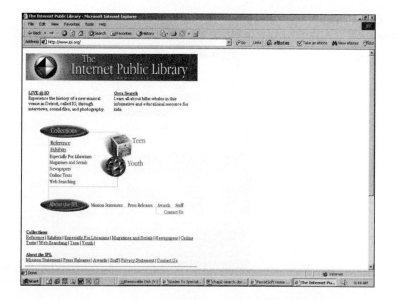

Specialized directories cover the kinds of data (for example, e-mail addresses, e-mail newsletters, and Web server information) that require special tools for effective searching or for accessing information. Some specialized directories are:

- Bigfoot (http://www.bigfoot.com/).

- Topica (http://www.topica.com/).

- 555-1212.com (http://www.555-1212.com/).

Search Techniques

We have come a long way since the advent of Archie and Veronica. In the early days of the World Wide Web the search for information, documents, and programs on the Internet would only involve scanning a little over 10,000 documents. Today, however, there are over 1 billion pages on the Internet (Waller, 2001), and it is estimated to be increasing at a rate of 25 pages every second of every day. Fortunately, there have been major advances in the search technology required to handle this information explosion, although it is incumbent on users to develop their Internet search skills to take full advantage of these improvements. At a bare minimum, the concepts of Boolean operators, word stems, wildcards, and spellings, and their relation to Internet searches, should be understood.

Boolean Operators

Boolean operators (named after the mathematician George Boole, who developed Boolean algebra) are fundamental to structured search techniques. Boolean operations are based on the user defining the keywords that are to be included and excluded in an online search. The Boolean operators AND, OR, NOT (or AND NOT), and NEAR dictate what words the user wants the search engine results to include or exclude, and whether the keywords should appear close to each other.

FIGURE 2.7
555-1212.com

Source: http://www.555-1212.com/

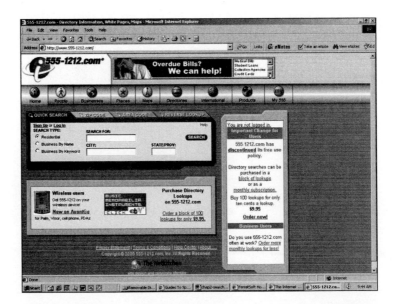

Example of the Boolean Operator AND

The Boolean operator AND identifies what search terms the user wants to appear in the results. If someone wanted to search for mammals that deliver their young as eggs, the search would be for *mammals* AND *egg laying animals* (the answer being Monotremes).

Example of the Boolean Operator OR

The Boolean operator OR indicates to the search engine that either or both search terms appear in the results. If a user is seeking documents on the topic of electronics, the topics may be as wide as any article with either the term *transistor* or *integrated circuit*. In this case the search term would be for *transistor* OR *integrated circuit*.

Example of the Boolean Operator NOT (or AND NOT)

The Boolean operator NOT (or AND NOT) prohibits the word after the search term from appearing in the results list of the search engine. Continuing the last example, a user may seek documents on the subject of electronics. However, on this occasion they would like to confine the results to documents that contain the term *transistor* and wish to exclude documents with the term *integrated circuit*. In this case the search could be for *transistor* AND NOT *integrated circuit*.

FIGURE 2.8
Graphical Example of the Boolean Operator AND

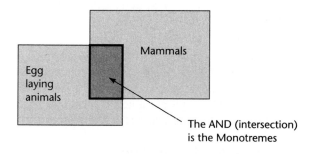

FIGURE 2.9
Graphical Example of the Boolean Operator OR

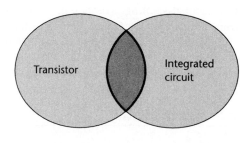

FIGURE 2.10
Graphical Example of the Boolean Operator AND NOT

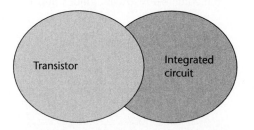

Example of the Boolean Operator NEAR

The Boolean operator NEAR requires that the search terms entered appear within a certain number of words of each other. Continuing from the last example, a user may seek documents that contain the terms *integrated circuit* and *radio*. In this case the search term entered would be for *integrated circuit* NEAR *radio*.

Word Stems and Wildcards

A user can widen or narrow the net of a search by incorporating word stems or **wildcards**. Word stems are the basis of larger words; for example, a word stem of *consumerism* would be *consume* and *consumer*. Using the Google search engine, these individual word searches would provide the following results:

- *Consume:* 886,000 matches.

- *Consumer:* 9,790 000 matches.

- *Consumerism:* 115,000 matches.

Truncation is the application of a wildcard to the word stem. The most popular wildcard used in computing is the asterisk (*). Thus *consume** would locate *consumed, consumer, consumerism, consumerist, consumers,* and *consumes.* Using the AltaVista search engine, the truncated word *consume** would result in 12,262,407 matches. It is important to know, however, that not all search engines accept word stemming or truncation.

Stoplist

Before planning a search, it is important to know that computer indexing software does not catalog on certain words, termed **stop words** or **stoplist words**. These common words include *a, about, and, as, before, of, if, in, is, it, never, not, the,* and *why.* The exclusion of these words may make a search query look less obvious as a phrase and may require a combination of words using a Boolean operator.

Consider the Spelling

It is possible to miss finding a document because of a word being misspelled or typed using regional spelling. Misspelling is impossible to predict and may require the use of a truncation search. Regional spelling differences are overcome by using the Boolean operator OR between the possible words, for example, *consumer behaviour* or *consumer behavior.* Table 2.3 shows some examples of the differences between Australian and American English.

Improving Your Search Skills

One of the best resources to help develop a Web researcher's skills is About.com (http://web-search.com/cs/howtosearch/index.htm/). This website lists "articles with strategies, tips and

FIGURE 2.11
Graphical Example of the Boolean Operator NEAR.

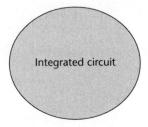
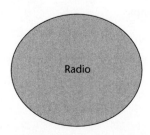

TABLE 2.3
Australian versus
American English
Terms and Spellings

Australian	American
Colour	Color
Behaviour	Behavior
Customise	Customize
Globalisation	Globalization
Boot	Trunk
Bonnet	Hood
Lift	Elevator

techniques, from beginner to advanced, as well as comparisons, advice and recommendations of search websites, and how-to/tutorial pages." The main areas covered are:

- Basics for beginners.
- Advanced search techniques.
- Scavenger hunts and Web search games.
- Search tutorials and workshops.
- Metasearch techniques and how-to.

Outsourcing a Search

If necessary, it is possible to hire someone to undertake an Internet search. One of the better services might be FIND/SVP (http://findsvp.com/). The Australian affiliate of this group is called Tell Me Now (http://www.tellmenow.com.au/). FIND/SVP offers custom research services and access to the "collective experience, specialized knowledge and research skills of over 1,100 consultants worldwide." Depending on the nature and scope of a user's inquiry, they can select among four main services:

FIGURE 2.12
About.com

Source:
http://websearch.about.com/cs/
howtosearch.htm/

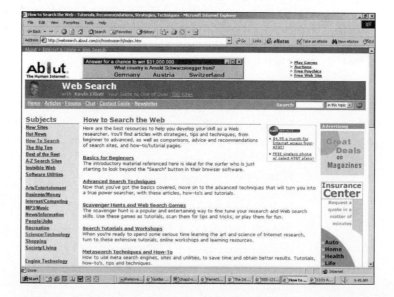

FIGURE 2.13
FIND/SVP

Source:
http://websearch.about.com/cs/
howtosearch/index.htm/

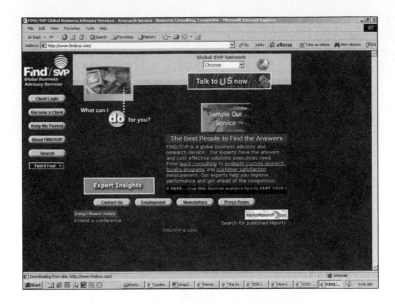

- Quick Consulting and Research Service.

- The Strategic Consulting and Research Group.

- The Customer Satisfaction and Loyalty Group.

- The Live Answer Desk.

Summary

The Internet and its offshoot, the World Wide Web, have grown to become the world's largest repository of information. The ability to easily and quickly find key documents and relevant data is a requisite skill for any knowledge seeker. This chapter has reviewed some of the best websites available for learning about search tools, techniques, and resources. There are thousands of search utilities from which to choose. In order to select the best engine for the task at hand, it is imperative that researchers have an intimate understanding of the nature, processes, and application of a full range of search utilities. Moreover, it benefits every Internet user to understand the fundamentals of constructing the most accurate and effective online queries.

Your online learning center has a case study on *Internet Search and Research* available now at www.mhhe.com/forrest.

Discussion Questions

1. Using the same keyword/s, conduct a series of searches on the Internet with four different search tools listed in this chapter. Compare and contrast the results reported by each tool and suggest reasons for any differences in the hit lists.

2. What is your favorite search tool and why?

3. What is a good website to refer to when searching for search tools and utilities?

4. What is a good website for learning all about search tools?

5. What is a good website to refer to for information on how to conduct searches?

6. Define or otherwise describe the following terms:

   (*a*) Subject catalog.

   (*b*) Annotated subject catalog.

(*c*) Searchable index.

(*d*) Meta-index.

7. What are the search steps you would take to conduct a search for the following:

(*a*) Scholarly topics.

(*b*) Scholarly information.

(*c*) Simple topics.

(*d*) General facts and figures.

Internet Project

Go to SearchAbility (http://www.searchability.com/) and browse through each of the guides offered:

- Guides to Specialized Search Engines Listed by Size.

- Guides A–Z.

- Giant Guides.

- Guides to Search Engines Focusing on Popular Topics.

- Guides to Academic Search Engines.

- Guides to Regional Search Engines.

- Guides to Search Engines for Children.

- Specialized Metasearches.

- About Specialized Search Engines.

Which guide (and search engines listed therein) do you perceive as most relevant and valuable for your research purposes?

Further Reading

Gilster, Paul (1996). *Finding It on the Internet: The Internet Navigator's Guide to Search Tools and Techniques,* revised and expanded, 2nd ed. New York: John Wiley & Sons.
Gould, Cheryl (1998). *Searching Smart on the World Wide Web: Tools and Techniques for Getting Quality Results.* California: Library Solutions Press.
Hock, Randolph (2001). *The Extreme Searcher's Guide to Web Search Engines.* Medford, New Jersey: CyberAge Books.

References

Dugas, Terry (1997). "Only Sissies Use Search Engines." *Using the Internet for College Research*, Section 204, Week 7, October 5 (http://www.naples.net/~dugast/LIS1003/week7a.htm/).
Locke, Christopher (2001). "Accelerating Toward a Better Search Engine." *Red Herring*, March 6 (http://www.herring.com/index.asp?layout=story&channel=10000001 &doc_id=1450018145/).
Sonnenreich, Wes (1997). "A History of Search Engines." (http://www.wiley.com /legacy/compbooks/sonnenreich/history.html/).
Sullivan, Danny (2001). "Avoiding the Search Gap." *Search Engine Report*, No. 54, pt. 1, May 2. Statistic cited from Booz-Allen & Hamilton study.
Waller, Richard (2001). "How Big Is the Internet." July 10 (http://www.waller.co.uk/web.htm/).

3

Personal Intelligence

One of the major problems brought on by the **information age** is just that—information. Simply put, there Is just too much of it. Moreover, every day the universal pool of information expands exponentially and so does the probability of suffering from information overload. Fortunately, the information explosion has been accompanied by significant advances in information management tools and techniques. In an era where personal and professional success depends on having the most recent and relevant information, knowing how to utilize these tools and techniques is essential.

By properly configuring their own personal intelligence management system, users will be able to gather information more effectively than other researchers. This chapter offers a variety of resources, tools, and techniques available through the Internet that can be used to construct an individual personal intelligence system.

Chapter objectives

This chapter aims to:

- Provide an understanding of the importance of personal intelligence in current times.

- Assist in identifying resources on the Internet that address personal intelligence requirements—in both a personal and a professional capacity.

- Give guidelines for exploring Internet marketing research resources.

- Develop the skills required to create an integrated personal intelligence system using a range of Internet-based resources.

What Is Personal Intelligence?

Intelligence is a multifaceted concept. The term has been defined as:
1. capacity for understanding; aptitude in grasping truths, facts, meaning, etc. [2.] knowledge of an event, circumstance, etc., received or imparted; news; information. [3.] the gathering or distribution of information, especially secret information which might prove detrimental to an enemy. (Macquarie Concise Dictionary, MacquarieNet 2002)

Personal intelligence refers to that information which is most relevant to an individual's personal and/or professional well-being. It involves gathering information that is of most importance to a person and applying that information to their personal and/or professional advantage. Information is used in the decisions, ranging from simple to critical, that are made every day throughout a person's life. It is important that people develop a coherent system of information collection, storage, and retrieval. Personal intelligence involves customizing information according to both personal and professional needs, so that an individual can operate in a more efficient manner. It can be derived from virtually any information source, such as local to international news, current affairs, financial or stock market reports, industry press releases, journal articles, newsletters, and convention proceedings. Personal intelligence can be achieved by modifying the access to information and personalizing its use for an individual's own purposes.

Prior to the Internet, acquisition of personal intelligence was primarily drawn from a limited set of print and broadcast media. The acquisition of personal intelligence today is entirely revolutionary in the breadth, depth, and relevance of information retrieval. Indeed, the user can access—and automatically scan and edit—*all* information resources that may contain pertinent bits of information. With such vast amounts of information readily accessible, it is vital for people to design and maintain an efficient daily routine of checking and updating their personal intelligence information stream.

The Internet offers numerous avenues for collection of information that will prove central to a user's personal and/or business interests. Many websites can be customized, or can allow registration with category-specific mailing lists. Websites can also encourage participation in chat or newsgroups dedicated to special topics. The Internet has greatly increased the opportunity (indeed, the necessity) for utilizing some form of electronic personal intelligence system to control and monitor information retrieval. People can eliminate the time wasted on labor-intensive and repetitive tasks by customizing and personalizing their information search strategies. Meeting the daily requirement of personal intelligence no longer has to be time-consuming or require an expensive investment in information resources.

Achieving Personal Intelligence: Finding, Downloading, Filtering, Displaying, and Managing Information

As outlined in the previous chapter, there are a multitude of search engines that can be employed in the search for information. However, having to search website-by-website can be a very "la-*bore*-ious" and time-consuming process. There are many useful research utilities and reference tools to simplify searches and maximize a user's efficiency and effectiveness in finding, downloading, filtering, displaying, and managing personal intelligence. ZDNet, for instance, provides a comprehensive listing of downloadable search tools and add-on browser utilities. More specific tools are discussed below.

Finding Information

With Atomica—a free downloadable browser add-on (available at http://www.atomica.com) a user can query information on any subject by typing the topic into a box and clicking "Answer." The information returned on a query includes (but is not limited to) general definitions, technical definitions and explanations, encyclopedic definitions, maps, relevant news, acronyms, foreign language translations, relevant websites, Internet keywords, and Internet search options. Aside from individual applications, Atomica is designed for businesses, offering consulting, training, and project services. Atomica's answer delivery technology can reduce the time a firm spends searching for information.

FIGURE 3.1
ZDNet

Source:
http://www.zdnet.com/searchiq/
searchtools/index.html/

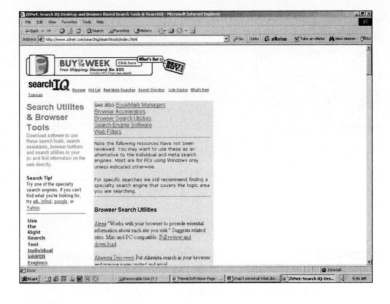

FIGURE 3.2
Atomica Search
Results for the Word
Marketing

Source:
http://www.atomica.com/

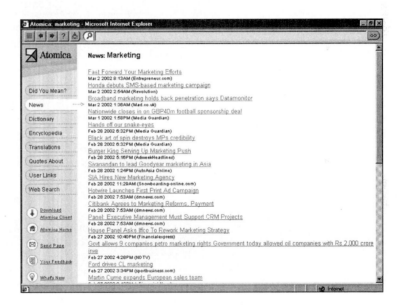

Table 3.1 lists a number of other tools and utilities that can assist in the search for relevant personal intelligence.

Exchanging Information

There are a number of ways to save time when exchanging information using the Internet. Table 3.2 lists a number of tools and **browser plug-ins** that will accelerate the speed of downloading files.

Many websites that provide information and utilities request that the user register, with users repeatedly asked to provide essentially the same information, such as name,

TABLE 3.1 Website Information Search Tools

Tool	Features
Alexa (http://www.alexa.com/) (free) IE, W	Alexa provides information regarding other websites related to the one the user is currently visiting, including traffic number, related links, and reviews.
UCmore (http://www.ucmore.com/) (free) IE, W	UCmore provides additional information based on the subject of whatever website the user is visiting. For example, visiting a travel website results in a menu of related websites displayed under Travel on the UCmore toolbar.
iRemember (http://seracsoftware.com /iremember.html/) (US$25) IE, N, M	iRemember indexes the websites visited by a user. When searching for an item seen during other Internet searches, the user can enter a few relevant words and iRemember will display websites previously visited that contain those words.

Key: IE = Microsoft Internet Explorer, N = Netscape, W = Microsoft Windows, and M = MacOS.
Source: Adapted from Lynch, 2001

TABLE 3.2 Tools to Accelerate Downloading

Tool	Features
NetSonic (http://www.netsonic.com/) (free) IE, N, W	NetSonic caches (stores) the main parts of websites (pictures, for instance) on the user's hard disk more effectively than the browser does, reducing the amount to be downloaded the next time it is visited. The program can also prefetch links on a website, so those pages are cached before the user visits them.
Download Accelerator (http://www.downloadaccelerator.com/) (free) IE, N, W	Download Accelerator claims to speed up downloads by up to 300 percent. Although an increase this great may not necessarily be seen, there can be a significant reduction in download time over a Digital Subscriber Line (DSL) connection. The program continues interrupted downloads if the user's server supports that capability.
Speed Download (http://homepage.mac.com/fred_cheung/) ($15) IE, M	Speed Download accelerates downloads by opening up to 32 simultaneous connections to the server providing a file, rather than transferring it over a single connection. Interrupted downloads can also be resumed without loss of data. It will work with Internet Explorer; however, check the program's documentation for advice.

Key: IE = Microsoft Internet Explorer, N = Netscape, W = Microsoft Windows, and M = MacOS.
Source: Adapted from Lynch, 2001

occupation, title, postal address, e-mail address, and passwords. However, users can save time and minimize effort by using certain Web tools.

Netscape Inbox Direct (http://home.netscape.com/ibd/index.html/) saves time by offering subscriptions to multiple mailing lists in an extensive range of categories including news, finance, business, technology, travel, sports, and entertainment. Inbox Direct eliminates the need to find and then visit individual websites to subscribe to their mailing lists by providing a single registration form used by Netscape to automatically register the user with the lists they choose. Preapproved by Netscape, the publications are generally of a high quality. New publications are continually being added, so it is worth checking for recent additions every month or so.

TABLE 3.3
Registration Tools

Source: Adapted from Lynch, 2001

Tool	Features
AI RoboForm (http://www.roboform.com/) (free) IE, N, W	AI RoboForm stores certain information the user chooses to provide, including log-in names, passwords, and credit card numbers. When a website requests information, the user clicks the Fill Forms button added to the browser and the program will fill in the blanks.
Gator (http://www.gator.com/) (free) IE, W	Gator saves time, especially for online shopping, by automatically filling in forms with standard information such as name, e-mail address, and credit card number. However, users should read the software privacy policy as Gator tracks the websites visited.
Web Confidential (http://www.web-confidential.com/) (US$20) IE, N, W, M	Web Confidential is considered to be the best form filler for Macintosh computers, although it will also work on Windows. It will store and handle confidential information including serial numbers, PINs, and credit card numbers.

Key: IE = Microsoft Internet Explorer, N = Netscape, W = Microsoft Windows, and M = MacOS.

Table 3.3 lists a number of other tools the user can employ to save time and effort in registering information.

Filtering Information

Taking control of the information received, as well as provided, is an important consideration for every Internet user. The proliferation of pop-up ads, blinking banners, and cookies has exacerbated the problem (and irritation) of information search and retrieval. Once more, a range of tools and utilities exists (such as those listed in Table 3.4) to keep a user's screen clear of superfluous solicitations and unwanted intrusions during Internet searches.

Displaying Information

In addition to saving time (and aggravation) in searching for information, users can maximize the amount of information they can simultaneously access, organize, and display. The researcher's task of evaluating and analyzing data can be greatly enhanced with the ability to quickly pull up, compare, and analyze multiple windows of information. Table 3.5 lists a few Web tools of assistance in customizing and optimizing the display of information.

Managing Information

Having searched for and found useful information on the Internet, a user needs to label and save it. For example, when researching the hundreds of websites for this text, the author captured, labeled, and archived selected websites and related information. A most useful tool employed for this task was eNotes (http://www.my-enotes.com/), a free enhancement for Microsoft's Internet Explorer. It adds an intelligent "cut and paste" capability that provides a quick and simple way to gather information from the Internet. When a user highlights anything of interest, eNotes automatically captures and organizes the material in a personalized Knowledge Cart™ (the collection of text and images the user has saved).

Info Select is a more general-purpose archiving tool. It is specifically designed to help manage Internet-based resources and any other random information. Info Select makes

TABLE 3.4 Information Filtering Tools

Tool	Features
AdShield (http://www.adshield.org/) (free) IE, W	AdShield prevents advertisement images, pages, and pop-up windows from being downloaded and displayed.
Ad-Aware (http://www.lsfileserv.com/aaw.html/) (free) IE, W	Ad-Aware scans a user's computer for the most common spyware programs such as Adware, Comet Cursor, and Web3000, helping users to find and remove programs that might be tracking their online behavior.
SurfSecret (http://www.surfsecret.com/) (30 days free, then US$29.99 to US$39.99) IE, N, W	SurfSecret eliminates the items left in a user's computer that indicate where they've been online, such as cache files, cookies, and even files left in the recycling bin. The Cookie Saver lets users choose which cookies they want to keep.
WebFree (http://www.falken.net/webfree/) (free for 30 days, then US$20) IE, N, M	WebFree lets users choose what they want to see on the websites they visit, allowing them to block flashing banners, images, cookies, and links.
WebWasher (http://www.webwasher.com/) (free for private users, or US$29 for single-user license) IE, N, W, M	WebWasher protects online privacy by filtering cookies and other items suspected of compromising a user's privacy. Users can also eliminate unwanted pop-up windows.

Key: IE = Microsoft Internet Explorer, N = Netscape, W = Microsoft Windows, and M = MacOS.
Source: Adapted from Lynch, 2001

TABLE 3.5 Information Display Tools

Tool	Features
Katiesoft (http://www.katiesoft.com/) (free) IE, N, W	Katiesoft lets users view multiple Web pages from within the same browser window. In addition to the usual browser navigation tools, this program provides quick access to Windows Explorer and Media Player programs.
BroadPage (http://www.broadpage.com/) (free) IE, W	BroadPage is a multipage browser that assists in viewing and managing multiple websites. Users can switch between as many as 100 windows by clicking on convenient tabs.
WebCascader™ (http://mathtechassociates.bizland.com/) (free for 300 launches, then US$15) IE, N, M	WebCascader™ is part multipage viewer, part bookmark organizer, letting users load all their favorite or related websites in a project with one click.

Key: IE = Microsoft Internet Explorer, N = Netscape, W = Microsoft Windows, and M = MacOS.
Source: Adapted from Lynch, 2001

organizing quick and easy by letting users drag and drop data into the categories they create. Figure 3.4 demonstrates an Info Select archive.

Other research utilities that enable the copying, archiving, and retrieval of websites and related information are shown in Table 3.6.

Bookmark Management

One of the fundamental components of Internet research is the **bookmark**. It serves as the central listing of the selected information resources of a user's research endeavors. Here again, effective management of and ready access to a list of important websites and Internet

FIGURE 3.3
eNotes

Source: http://www.my-enotes.com/

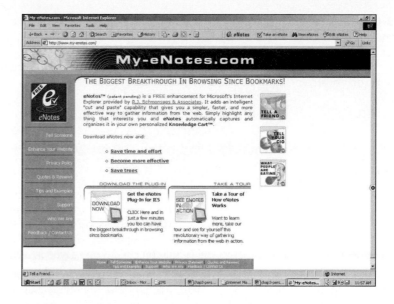

FIGURE 3.4
An Info Select Archive

Source:
http://www.miclog.com/isover.htm

resources can greatly augment research efforts. Table 3.7 lists three tools that can help in this regard.

A variation on these types of tools is Mind-it (http://mindit.netmind.com/), which acts as a personal Web assistant. If a user needs to stay informed of any changes to information and content on a specific website, Mind-it will monitor the website and e-mail the user when relevant changes occur.

Personalizing and Customizing Browsers

Not all Internet tools need to be related to researching. For researchers who spend a lot of time online, there are a number of options for customizing the appearance of their browser. Table 3.8 lists some tools that let users change a browser's look, design, and texture.

TABLE 3.6 Information Management Tools

Tool	Features
Octopus (http://www.octopus.com/) (free) IE, W	Octopus compiles content from various websites into one browser page called a "View." News junkies will love Octopus because of the ease with which content from many websites can be delivered to only one Web page.
SurfSaver (http://www.surfsaver.com/) (free, US$29.95 for pro version) IE, N, W	SurfSaver allows users to save websites in searchable folders on their hard disks. This is an excellent tool for those researchers who need to save Web pages from the Internet locally and then recall them quickly.
netXtract (http://www.netxtract.com/) (free for 30 days or US$29.95) IE, W	netXtract streamlines Internet research by automatically creating an index for the website being displayed by Internet Explorer. By clicking on an index entry, the user can see all the phrases that include that word and jump to any context of interest. Relevant information can also be saved in a database.
WebCopier (http://www.maximumsoft.com/) (free or full version for US$24.95) IE, W	WebCopier enables the partial or full download of websites to a hard disk for viewing off-line. Users can also schedule a time for the program to download Web pages.

Key: IE = Microsoft Internet Explorer, N = Netscape, W = Microsoft Windows, and M = MacOS.
Source: Adapted from Lynch, 2001

TABLE 3.7 Bookmark Management Tools

Tool	Features
Blink (http://www.blink.com/) (free) IE, N, W, M	Blink enables access to a user's bookmarks, or favorites, from any computer connected to the Internet. Users can also share bookmarks and access ones posted by other users.
HotLinks (http://www.hotlinks.com/) (free for 30 days, then US$19.95 per year) IE, N, W, N (limited features)	HotLinks allows users to access their bookmarks from any Windows system at any Internet connection. In addition, users can find websites similar to those they visit, arrange links by category, and e-mail links to others.
URL Manager Pro (http://www.url-manager.com/) (US$25) IE, N, M	URL Manager Pro lets users drag links from their browser to the URL Manager window to add websites to their collection. URLs can be organized in a hierarchical structure, and bookmarks can be stored in folders.

Key: IE = Microsoft Internet Explorer, N = Netscape, W = Microsoft Windows, and M = MacOS.
Source: Adapted from Lynch, 2001

Research Tools

Long before the Internet, every researcher had their standard desk references that aided the tasks of gathering information, analyzing it, and preparing a report: dictionaries, thesauruses, Bartlett's quotations, encyclopedias, and the like. As expected, all these tools and more are now immediately accessible on the Internet. The following are some of the most complete and powerful research utilities available.

TABLE 3.8   **Browser Customization Tools**

Tool	Features
NeoPlanet (http://www.neoplanet.com/) (free) IE, W	NeoPlanet allows users to change the "skin" of their browser, for example, replacing Microsoft gray with neon blue, turning dull buttons into shiny metallic knobs, or using splotches of color. There are more than 500 skins available.
Internet Explorer Personalizer (http://accesscodes.hypermart.net/) (free) IE, W	Internet Explorer Personalizer enables the retitling of a user's browser and lets them replace elements such as the Internet Explorer logo, toolbar background, and search button.
Hotbar (http://www.hotbar.com/) (free) IE, N, W	Hotbar allows users to personalize their browser's toolbars using thousands of "skins" in themes including nature, sports, romance, and children. Hotbar also adds buttons to your browser for quick access to news and other services.

Key: IE = Microsoft Internet Explorer, N = Netscape, W = Microsoft Windows, and M = MacOS.
Source. Adapted from Lynch, 2001

Refdesk (http://www.refdesk.com/) claims to be "the single best source for facts on the Net," backing up this assertion with a myriad of information sources and services. Resources range from nearly a dozen encyclopedias and dictionaries to a vast array of news links. There is also a reference resources area containing links to the top 10 Refdesk pages, indispensable websites, and journalists' tools, just to name a few. This is an excellent website for users requiring reference information or direction in a specific field of personal intelligence. Refdesk is a good first stop for secondary information for any research and/or to keep informed about current news and events.

Where to Do Research (http://www.wheretodoresearch.com/) provides quick access to over 100 subject areas and over 6,000 external links.

Research-It! (http://www.iTools.com/research-it/researchit.html/) is an iTools website that groups a whole range of extremely useful features into the one place. The following are some of the functions offered:

- Dictionary definitions.

- Translation of words into multiple languages.

- Stock quotes.

- Thesaurus entries.

- Quotations.

- Maps.

- Currency conversion.

- Shipping and postal info (U.S. only).

- Lists of discussion groups.

- General facts.

Dictionary.com (http://www.dictionary.com/) is not just an online dictionary, despite its name. In addition to providing definitions from a wide range of dictionaries, the website contains, among other things, writing resources, translators, a Web directory, and links to

FIGURE 3.5
Refdesk

Source:
http://www.refdesk.com/

FIGURE 3.6
Where to Do Research

Source:
http://www.wheretodoresearch.
com/

other relevant websites. Thesaurus.com (http://www.thesaurus.com/) is a companion to this website and is shown in Figure 3.8.

Encyclopedia.com (http://www. encyclopedia.com/) is a free service that provides users with direct access to the Electric Library database, which has over 50,000 articles as well as links to millions more articles and pictures.

FindArticles.com (http://www.findarticles.com/) provides researchers with a large archive of published articles dating back to 1998 from more than 300 magazines and journals. Each of the hundreds of thousands of articles (which are constantly updated) can be read and printed in full for free.

World Lecture Hall (http://www.utexas.edu/world/lecture/) publishes links to websites created by universities and colleges worldwide that are using the Internet to deliver course

FIGURE 3.7
Research-It!

Source:
http://www.itools.com/research-it/

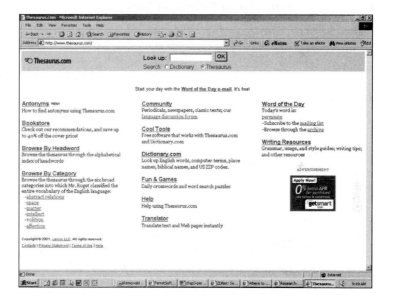

FIGURE 3.8
Thesaurus.com

Source:
http://www.thesaurus.com/

materials in any language. Some courses are delivered entirely over the Internet, while others are designed for students in residence. Many fall somewhere in between, and all can be visited by anyone interested in courses available on the Internet, including course developers and curious students.

Gathering News and Information

Portals

Portals provide a "doorway" to the Internet and enable the user to personalize the information they want presented. This may include local news, international news, stock quotes, weather, sports, and horoscopes. In addition, shopping, communications, search engines, links to useful pages, and other related services are offered on many websites. These services are usually provided for free with the hope that users will make the website their home page (or at least visit it on a regular basis—so as to generate traffic for advertising purposes). The following are some of the major portals on the Internet and make excellent "front-end" resources through which users can obtain and organize personal intelligence.

- Excite (http://live.excite.com/).

- Yahoo! (http://www.myyahoo.com/).

- Bigpond (http://www.bigpond.com/).

- WebWombat (http://www.webwombat.com.au).

- Netscape (http://www.mynetscape.com/).

- Lycos (http://www.lycos.com/).

- MSNBC (http://www.msnbc.com/).

- Walt Disney Internet Group (WDIG) (http://www.go.com/).

Personalized Retrieval Services

A number of companies specialize in personalized information research and retrieval services. Compared with the portals, the depth of coverage is often greater and can be defined with more precision. Individual.com's Personal NewsPage (http://www.individual.com/) purports to be "the world's leading provider of free, individually customized news, information, and services over the Internet."

IntelBrief's (http://www.intelbrief.com/) self-professed goal is to "provide insight into the pressing, urgent issues of today and tomorrow, distilled into brief, cogent overviews." The website provides the researcher with an abundance of articles and newsfeeds (from over 2,000 sources) on a wide range of intelligence topics organized into 200 categories such as:

- Business intelligence.

- Military intelligence.

- Government intelligence.

- Investing intelligence.

- Technology intelligence.

- Regional intelligence.

Market Guard 24/7 (http://www.marketguard247.com/) is a scheduled retrieval service of relevant competitor and Internet news. The Market Guard 24/7 reporting service monitors competitors' websites and the Internet for recent news articles, bulletin postings, press releases, search engine listings, and news wire updates about any given companies, products, and events.

eWatch (http://www.ewatch.com/) is a news service that tracks specific information (primarily business-related) on the Internet, including newsgroups and list servers. It is not cheap and may be more suited to business subscribers; however, it appears to collect high-quality information.

ENews (http://www.enews.com/) is a one-stop source for subscriptions to more than 100,000 magazines, newsletters, and newspapers from more than 400 publishers.

FIGURE 3.9
Example of a CRAYON Personalized Newspaper

Source:
http://www.crayon.net/using/sample/

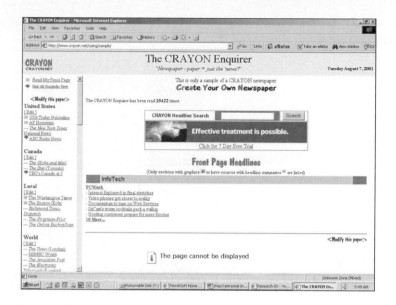

CRAYON (http://www.crayon.net/) was one of the first interactive and information-integrating tools available on the World Wide Web. Its name was derived as an acronym for CReAte Your Own Newspaper, and indeed this is exactly what users can do. Picking from hundreds of options, the website allows users to create a customized Web page that is their own newspaper compiled from almost any major papers and news sources in the world, complete with the user's own title.

CNNFN (http://www.cnnfn.com/) is a financial news network that also provides industry-specific news and information using the resources of U.S. communications company CNN (Cable News Network). The website can be personalized and includes an "On Track" feature that tracks news articles selected and defined by the user.

News Online (http://www.newspapers.com/) provides the user with indexes of and access to tens of thousands of media websites from around the world.

E-Zines

E-zines consist of magazine-like material presented in an electronic format. This format allows articles to be changed or updated at any time—monthly, weekly, daily, or even hourly. The electronic nature of the Internet is ideal for content publishers. Volumes of back issues or other information can be stored easily and cheaply in digital form for easy access by Internet users. A keyword search can usually be undertaken to locate material in this vast store of archived information.

E-Business

Rather than doing all the searching themselves, a user may find that a much easier way to amass personal intelligence is to have it digested for them or, even better yet, automatically e-mailed to them. There are a number of excellent e-business news websites that constantly monitor the Internet for new and interesting developments, websites, and features that could prove to be of personal and/or professional importance. These websites also have e-mail, e-zines, electronic newsletters (e-newsletters), and newsfeed services that can be subscribed to—some for a fee, most for free.

FIGURE 3.10

Internetstats.com

Source:
http://internetstats.com/

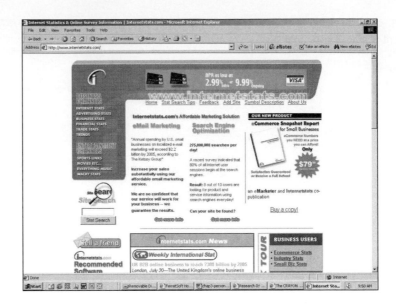

Iconocast (http://www.iconocast.com/) is "a new media company that specializes in news and analysis." For those individuals interested in Internet marketing strategy, Internet marketing research, Internet marketing advice, Internet marketing resources, and/or revolutionary "infotainment" events, a subscription to the weekly Iconocast e-newsletter is recommended.

TheStandard.com (http://www.thestandard.com/) is the newsmagazine of the Internet economy, with news, analysis, commentary, and other features.

If you need to quickly and easily obtain facts or figures regarding Internet, advertising, business, financial, or trade statistics or trends, Internetstats is definitely one website to bookmark. Internetstats.com (http://internetstats.com/) is an excellent one-stop website for business and market information, statistics, trends, and news.

Other comprehensive e-business news and information services include:

- CNET Digital Dispatch (http://www.cnet.com/).

- HotWired (http://hotwired.lycos.com/).

- TechWeb (http://www.techweb.com/).

E-Marketing

The following resources are directly relevant to marketing professionals and provide current updates on Internet marketing, technology, and research:

- Internet Marketing Center (http://www.marketingtips.com/).

- ZDNet (http://www.zdnet.com/).

- Guerrilla Marketing Online (http://www.gmarketing.com/).

- Larry Chase's Web Digest for Marketers (http://wdfm.com/).

- Web Marketing Today (http://www.wilsonweb.com/wmt/).

- Inside 1to1 (http://www.1to1.com/Building/CustomerRelationships/entry.jsp).

- Media Central's Inside.com (http://www.mediacentral.com/).

- Asian Internet Marketing (http://www.aim.apic.net/).

- eMarketing Digest (http://www.webbers.com/emark/).

  Essentially, any marketing e-zine that exists can be located at the following websites:

- Google (http://directory.google.com/Top/Business/Marketing/Internet_Marketing/Resources/Publications/).

- "All the secrets" (http://www.ozemedia.com/articles/index.htm).

- Digital Women (http://www.digital-women.com/ezines.htm/).

Marketing Research Information and Resources

When searching for marketing information on the Internet there are a number of websites that have assembled, sorted, indexed, and hyperlinked a wealth of resources for the convenience of users. Akin to your desktop address book, these metadexes are one-stop compendiums of marketing-related resources.

World Opinion (http://www.worldopinion.com/) proclaims itself "The World's Market Research Website," and provides up-to-date news and comprehensive information on the market research industry. This website offers thousands of marketing research reports and is perhaps the premier website for the marketing research industry.

Aspy P. Palia, professor of marketing, University of Hawaii at Manoa, provides a website with links to international marketing resources at (http://www.cba.hawaii.edu/aspy/aspymktr.htm/). Professor Palia has compiled what is certainly one of the most comprehensive metadexes on marketing on the Internet. Links to scores of marketing information resources and services are divided into numerous categories, for example:

- International marketing associations, journals, and organizations.

- Internet marketing information and resource websites.

FIGURE 3.11
World Opinion

Source:
http://www.worldopinion.com/

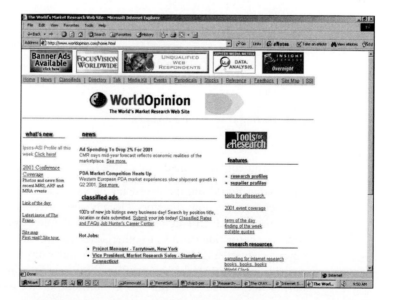

FIGURE 3.12
Aspy P. Palia's Useful
Marketing Websites

Source:
http://www.cba.hawaii.edu/aspy
/aspymktr.htm/

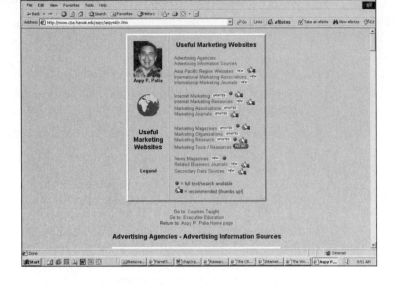

FIGURE 3.13
Advertising World

Source:
http://advertising.utexas.edu/
world/

- Marketing research companies.

- News magazines.

- Government, syndicated, commercial and database sources of information.

Advertising World (http://advertising.utexas.edu/world/) claims to be "the ultimate marketing communications directory." Run by the University of Texas, it is a great resource for marketing and advertising professionals, academics, and students. This website offers an extensive collection of links to other advertising-related websites, covering such diverse topics as advertising design, resources, job opportunities, agencies, and advertising law.

Volition.com's marketing website (http://www.volition.com/market.html/) is essentially a list of lists with links to a multitude of websites, such as advertising, online

FIGURE 3.14

Volition.com

Source:
http://www.volition.com/market
.html

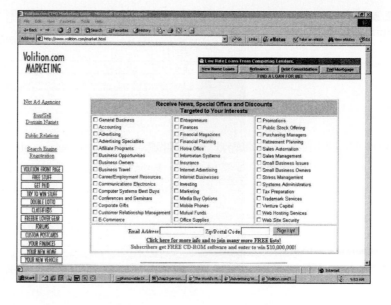

FIGURE 3.15

Tilburg University

Source:
http://marketing.kub.nl/journal1
.htm/

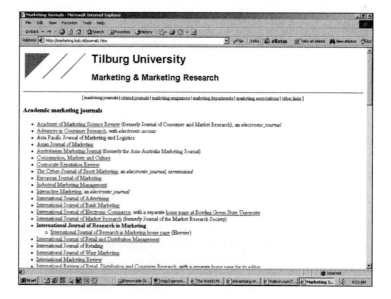

journals, e-mail discussion lists, marketing courses, e-zines, market research, education resources, and company lists.

Tilburg University (http://marketing.kub.nl/journal1.htm/) provides an extremely rich marketing metadex that includes an excellent listing of marketing-oriented journals on the Web.

MouseTracks (http://www.nsns.com/MouseTracks/) has been compiled by Dr. Charles Hofacker of the Florida State University. This website has been tracking marketing-related websites "for the entire history of marketing on the Internet." MouseTracks has lots of useful links to marketing-related websites, grouped into categories such as Hall of Malls, Conference Calls, Syllabits, and the List of Marketing Lists. It presents commentary on some of the more interesting marketing activities and resources on the Internet.

FIGURE 3.16

ResearchInfo.com

Source:
http://www.researchinfo.com/

ResearchInfo.com (http://www.researchinfo.com/) is a valuable source of information on the market research industry that includes the Market Research Roundtable, a discussion forum. This website also has a directory of market research companies, an employment board, a Research Software Archive, a Market Research Library, Legislative Watch, and up-to-the-minute business news and market research company stock quotes.

Quirks Marketing Research Review (http://www.quirks.com/) remains a good source for information on marketing research. In addition to case studies, job postings, and directories of custom research providers, Quirks provides centralized access to over 40,000 research reports that can be purchased for varying fees.

Summary

Personal intelligence involves the gathering, processing, and application of information that is directly relevant to one's personal and professional well-being. An effective personal intelligence system should employ a combination of resources. By applying the methods and utilizing the resources outlined in this chapter, a user will be able to resolve many of their critical info-management problems. For example:

- Marketers can use a personalized news retrieval service to keep up with the latest industry information and trends.

- Bookmark management tools can be utilized to notify users when specified websites are updated, saving people time in checking the websites themselves.

- The complex task of searching for marketing-related information can be simplified by using a metadex.

- By using a portal, a user can personalize a home page to display only the news and information they are specifically interested in.

Your online learning center has a case study on *Personal Intelligence* available now at www.mhhe.com/forrest.

Discussion Questions

1. Why do you think it is important to configure your own personal intelligence system?
2. Name one information management tool you can use to do each of the following: find, download, filter, display, and manage personal intelligence.
3. Identify some ways you can archive information accessed on the Internet.
4. Create your own personal intelligence system. Begin with some of those outlined in this chapter and add more of your own.
5. Review the metadexes listed in this chapter. Which do you believe is the most comprehensive?

Internet Project

Go to CRAYON (http://www.crayon.net/) and create your own electronic newspaper. Design your front page and select which newspapers and features you want. You have close to 1,000 sources from which to choose. This will be an indispensable personal intelligence tool for gathering and managing information from the Internet. When you are finished, demonstrate which features you have chosen and explain why.

Further Reading

MarketResearch.com (2001). *Finding Market Research on the Web*, August, Rockville, Maryland: MarketResearch.com.
Schlein, Alan M. (2000). *Find It Online: The Complete Guide to Online Research*. Tempe, Arizona: Facts on Demand Press.

References

Dictionary.com (http://www.dictionary.com/).
Lynch, Jim (2001). "Build a Better Browser." *Access Magazine*, March 25, pp. 8–10.

Chapter 4

Environmental Intelligence

This chapter examines the nature of **environmental intelligence** as it applies to marketing strategy. Marketing researchers need to maintain constant surveillance for any and all changes in the environment that may impact, favorably or unfavorably, on business conditions. By setting up an online environmental scanning system, the Web-wise researcher can maintain a constant vigil over the vast, information-laden Internet landscape.

Chapter objectives

This chapter aims to:

- Define environmental intelligence.

- Explain the phenomenon of environmental scanning and why it is an essential analysis that should be carried out by every organization.

- Demonstrate the utility of the Internet as a means for gathering environmental intelligence for marketing management.

What Is Environmental Intelligence?

Environmental intelligence is information about critical aspects and events in the macro-environment. The key macro-environmental elements examined include the politico-legal, economic, sociocultural, and technological environments (often characterized by the acronym PEST). Some researchers include the *physical* environment in their monitoring activities as well. This is because chronic and acute weather patterns and related ecological factors such as pollution, product biodegradability, and "environmental-correctness" (being informed about the environment and acting on this information) can and do have a profound impact on brand perceptions and product sales.

The relationship between an organization and the environment is highly interactive and has a direct bearing on an organization's viability. Constant monitoring and analysis of the macro-environment are critical if an organization wants to detect trends and events that

FIGURE 4.1 Macro-Environment Variables

Source: Sesolak, 1996

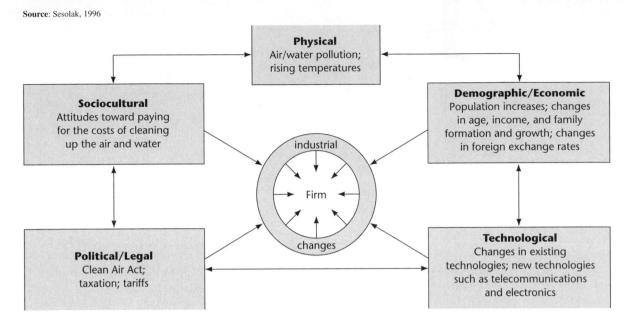

pose marketing threats and/or opportunities to business. Figure 4.1 depicts the interrelationship between a firm and the macro-environment.

In order to discern those trends and events that will affect the performance or survival of the organization either directly or indirectly, environmental intelligence should be undertaken as a formalized and ongoing activity. The following six steps are involved in conducting environmental analysis (Aguilar, 1967).

1. Audit the environmental influences.

2. Assess the nature of the environment.

3. Identify key environmental forces through structural analysis.

4. Identify competitive position.

5. Identify key opportunities and threats.

6. Devise a strategic position.

Defining Environmental Scanning

Environmental scanning may best be viewed as a process wherein information on key environmental variables is gathered, evaluated, and incorporated into everyday decision making and long-term strategic planning. In today's global village, trends, events, and emerging issues from anywhere can, at any time, impact significantly on an organization's ability to meet its immediate mandate or achieve its strategic goals.

Environmental scanning is the acquisition and use of information about events, trends, and relationships in an organization's external environment, the knowledge of which would assist management in planning the organization's future course of action. . . . Environmental scanning includes both looking at information (viewing) and looking for information (searching). It could range from a casual conversation at the lunch table or a chance observation of an angry customer, to a formal market research program or a scenario planning exercise. (Choo, 1995)

Environmental scanning can vary in *scope* as well as *style*. With respect to scope, environmental scanning can take a wide-angle look "at the total environment so as to develop a broad picture, and identify areas that require closer attention. Or, scanning can zoom in on specific areas and analyze them in detail" (Choo, 1995). In addition to adjusting its scope, an organization can vary the style it employs in information collection. Table 4.1 delineates four distinct styles of scanning, originally suggested by Aguilar (1967):

Environmental Scanning on the Internet

All formal environmental scanning systems consist of five generic components:

1. Resources to scan. Traditional sources of environmental information include:

   (*a*) Media. Journals, reports, books, magazines, newsletters, newspapers, TV, radio.

   (*b*) Professional. Meetings, industrial conferences, board meetings.

   (*c*) Personal. Colleagues, friends, employees.

TABLE 4.1
Styles of Environmental Scanning

Style	Definition	Examples
Undirected viewing	Browsing through information with little other purpose than exploration. The sources of information are many and varied. Screening is generally superficial, and most information is quickly and easily dropped from attention.	Flipping through TV channels or pages of a magazine or "surfing" the Internet.
Conditioned viewing	Directed exposure, not involving active search, to a more or less clearly identified area or type of information. It frequently serves to signal a warning that more intensive scanning should be instituted. Conditioned viewing differs from the undirected type principally in that the researcher is sensitive to particular kinds of data and is ready to assess their significance as they are encountered.	Browsing the sections of newspapers, periodicals, or websites that report regularly on topics of interest.
Informal search	A relatively limited and unstructured effort to obtain specific information or information for a specific purpose. It differs from conditioned viewing principally in that the information wanted is actively sought. Informal search can take many forms, ranging from soliciting information to increasing the emphasis on relevant sources, or to acting in a way that will improve the possibility of encountering the desired information.	Keeping an eye on the market to monitor the results of some new product pricing policy or searching the Internet by category and with general keywords.
Formal search	A deliberate effort—usually following a preestablished plan, procedure, or methodology—to secure specific information or information relating to a specific topic.	Systematically gathering information to evaluate a prospective corporate acquisition or searching with exact keywords.

Source: Aguilar, 1967

2. People to scan the resources and identify and extract relevant information.

3. People to assess the organizational implications of the extracted trends and issues.

4. People to analyze and prioritize implications as to their strategic importance.

5. People to conceive and take action on the items of strategic significance.

The Internet impacts all components of the environmental scanning system. First and foremost, the Internet's search engines and intelligent agents are unparalleled in their speed and ability to cull information. Second, with more timely and accurate information, analysts should be better able to track trends and interpret issues, and generally become more adept in responding to market needs and macro-environmental forces. Third, the Internet enables the organization's knowledge network to expand, as more people in the organization tap into external knowledge and as connections are made with relevant expertise and advice outside the organization. Effective use of the Internet increases the timeliness and the relevancy of information used in decision making. Accordingly, the Internet may prove to be the most essential component in a researcher's environmental scanning system.

Macro-Environmental Websites

When constructing an Internet scanning system to monitor changes in the macro-environment, websites should be selected according to a mixed scanning strategy. That is, websites selected should be "high-order," and scan the total environment, as well as "low-order," which is where specific areas are covered in detail. Accordingly, low-order websites will be geographically distinct and/or industry, product class, and brand specific. The following sections define each macro-environmental sector and highlight websites that can be used in monitoring and analysis.

Integrated/Global Information Resource Websites

There are a number of websites that provide the environmental intelligence researcher with a wealth of data on all aspects of the macro-environment. Some websites—such as globalEDGE™, UNESCO, Global Trends 2015, and World Factbook—cover the entire world; others—such as FedStats, J GUIDE, and LANIC—provide comprehensive coverage of macro-environmental variables for the United States, Japan, and Latin America, respectively.

Self-defined as "a global business knowledge web-portal that connects international business professionals worldwide to a wealth of information, insights and learning resources on global business activities," globalEDGE™ (http://globaledge.msu.edu/index.asp/) is produced by Michigan State University and serves as a promotional vehicle for its Internet-mediated certificate and degree programs. The researcher will find that the website provides a plethora of international business links to:

• News and periodicals.

• Specific regional/country data and information.

• Indexes of business resources.

The United Nations Educational, Scientific, and Cultural Organization (UNESCO) can be found at http://www.unesco.org/ and provides information on publications, statistics, UNESCO partners, information services, and current events.

FIGURE 4.2
globalEDGE™

Source:http://globaledge.msu.
edu/ibrd/ ibrd.asp/

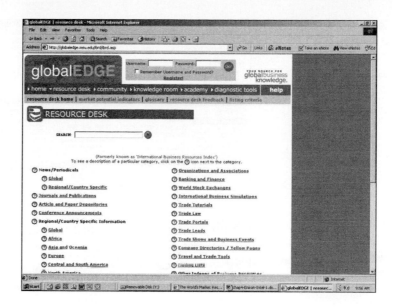

There are numerous government websites from around the world that provide consumer intelligence data. Yahoo! provides a list of several of these services (http://www. yahoo.com/Government/Statistics/).

Global Trends 2015 (http://www.cia.gov/cia/publications/globaltrends2015/) is a report published in December 2000 under the authority of the director of the Central Intelligence Agency (CIA). Global Trends 2015 provides a comprehensive analysis of the future. The report's "purpose is to rise above short-term, tactical considerations and provide a longer-term, strategic perspective. Judgments about demographic and natural resource trends are based primarily on informed extrapolation of existing trends. In contrast, many judgments about science and technology, economic growth, globalization, governance and the nature of conflict represent a distillation of views of experts inside and outside the United States Government."

World Factbook (http://www.odci.gov/cia/publications/factbook/index.html/) makes available information on the geography, demographics, government, and economy of countries, territories, and regions of interest to researchers (for example, Antarctica and the Gaza Strip).

A number of websites provide comprehensive statistics and profiles of consumers' demographic characteristics. The first of these is The Dismal Scientist (http://www.dismal.com/), which provides timely economic information, with comprehensive data and analyses at U.S. metropolitan, state, and national levels. This authoritative website also has data and analyses of global issues, including situations facing Asia, South America, and Europe. Users can rank states and metropolitan areas on more than 100 economic, socioeconomic, and demographic categories.

Online Intelligence Project (http://www.interaccess.com/intelweb/) specializes in international information, especially news and commerce, and provides hundreds of links to databases and info-resources for every region and country in the world.

FedStats (http://www.fedstats.gov/) contains official statistical information, which is available to the general public and is put together by over 100 U.S. federal agencies. Information is sorted by topics listed alphabetically, or by subject area, agencies, keywords, or press releases. According to FedStats, "the statistical information is maintained and updated by federal agencies on their own Web servers." Businesses can use this website to

FIGURE 4.3
The Dismal Scientist

Source:
http://www.dismal.com/

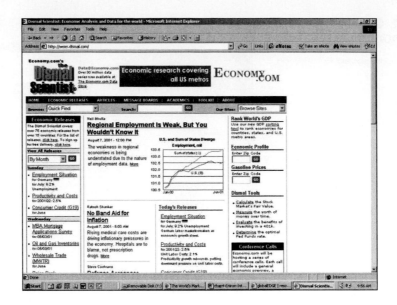

obtain general information on their industry and examine overall trends or acquire information on their target market.

J Guide: Stanford Guide to Japan Information Resources can be found at http://bases.stanford.edu/USATMC/jguide/. Produced by the Stanford University U.S.–Asia Technology Management Center, this website provides a multitude of links to a complete range of information and resources on Japan. The following are some of the topics included at this website:

- Arts and entertainment.

- Business and economy.

- Computers and the Internet.

- Education and academia in Japan.

- History.

- Language and literature.

- Government and politics.

- Law and regulation.

- Society and culture.

- Travel and living in Japan.

- News and media.

LANIC (Latin American Network Information Center) can be found at http://www.lanic.utexas.edu/. This University of Texas website provides an extensive source of information on Latin America and lists itself as the most complete library of Latin American studies on the Internet. There are country and subject directories, and information available includes statistics, trade, newspapers, references, economies, history, and libraries.

The Politico-Legal Environment

The politico-legal environment has a direct and significant effect on marketing. Product and service standards, business practices, packaging, and advertising are all strictly regulated. Marketers must know and obey the law, with no exceptions. Legislation affecting business is increasing in its complexity and is constantly changing. Regulation occurs at all levels of government—federal, state, and local—and can occur within nongovernment agencies such as the Better Business Bureau and professional review boards (for example, the Australian Direct Marketing Association [ADMA] at http://www.adma.com.au/ and the Australian Association of National Advertisers [AANA] at http://www.aana.com.au/public.htm). Public and private consumer interest groups may also monitor an industry's marketing practices and thus influence marketing activities. All of these official, professional, and grassroots regulatory bodies can be monitored through a multitude of websites that cover the gamut of the politico-legal environment. When it comes to finding almost any law at any level in most developed countries, the Internet is at its best.

Legal Information Websites

Administered by the University of Indiana, the World Wide Web Virtual Law Library (http://www.law.indiana.edu/v-lib/) is part of The Virtual Library, which is the oldest catalog on the Web and was started by Tim Berners-Lee, the developer of the World Wide Web itself. This website provides the researcher with a comprehensive set of search tools to retrieve legal documents and also offers a general set of law-related links.

The University of Texas hosts the Law and Politics Internet Guide (http://ccwf.cc.utexas.edu/~rmr513/lpig.html/). This is a most comprehensive website that provides links to:

- Legal portals.
- Legal resources.
- Foreign and international law.
- Legal research.

FIGURE 4.4
World Wide Web Virtual Library

Source:
http://conbio.net/vl/database/

- Law study.

- Foreign/international law journals.

- Treaties.

- Lawyers and law firms.

- Associations.

- Forms.

- Law books and book reviews.

- Law libraries.

- Paralegal legal employment.

- U.S. judicial.

- Government, politics, and policy.

- Criminal justice.

- Tax information.

- Consumer information.

The United States House of Representatives Internet Law Library (http://lectlaw.com/inll/1.htm) contains fully text searchable versions of all the basic documents of U.S. law. It also provides access to thousands of other Internet-based law resources, organized by subject or jurisdiction.

Another comprehensive website is American Law Sources On-line (http://www.law-source.com/also/). In addition to providing resources and reviews of the American legal system, this website features links and resources focusing on the legal systems of Canada and Mexico.

Lexis Nexis has a legal express information service (http://www.michie.com/) that provides links to a wide range of legal websites and resources. For Australian information, the Australia Legal Information Centre (http://www.wwlia.org/as-home.htm/) provides fast access to the latest Australian and international legal, law, court, and legislative information on the Internet.

At the Better Business Bureau website (http://www.bbb.org/) researchers can access the thousands of branches of the Better Business Bureau throughout the world.

FindLaw (http://www.findlaw.com/) claims to be "the highest-trafficked legal website, providing the most comprehensive set of legal resources on the Internet." Indeed, it does provide direct access to the U.S. federal and all 50 states' Case and Code Law. In addition, the website provides legal news, web-search utilities, message boards, and mailing lists.

An excellent guide to websites covering politics is provided by Where to Do Research (http://www.wheretodoresearch.com/). Herein, researchers will find links to international information on political candidates and parties, publications, research and polling centers, democracies, newspapers, reference material, and the like.

The Economic Environment

The **economic environment** is monitored for business cycles, variations in inflation and interest rates, prices, investments, savings, and income and employment levels. The interaction among these variables determines the general economic conditions that in turn directly affect the buying power and spending patterns of consumers (see Table 4.2).

Some indicators of buying power are:

FIGURE 4.5
Australia Legal Information Centre

Source:
http://www.wwlia.org/as-home.htm/

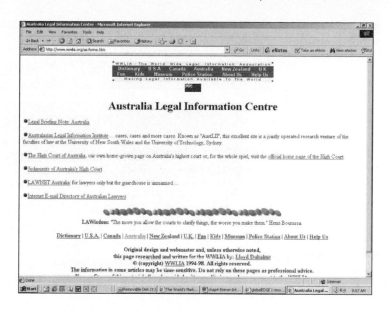

FIGURE 4.6
FindLaw

Source:
http://www.findlaw.com/

- *Effective buying income (EBI).* Income left after paying taxes (similar to disposable income).

- *Buying power index (BPI).* A weighted index consisting of population, effective buying income, and retail sales data.

Total buying power remains contingent on the interrelationship between income and prices, and savings and credit. It has been demonstrated how patterns of expenditure vary with income levels (Kotler, 1998). The following are examples of Internet sources that will assist the researcher in monitoring these key economic variables and statistics.

Economic Information Websites

The Bureau of Labor Statistics is a key resource for information on U.S. household income, employment, and related data.

FIGURE 4.7
Where to Do Research

Source:
http://www.wheretodoresearch.com/

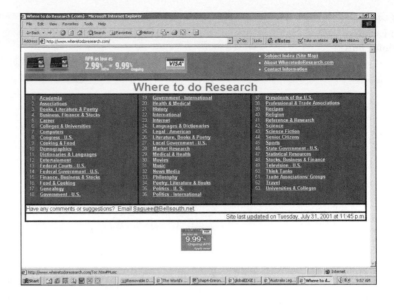

TABLE 4.2
General Economic Conditions

Economic Condition	Characteristics
Prosperity	Low unemployment, high total income, and high buying power
Recession	Rising unemployment, declining total buying power, stifled consumer and business buying
Depression	High unemployment, low total disposable income, lack of consumer confidence in economic recovery

The goal of Dr. Ed Yardeni's Economics Network (http://www.yardeni.com/) is to become the number one source of economic and financial information. This website includes a section dedicated to monitoring and analyzing Alan Greenspan's public statements as well as various links to information such as government statistical and economic data, and stock information. The website can also be viewed in different languages.

The Australian Bureau of Statistics (ABS) (http://www.abs.gov.au/) is Australia's official statistical organization. The ABS provides an extensive range of reports and analytical papers that examine Australia's key economic and social indicators including the latest consumer price index, gross domestic product, unemployment rate, retail trade, average weekly earnings, estimated resident population, and company profits.

Eurostat (http://europa.eu.int/comm/eurostat/) provides a complete database of statistics pertaining to its member countries' economy and finances as well as population, social conditions, industry and trade, transport, and technology.

As was found to be the case with the politico-legal environment, an abundance of websites exist that will provide the market researcher with almost any piece of information desired with respect to macro-economic factors. Indeed, it can be noted that relevant economic data are proffered on additional websites for countries such as Canada, Japan, Taiwan, the United Kingdom (U.K.), Singapore, South Africa, the Philippines, Central and South America, Germany, Mexico, and Italy.

FIGURE 4.8
Bureau of Labor
Statistics

Source: http://stats.bls.gov/

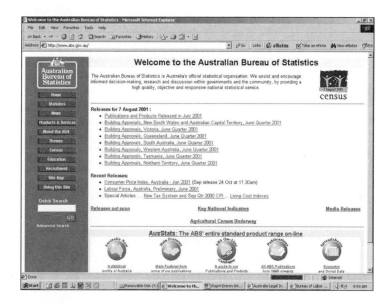

FIGURE 4.9
Australian Bureau of
Statistics

Source: http://www.abs.gov.au/

The Sociocultural Environment

The **sociocultural environment** is an amalgamation of people's attitudes, interests, values, norms, customs, beliefs, aesthetics, and lifestyles. This environment exerts a profound influence on people's perceptions of and preferences for any and every product and service. Indeed, as Kotler et al. (1998) noted, sociocultural values impact people's views of:

- *Themselves.* How they gratify their needs, instant versus delayed gratification, and hedonic consumption.

- *Others.* Degrees of trust, respect, and openness.

- *Organizations.* Institutional loyalty.

- *Society.* "Life-ways," movers and shakers, takers, changers, and the like.

- *Nature.* Environmentalists and those who want/need natural products and ingredients.

- *The universe.* Spiritualists and religion.

A marketing manager must be cognizant of long-term cultural trends, as well as the latest social fads and fashions. Sociocultural change tends to evolve slowly but has far-reaching effects.

> Trends are predictive because they start small, then gather momentum. If you can connect
> the dots between the inception of a trend and the impact it will have on your business, then
> you can fine-tune your product to fit the trend. (Popcorn, 1991)

For the past three decades, a number of social movements have united and gathered continual momentum: civil rights, followed by women's rights, environmentalism, consumer rights, political correctness, and the opposing forces of nationalism and multiculturalism. In association with these movements, consumers also exhibited growing concern with health and nutrition, personal security, and self-indulgence. Once each of these trends evolved, they influenced the nature and scope of products and services desired by consumers.

Within every society, the sociocultural environment will affect different subgroups of people in different ways. Assessing the variation across subgroup segments is often one of the greatest challenges marketing managers will face when planning strategies, especially for international markets. Beyond its effect on specific issues and items, the sociocultural environment influences the entire business climate and general *zeitgeist* ("spirit of the times") of society. The consumer and environmental movements are social forces within the environment, exerting legal, moral, and economic pressures on business. The public's confidence in the economy and their trust in business and government influence sales and legislation, which in turn regulate business practices and marketing strategies.

Tracking social and cultural values is critical if the marketer wants to keep a business or product "on-trend."

> Bear in mind, however, that each trend is merely one fraction of the whole. Don't veer too
> far in any one direction with only one trend or another. To make your product or business on-
> trend, you'll need to understand how the trends work together to define the future. If trends
> seem to contradict each other, it's inevitable. Trends merely reflect the coming consumer
> moods, and consumers are people—full of contradictions. (Popcorn, 1991)

Sociocultural Information Websites

One service listed on the Internet that can be considered for outsourcing the scanning and analysis of the sociocultural environment is Iconoculture (http://iconoculture.com/). As noted on their website, "Iconoculture offers its services through consulting and presentations, a book (*The Future Ain't What It Used to Be*), a bi-monthly newsletter, and as television and radio commentators." *Iconoculture*'s self-professed philosophy is "not only to identify current and emerging trends, but also to decode the consumer values and attitudes driving the trends [and] translate trend information into culturally acute strategic plans, scenario planning, new products, brand positionings and brandnames."

Imagitrends (http://pages.prodigy.net/imagiweb/index.htm/) offers a unique service with their TrendPaks, available for a US$885 subscription fee. They read over 500 journals and publications each month, as well as covering conferences, interviews, and popular books. They then condense the information from these into a TrendPak, which contains several reports and includes an abstract containing background, trends, forecasts, and countertrends.

If a researcher is interested in finding out what Australians think about current political, economic, and social issues, there are the Morgan Polls (http://www.roymorgan.com.au/)

FIGURE 4.10
Iconoculture

Source:
http://iconoculture.com/index2.
html/

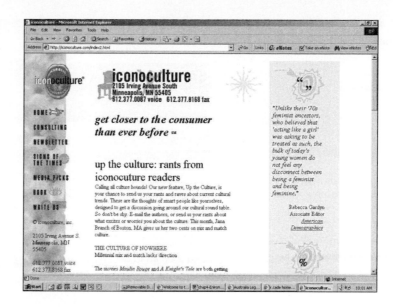

provided by Roy Morgan Research. With new releases published every week, the Morgan Poll tracks a wide range of issues. The website also contains a searchable archive of previous polls.

The National Network of State Polls (NNSP) (http://www.unc.edu/depts/nnsp/archives.htm/) has an archive of hundreds of state-level studies and includes data from the Institute for Research in Social Science (IRSS) Public Opinion Poll Question Database. Researchers can explore the survey databases by keyword search, date, and U.S. state. According to their website, an "index displays the full question text and marginals for each item retrieved. It is useful to researchers who wish to look up marginals for particular items, as well as to those who wish to examine previously asked questions for the purpose of designing their own questionnaires. The index is accessible at no charge to any researcher with an Internet connection."

As described at the IRSS website (http://www.irss.unc.edu/data_archive/):

IRSS maintains one of the oldest and largest archives of machine-readable data in the U.S. It is the exclusive national repository for Louis Harris public opinion data. Other major sources of data include the Roper Center's International Survey Library Association (ISLA), which provides access to most nonproprietary public opinion data; the Inter-university Consortium for Political and Social Research (ICPSR), which stores and distributes data from both individual researchers and most federally funded social science studies. IRSS maintains a variety of public opinion data, which is described below. Many of these data can be accessed on IRSS's Public Opinion Poll Question Database. Researchers interested in public opinion data and research can also subscribe to the Public Opinion Research e-mail list (*por*), maintained by IRSS.

Since 1965, IRSS has operated the Louis Harris Data Center, the national depository for survey data collected by Louis Harris and Associates, Inc. More than 1,000 Harris Polls from as early as 1958 are archived at the Center, containing over 60,000 questions asked of more than 900,000 respondents. Respondent groups range from national cross-section samples to such special populations as Vietnam veterans, Hispanics, teenagers, and the elderly. The surveys also cover a diverse range of topics, such as aging, environmental issues, leisure and the arts, business, foreign affairs, presidential ratings, health care, attitudes toward government, and crime. Many questions have been repeated over time, allowing researchers to track changes in opinions and attitudes. In 1991, IRSS became the national headquarters

FIGURE 4.11
Roy Morgan
Research

Source:
http://www.roymorgan.com.au/

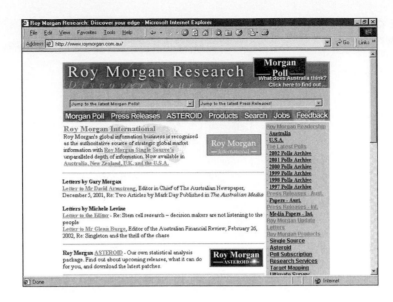

for the National Network of State Polls, a 57-member organization devoted to promoting high-quality public opinion polls of state populations. IRSS has encouraged members of the organization to archive their state poll data at IRSS. The archive contains over 40,000 items from more than 450 studies, contributed by 28 survey organizations.

United Nations Global Trends (http://www0.un.org/cyberschoolbus/globaltrends/index.asp/) is a place where users can find a wide range of global data and regional statistics on population, health, agriculture, economic development, climate and the environment, as well as various social indicators.

United Nations Social Indicators (http://www.un.org/Depts/unsd/social/main2.htm/) includes global indicators of population, youth and elderly populations, housing, education, and literacy. Population Reference Bureau (http://www.prb.org/) provides a wide range of global demographic information on population issues.

The U.S. Census Bureau (http://www.census.gov/) has a News Web page that provides a quick review of new releases by date or subject. The website also includes a search facility and subject listings that can be used to locate the data required. However, many of the files are in PDF format, meaning it is necessary to download the files and view them using the free, downloadable Adobe Acrobat Reader program. Users can also subscribe to a mailing list that keeps the reader informed about the latest news from the U.S. Census Bureau. If the visitor has any inquiries about the subjects or issues covered at the website, there is a list of experts who can be contacted for advice. New users are probably better off starting at the News section, as much of the information contained at the website can be linked to from here.

Asian Demographics (http://www.asiandemographics.com/) offers detailed information about the demographic and socioeconomic trends of 12 Asian countries. The company also provides demographic profiles, demographic forecasts, and household income models of each country for a fee. For those interested in trading in Asian markets, this website is a great resource.

As an extension of the magazine *American Demographics* this website of the same name (http://www.inside.com/default.asp?entity=AmericanDemo/) is an excellent source of research reports on and analysis of key demographic segments, patterns, and trends.

FIGURE 4.12
Population Reference
Bureau

Source: http://www.prb.org/

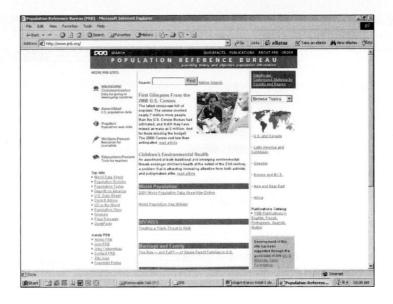

Other resources monitoring what consumers think are:

- Gallup (http://www.gallup.com/).

- Roper Starch Worldwide (http://www.roper.com/).

- The Roper Center for Public Opinion Research (http://www.ropercenter.uconn.edu/).

- Yankelovich (http://www.yankelovich.com/).

- The Australian Bureau of Statistics (http://www.abs.gov.au/).

The Technological Environment

The **technological environment** is not only the most dynamic force shaping human destiny (Kotler et al., 1998) but also the most potent force shaping marketing research and strategy. Technological innovations in product development, manufacturing, and marketing make new products available every day and other products obsolete overnight.

> If there's one critical component in your success tomorrow, it's how you think about the future today: Because of recent technological advances, the pace of change will accelerate astronomically. Don't do what many sales and marketing professionals do—wait until their competition outstrips them before they admit they need to make a change, too—instead, use the forces that are driving permanent change to your competitive advantage. (Burrus, 1998)

Technological Information Websites

For the researcher who wants/needs to keep track of the latest developments in any domain of technology, patent information available through the United States Patent and Trademark Office is a good source of intelligence.

Technology Review, Inc. (http://techreview.com/) is a Massachusetts Institute of Technology (MIT) enterprise that promotes the understanding of emerging technology and its impact on the world. The centerpiece of the company is *Technology Review*, which MIT considers to be a magazine of innovation. The purpose of this magazine is to help an expanding community better grasp how new technologies are shaping the world. The editors

FIGURE 4.13
**United States Patent
and Trademark
Office**

Source: http://www.uspto.gov/

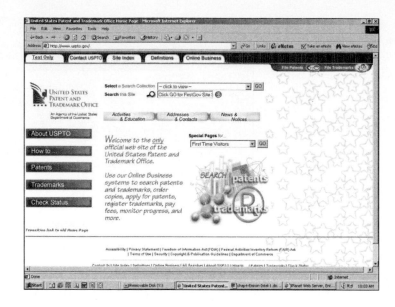

at *Technology Review* believe that in the foreseeable future three areas of emerging technology will be the most significant: information technology, biotechnology, and nanotechnology (the creation of tools and devices on the very smallest scale—the scale of atoms and molecules). It is these three broad areas that are at the heart of *Technology Review*'s mission.

Science, Technology, and Innovation Systems Policy Information Map (STIMAP) (http://STIMAP.matrixlinks.ca/) is a treasure trove of information on technology. The researcher can use the STIMAP search engine to locate links relating to technology in specific countries and keyword search on its index of leading science, technology, and innovation policy websites. Herein, the user can find:

- Major policy documents.

- Government departments and science, technology, and innovation policy advisory bodies.

- Scientific academies and associations.

- Policy research and teaching institutions.

- Science and technology institutions and networks.

- Science and technology-related business organizations.

- The International Science System.

- Public awareness of science, science museums, and the like.

Science and Technical Information Network (STN Easy) (http://stneasy.cas.org/) is a fee-based service that has scientific and patent information amassed in 200 databases representing virtually every industry.

Often some of the best marketing research resources can be found in the hundreds of university courses and subjects that are available online. With respect to tracking technological trends and evaluating each trend's impact on marketing, an excellent resource is Duke University Professor John M. McCann's CyberTrends (http://www.duke.edu/~mccann/cyb-quot.htm/). Professor McCann has identified dozens of trends, termed

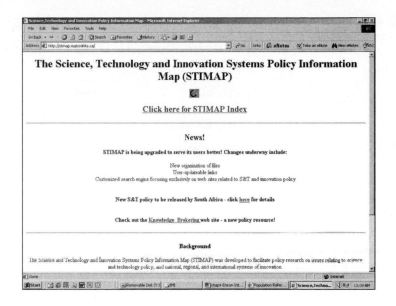

FIGURE 4.14
Science, Technology, and Innovation Systems Policy Information Map (STIMAP)

Source:
http://STIMAP.matrixlinks.ca/

"CyberTrends," which he has classified into several broad classes (technologies, digital dawn, the way we live, the way we work, media, and marketing) and then into trends or topics within each class.

The Physical Environment

Biogenetically altered foods, the environmental impact of packaging, increased pollution levels, and energy shortages have for the past two decades significantly impacted on consumers' attitudes and lifestyles. Indeed, an entirely new branch of marketing known as "green marketing" has manifested itself in response to consumers' concerns for these and other environmental issues. Thus, for the "environmentally correct" marketer environmental intelligence would necessarily include information on the **physical environment**. Some of the best and most comprehensive resources on the environment include the following.

Physical Information Websites

Global Environment Business (http://www.tomorrow-web.com/) has an electronic edition called *Tomorrow* with:

• *News and Trends.* The latest developments in the global environment business.

• *Sector Surveillance.* Industry sustainability outlooks and corporate environmental reports.

• *Tomorrow's Agenda.* An events calendar of upcoming environment conferences.

• *Tomorrow's Network.* A directory of corporate environmental managers, green business networks, and organizations.

See also:

• People & the Planet (http://www.peopleandplanet.net/).

• International Homepage of Greenpeace (http://www.greenpeace.org/index.shtml/).

• Overview of the Environmental Movement in Europe (http://www.eeb.org/).

FIGURE 4.15
Professor John M.
McCann's
CyberTrends

Source:
http://www.duke.edu/~mccann/
cyb-quot.htm/

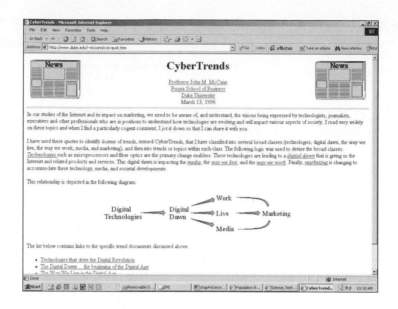

FIGURE 4.16
Tomorrow by Global
Environment
Business

Source: http://www.tomorrow-
web.com/

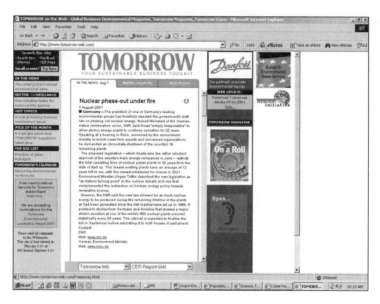

Summary

Marketing researchers need to constantly monitor the macro-environment for any and all changes that may impact on business conditions. Environmental intelligence is information about changing macro-environmental variables that are incorporated into an organization's marketing strategy. The macro-environment is composed of politico-legal, economic, sociocultural, technological, and physical sectors.

Environmental scanning may be best viewed as a process wherein information on key macro-environmental variables is gathered, evaluated, and incorporated into everyday decision making and long-term strategic planning. Scanning the environment is vital for every business as it can determine the difference between simply surviving and thriving. Environmental scanning gives organizations an edge over its competitors in a complex and rapidly changing business climate. Environmental scanning can vary in *scope* as well as *style*. In scope, environmental scanning can be high or low level. In style, environmental scanning can range from undirected to conditional, and from informal to formal.

Your online learning center has a case study on *Environmental Intelligence* available now at www.mhhe.com/forrest.

Discussion Questions

1. Define environmental intelligence.
2. Explain the process of environmental scanning.
3. What areas of an organization's overall business domain should be scanned?
4. What types of decisions depend on the organization's scanning activities?
5. How has the Internet impacted environmental scanning?

Internet Project

Select one particular product class or specific industry and conduct an environmental scan of the macro-environment using the Internet. Prepare an executive summary of your findings and conclude with any immediate, short-term (less than five years), and long-term (greater than five years) marketing strategy recommendations.

Further Reading

Halliman, Charles (2001). *Business Intelligence Using Smart Techniques: Environmental Scanning Using Text Mining and Competitor Analysis Using Scenarios and Manual Simulation*. Houston, Texas: Information Uncover.

References

Aguilar, F. (1967). *Scanning the Business Environment*. New York: MacMillan.

Burrus, D. (1998). "Use Technology to Outpace Your Competition." Cited from Burrus Research Associates, Inc. (http://www.speaking.com/articles/articles,b/burrusarticle2. html/).

Choo, Chun Wei (1995). "Information Management for the Intelligent Organization: The Art of Scanning the Environment." *ASIS Monograph Series*. Medford, New Jersey: Information Today/Learned Information (http://choo.fis.utoronto.ca/FIS/IMIO/IMIO4. html/).

Kotler, P., Armstrong, G., Brown, L., & Adam, S. (1998). *Marketing*. Sydney: Prentice Hall.

Morrison, James L. "Establishing an Environmental Scanning Process." Edinboro University (http://horizon.unc.edu/projects/seminars/Edinboro/page13.asp/).

Morrison, James L., & Held, William G. (1989). "Developing Environmental Scanning/Forecasting Systems to Augment Community College Planning." *VCCA Journal*, Spring/Summer, Vol. 4, No. 1, pp. 12–20 (http://www.br.cc.va.us/vcca/mor.html/).

Popcorn, F. (1991). *The Popcorn Report: Faith Popcorn on the Future of Your Company, Your World, Your Life*. New York: Harper Business (http://www.faithpopcorn.com/).

Sesolak, S. (1997). Subject outline chapter of *Introduction of Marketing* online (http://www.waukesha.tec.wi.us/busocc/market/)

Stanton, W., Miller, K., & Layton, R. (2000). *Fundamentals of Marketing*. Sydney: McGraw-Hill.

Chapter **5**

Consumer Intelligence

Knowing who your customers are and what, why, when, and where they consume your product or service is essential for every marketer. Obtaining consumer intelligence can help companies better understand and anticipate the behavior of consumers and thus enable them to formulate the most effective marketing mix. Formulating the right marketing mix mandates that researchers constantly monitor consumers' perceptions, preferences, purchases, and satisfaction.

Getting to know a customer has become increasingly important in an age where the consumer's every move can be closely monitored. In order to gain a competitive advantage, many companies are now committed to building long-term relationships with their clientele. Indeed, some scholars argue that **one-to-one marketing**—an advanced form of relationship marketing with an emphasis on customization—is a key strategy that can set an organization apart from its competitors (Peppers & Rogers, 1997).

How the Internet can provide the information a company needs to build its consumer intelligence quotient is the focus of this chapter.

Chapter objectives

This chapter aims to:

- Provide an understanding of the importance of consumer intelligence in the global economy.

- Develop an appreciation of how the Internet has created a greater need and opportunity for consumer intelligence.

- Give an insight into why the Internet and associated interactive technologies are powerful tools in gaining information about consumers.

- Explore the underlying principles of consumer research.

- Develop the ability to conduct consumer research using the Internet.

What Is Consumer Intelligence?

Consumer intelligence is the analysis followed by the synthesis of information on consumer tastes, needs, desires, preferences, purchases, attitudes, interests, opinions, and product and service consumption patterns. Consumer intelligence must be a central and on-going endeavor. In keeping with the tenets of "total quality management," consumer intelligence should be considered a responsibility of all employees. Nonetheless, it remains incumbent on the marketing manager to analyze and apply the gleanings of the aggregated data. Higher levels of consumer intelligence should equate to more effective marketing strategies and higher levels of sales and consumer satisfaction.

Consumer Intelligence and the Internet

As predicted by Anselmi (1997), market research on customer satisfaction and customer choice processes has increased in the past few years. One of the key tools that have been used to conduct this research is the Internet, which has given researchers the opportunity to access more information about consumers and with greater accuracy than ever before.

The Internet (and the array of new technologies that accompany it, such as integrated databases and customized production capacity) presents marketers with significant opportunities. It provides researchers with the ability to track the motivations and movements of consumers on an ongoing and real-time basis. Accordingly, computerized interactions enable organizations to learn more about their customers and to serve them better than ever before. As a consumer intelligence gathering tool, the Internet is a boon to marketing professionals.

Moreover, the emergence of the Internet has precipitated a power shift from vendors to buyers. Buyers now have the potential for exercising more control over the purchasing process. This is due to the increased information available to the consumer via the Internet. The global nature of the Internet, which enables companies from around the world to compete directly with each other, has compounded this effect. Such a rapidly changing business environment, fraught with new threats and increased competition, demands that companies know all they possibly can about their customers' changing desires and perceptions. Today, the key to success is as much in retaining customers as in obtaining them.

As depicted in Figure 5.1, the Internet has given rise to the popular new concept of one-to-one marketing, which stems from increased competition and customer empowerment and the consequent need for better customer retention that translates into long-term survival for companies.

The emergence of Internet marketing is an example of how many organizations have capitalized on a technological trend to better service their customers. The Internet now constitutes an integral component of most firms' planning, research, forecasting, scanning, operations, and distribution. The Internet gives market researchers rapid access to consumer intelligence data from all over the world. Numerous services exist that offer a wide range of information about consumers. On the Internet, users can find business reports, trade journals, government websites, databases, census data, and consumer surveys. Additional resources are available that measure consumer usage of products and/or media. Some of these services are free, but many will charge fees depending on the amount and type of information required. However, purchasing secondary data is often faster and less expensive than collecting primary data. The websites in this chapter are some of the more informative and widely used services available.

Internet Resources Related to the Cornerstones of Consumer Research

Kotler (1994) delineated the seven cornerstones of consumer research, which have come to be referred to as the Seven Os:

FIGURE 5.1
The Dynamics of
Internet Marketing

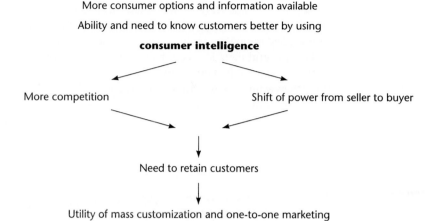

1. *Occupations.* What constitutes the markets?

2. *Objects.* What does the market buy?

3. *Objectives.* Why does the market buy?

4. *Organizations.* Who participates in the buying?

5. *Operations.* How does the market buy?

6. *Occasions.* When does the market buy?

7. *Outlets.* Where does the market buy?

This chapter will utilize this scheme to categorize the variety of websites available for accessing and acquiring intelligence on consumers.

Occupations—What Constitutes the Markets?

> In any market, companies need to know who are the potential consumers of their products. Are they predominantly teenagers or the aged? Are they females or males? Do they have high or low income? Such demographic issues need to be analyzed by marketers. (Kotler, 1994)

Information on consumer demographics is available for virtually every country, state, and city in the world. The following are the most comprehensive websites providing the market researcher with international indices.

Researchers will find InfoNation (http://www.cyberschoolbus.un.org/infonation/info.asp) a useful website where they can readily compare and contrast statistical data on all the member states of the United Nations.

United Nations Global Statistics (http://www.un.org/Depts/unsd/global.htm/) provides a detailed description of the international statistical services in the United Nations publication *Directory of International Statistics*. Countries have many sources of statistics such as central statistical offices, ministries, and national banks. A listing of national statistical offices—and their general statistics, publications, and websites—is also given at the UN Statistics Division's website (http://www.un.org/Depts/unsd/).

United Nations Global Trends (http://www0.un.org/cyberschoolbus/globaltrends/index.asp/) allows access to a wide range of global data and regional statistics on population, health, agriculture, economic development, climate and the environment, and various social indicators. United Nations Social Indicators (http://www.un.org/Depts/unsd/social/main2.htm/) includes indicators of population, housing, education, and literacy.

World Factbook (http://www.odci.gov/cia/publications/factbook/index.html/) provides information on the geography, demographics, government, and economy of countries, territories, and regions of interest (for example, Antarctica and the Gaza Strip).

Other useful metadexes on demographics, psychographics, and geographics follow, including Iowa State University's Greenlee School of Journalism and Communication (http://www.jlmc.iastate.edu/facilities/reading/2research/2demog.html/), which provides a short but useful delineation of links to websites offering demographic, psychographic, and geographic data.

FIGURE 5.2
InfoNation

Source:
http://www.cyberschoolbus.un.org/infonation/info.asp

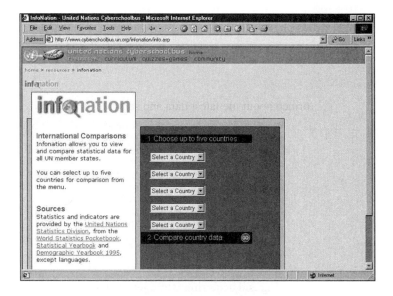

FIGURE 5.3
Abbott Wool's Market Segment Resources

Source: http://www.awool.com/

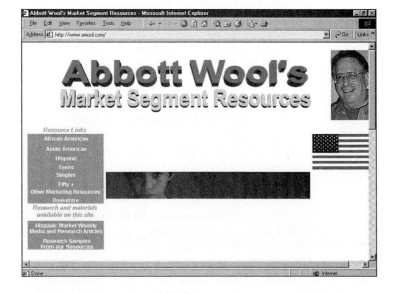

Abbott Wool's Market Segment Resource Locator (http://www.awool.com/) provides a wide range of links to market segmentation resources on the Internet focusing on groups such as African Americans, Asian Americans, Hispanics, fifty-plus, teenagers, and singles.

The U.S. Census Bureau (http://www.census.gov/) has a "News" page that provides a quick review of news releases by date or subject. The website includes a search facility and subject listings that can be used to locate the data desired. However, as many of the files are in PDF format, it is necessary to download them and use the free program Adobe Acrobat Reader to view them. Users can also subscribe to a mailing list that keeps the reader informed about the latest news from the U.S. Census Bureau. If the visitor has any inquiries about the subjects or issues covered at the website, there is a list of experts who can be contacted for advice. New users are probably better off starting at the News section as it contains links to much of the other information found at the website.

USA Data (http://www.usadata.com/) provides a wide range of market-specific information on topics that include consumer demographics, Internet usage, shopping, lifestyle issues, transportation, and health. There is a Free Data section that gives users a general overview of the sort of information available from USA Data. However, full access to all USA Data information requires a subscription fee. Alternatively, payments can be made for access to individual reports. The company also offers a mailing list to keep subscribers informed about the latest data and services available.

Asian Demographics (http://www.asiandemographics.com/) offers detailed information about the demographic and socioeconomic trends of 12 Asian countries. The company also provides demographic profiles, demographic forecasts, and household income models of each country for a fee. For those interested in trading in Asian markets, this website is a great resource.

The Australian Bureau of Statistics (ABS) (http://www.abs.gov.au/) provides national, state, area, or household specific details on the Australian population with regard to consumer expenditure and demographics. Much of the information is based on census data, and there are usually fees involved for accessing it.

FIGURE 5.4
U.S. Census Bureau

Source: http://www.census.gov/

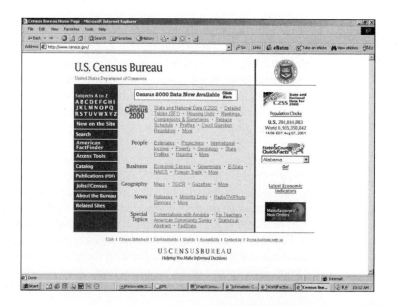

FIGURE 5.5

Asian Demographics

Source:
http://www.asiandemographics.
com/

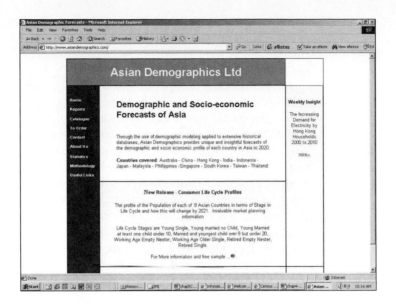

Geo-Demographic Segmentation Tools

Geo-demographic segmentation systems combine demographic descriptors with geographic coordinates. Geo-demographic analysis groups consumers according to various sets of common characteristics such as income, education, family, employment, and postal code criteria. These groupings are then classified as "neighborhood" lifestyle clusters and are often embellished by overlaying consumer buying and media consumption habits. Some of the most prominent among the geo-demographic research services are discussed below.

ESRI Business Information Solutions (http://www.esribis.com/) produces the ACORN segmentation system. This website provides an explanation of ACORN, as well as some free sample data, such as a snapshot of the dominant profile type in any U.S. town when a user enters a particular zip code. Population figures are available for the zip codes, as are percentages for race and sex. Data on businesses, lifestyles, consumer spending, purchase potential, shopping centers, traffic volumes, and crime statistics are available in a variety of formats including hard copy and Internet reports, maps, electronic media, software, books, and lists. There is also an Ask the Expert section that provides basic information about demographics, trade areas, and research.

Claritas (http://www.claritas.com/) claims to provide the latest and best data, systems, and precision marketing solutions available. It offers a wide range of segmentation tools that marketers can use to guide their marketing programs. Termed "precision marketing," Claritas's data collection and connection tools aim to integrate demographics, specialized data, customer data, and geography, mapping, and marketing experience to help precisely define, analyze, understand, and target consumer markets. Their segmentation tools include PRIZM, Claritas Dimensions, and P$YCLE, all of which combine detailed demographics with product, media, and lifestyle preferences to create portraits of a firm's targets. These data can assist marketers to segment and locate target groups, plan media buys, select direct mail lists, map product usage versus potential, and evaluate website locations and trade areas.

PRIZM, for example, is a market segmentation system that places every U.S. neighborhood into one of 62 clusters defined on the basis of demographics, psychographics, and behavior. This website provides information about geo-demographic segmentation techniques and lets researchers use the PRIZM Zip Code Look-Up Program to find information about

FIGURE 5.6
ESRI Business
Information Solutions

Source:
http://www.esribis.com/

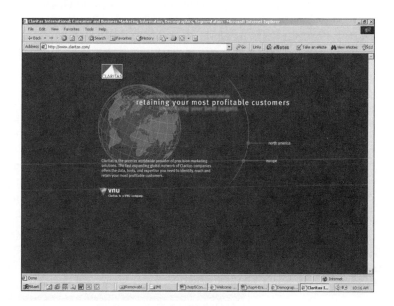

FIGURE 5.7
Claritas

Source:
http://www.claritas.com/

the lifestyle behaviors and purchasing preferences in any zip code in the United States (requires free registration).

MasterCard-TDS Shopper Clusters (http://www.mastercard.com/au/about/press/990218b.html) is the first segmentation system based on a unique model linking actual shopping behavior with consumer demographics, lifestyle preferences, and media habits. Created by Transactional Data Solutions, the TDS Shopper Clusters system merges data from nearly 650,000 MasterCard customers with 30,000 person-lifestyle surveys conducted by Simmons (a major syndicated marketing data company) to create a powerful tool for understanding consumers.

The Shopper Clusters system features 34 clusters across 10 buyer groups based on an analysis of nearly 2.7 million MasterCard transactions. The clusters are classified according to cardholders' store preferences, household incomes, and levels of urbanization (whether they live in cities, suburbs, small towns, or rural areas). The buyer groupings, in turn, are formed from clusters that have similar income levels, buying behaviors, geographic concentrations, and retail category preferences. The clusters and groups are then organized along a descending hierarchy of spending power that is grounded chiefly in measures of household income, transaction amounts, and frequency of purchases.

Psychographic Segmentation

SRI Consulting Business Intelligence's Values and Lifestyles (VALS™) program (http://future.sri.com/vals/) provides member companies with "a powerful psychographic segmentation system that can improve . . . profitability." This group offers four types of VALS™ information packages: VALS™ (Understanding American Consumers), Geo-VALS™ (Extending the Power of VALS™), CAT (Consumer Acceptance of Technology), and Japan-VALS™ (Specific to the Japanese Consumer). Additionally, this website has a link to a VALS™ survey that can be completed online.

In addition to VALS™, SRI offers a number of other information services. SRI Consulting Business Intelligence's (http://future.sri.com/) motto is "Bring the Future into Focus." Their website provides various types of consumer intelligence through links to its different group-products, including the following:

The Business Intelligence Program (B.I.P.) group provides research on new markets. "Using a framework of seven Defining Forces," it identifies "how organizations can profit from emerging opportunities created by change." The Consumer Financial Decisions (C.F.D.) group provides financial services companies with consumer information through MacroMonitor Marketing Reports.

The Explorer group provides "informed analysis of and marketing information about 40 emerging technology areas." The Digital Futures (D.F.) group helps "businesses understand how customers and competitors will respond to new products and services in the digital market place." This group publishes articles based on Content and Applications, Networks and Services, and End-User Devices. Articles such as "DVD-Video: Sunset for VHS Movies" give information concerning the DVD adoption forecasts and "explore DVDs competitive and complementary role in the markets for movie rental video-game machines, VCRs, and PVRs."

FIGURE 5.8
SRI's Values and
Lifestyles (VALS™)

Source:
http://future.sri.com/vals/

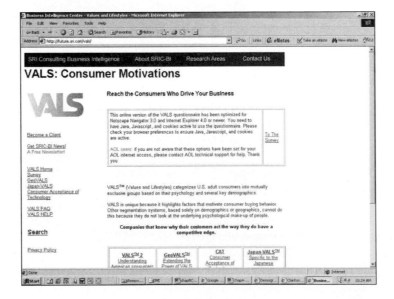

Technographic Segmentation

Traditional consumer research largely focused on demographic and psychographic data collection. While demographics and psychographics are still important components of market research, there is a need for marketers to combine this type of information with measurements of individual ownership and use of interactive technologies (Forrest, Kinney & Chamberlain 1996). The pivotal influence of technology on consumers' purchase behavior in the information age demands that additional information about consumers be obtained, particularly concerning the centrality of technology in their lives. Segmentation on the basis of this type of information is known as consumer **technographics** (Forrest, 1985) and refers to segmentation based on consumers' motivations, usage patterns, and attitudes toward technology (Potter et al., 1988).

For an example of technographics in action, visit the Forrester Research website (http://www.forrester.com/), which provides a series of reports on market trends with special focus on the impact of emerging technology on consumers, business, and society. Forrester aims to explain how technology will impact business and offers guidance on how companies can take advantage of it. As a registered guest, the user can access sample reports and read excerpts of publications from all of Forrester's research services. There are also several insightful publications and briefs available for free. Users can search the Forrester database by year, author, company, product, technology, or even specify a topic of interest. Full access to Forrester's resources is, however, subscription-based.

Objectives—Why Does the Market Buy?

It is especially important for marketers to be familiar with trends as they usually represent windows of opportunity for product and market development. By understanding trends within the marketplace, companies can modify their marketing mix to adapt to the needs and wants of their target markets. (Kotler, 1994)

Marketing researchers and managers must constantly monitor the environment for changing and evolving consumer tastes and desires. Again, the Internet offers a wide range of websites that have consumer trends data, some of the more robust of which are listed below.

Visitors to the Consumer Trends Institute (http://www.trendsinstitute.com/) will find an ongoing series of consumer reports available for purchase, as well as a variety of related

FIGURE 5.9
Forrester Research Technographic Segmentation Model

Source: Forrester Research, Inc. (http://www.forrest.com/jump/tech01.htm/)

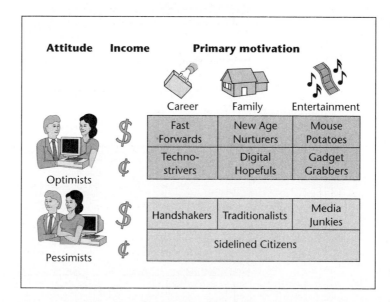

features that provide information on consumer trends, preferences, and typologies. For example, the Trends link provides information on the Consumer Trends Institute's prediction for the "Top Trends for 2002" as well as information about various generations of consumers with "Understanding Consumers" (focusing on baby boomers and generations X and Y). "Brain Snacks" provides insights into what peers and competitors are saying and the newest lingo from the streets to the boardroom, while the "Innernet" provides the inner thoughts, behaviors, opinions, and values of consumers.

As discussed in Chapter 4, Faith Popcorn views trends as:

> . . . merely one fraction of the whole. Don't veer too far in any one direction with only one trend or another. To make your product or business on-trend, you'll need to understand how the trends work together to define the future. If trends seem to contradict each other, it's inevitable. Trends merely reflect the coming consumer moods, and consumers are people—full of contradictions. (Popcorn, 1991)

Faith Popcorn (http://www.faithpopcorn.com/)—best-selling author of *Clicking*, *The Popcorn Report* and *EVEolution*—is the founder of BrainReserve, the futurist marketing consultancy established in 1974. Recognized as America's foremost trend expert, she has identified such sweeping societal concepts as "Cocooning," "Cashing Out," "Anchoring" and "Pleasure Revenge." As key strategist for BrainReserve, Faith Popcorn applies her insight regarding cultural and business trends to help BrainReserve clients reposition established brands or companies, develop new products, and define areas of new business opportunity.

Electronic Consumer Evaluations of Products and Services

One unique development due to the Internet is the emergence of consumer sound-off websites, which allow consumers to register their opinions and experiences with any given product or service. Accordingly, these websites serve as an invaluable resource for researchers interested in why some products are more popular and are perceived as better than others.

ePublicEye (http://www.epubliceye.com.sg/) touts itself as an independent third party, allowing consumers to rate e-business for reliability, privacy, and customer satisfaction. Through a "seal and monitoring" feature of its Open Customer Satisfaction Reporting Sys-

FIGURE 5.10
Consumer Trends Institute

Source:
http://www.trendsinstitute.com/

FIGURE 5.11
Faith Popcorn

Source:
http://www.faithpopcorn.com/
trends/trends.htm/

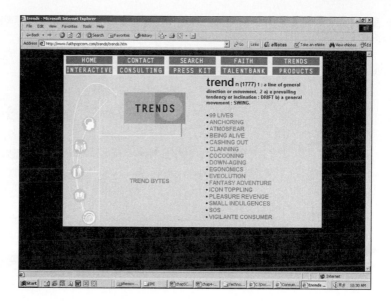

tem, consumers can "identify companies that are reliable and committed to customer satisfaction." ePublicEye then uses this information to provide a service to merchants that allows them to better understand their customers' needs. This website enables an indirect yet powerful dialogue between consumer and merchant. ePublicEye feels less like a business and more like a natural, intermediate step within the communication process.

Service Intelligence (http://www.serviceintelligence.com/) has an area devoted to customer stories of unpleasant experiences with airlines, banks, restaurants, and other service businesses. However, "hero" stories are also included.

Planet Feedback (http://biz.planetfeedback.com/biz/) holds itself out to be the public venue through which consumers can convey their feelings on how they have been treated by both large and small companies. Visitors are invited to compliment or complain, and many examples are posted. There are various categories under which visitors can lodge their comments—after they have registered and provided their demographic profile.

Beyond these sound-off websites, the American Customer Satisfaction Index (ACSI) is the premiere national economic indicator of customer satisfaction with the quality of goods and services available to household consumers in the United States. As delineated at their website, the American Consumer Satisfaction Index (http://www.bus.umich.edu/research/nqrc/acsi.html/):

> . . . is produced through a partnership among the University of Michigan Business School, the American Society for Quality, and the CFI Group. The University of Michigan Business School's National Quality Research Center, which developed the methodology used, compiles [and] analyzes the ACSI data. Each quarter, scores for one or two sectors of the U.S. economy are updated. Quarterly results include scores for individual firms, industries, economic sectors and the U.S. economy as a whole.

Objects, Occasions, Outlets—What, When and Where Does the Market Buy?

It is important to know where consumers prefer to purchase certain products. Is there a trend toward using a particular type of product? Will the market accept new products or changes to

FIGURE 5.12
Planet Feedback

Source:
http://biz.planetfeedback.com/
biz/

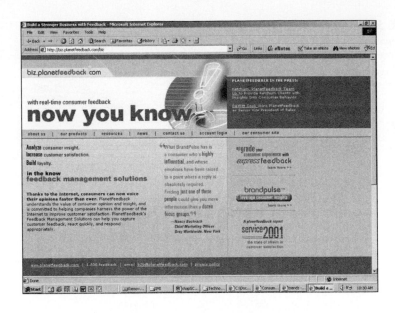

FIGURE 5.13
**American Consumer
Satisfaction Index**

Source:
http://www.bus.umich.edu/
research/nqrc/acsi.html/

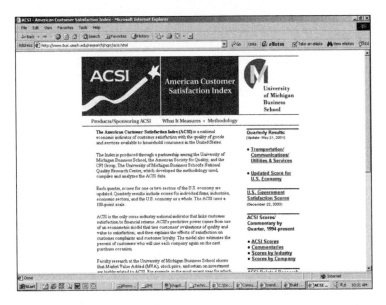

existing products? . . . Many products are needed or only available on a seasonal basis. . . .
Alternatively, there may be a sudden surge of demand for a particular type of product
stimulated by social influences. Hence, marketers must be quick to identify trends,
occasions, fads and other patterns of fluctuating demand. (Kotler, 1994)

Market researchers who desire to track consumer shopping habits and preferences will
find that all the major market research companies and syndicated data services that supply
this information can be accessed through the Internet. Among these are the following:

With more than 9,000 clients in over 100 countries, ACNielsen (http://www.
acnielsen.com/) is one of the world's leading market research companies. At the ACNielsen
website, researchers have access to information on the lifestyle, culture, politics, infrastructure, and economy of over 90 countries. As listed on their website, ACNielsen's research services include:

- *Retail measurement.* Continuous tracking of consumer purchases at the point of sale through scanning technology and in-store audits. Clients receive detailed information on actual purchases, market shares, distribution, pricing, and merchandising and promotional activities; this information is available in more than 80 countries.

- *Consumer panel services.* Detailed information on actual purchases made by household members, as well as their retail shopping patterns and demographic profiles. The service covers 126,000 households in 18 countries.

- *Customized research services.* Quantitative and qualitative studies that deliver information and insights into consumer attitudes and purchasing behavior. Other studies measure customer satisfaction, brand awareness, and advertising effectiveness. Simulated test-marketing services are used to launch new products or reposition existing brands. This service is available in more than 60 countries.

- *Media measurement services.* Information on international television and radio audience ratings, as well as advertising expenditure and print readership measurement. This information serves as the essential currency for negotiating advertising placement and rates. TV ratings are available in 18 countries, radio ratings in 12 markets, and advertising expenditure measurement in 31 markets.

Information Resources, Inc. (IRI) (http://www.infores.com/) considers itself to be a leading sales and marketing research partner in the expanding global consumer goods industry. Its aim is to provide clients with consumer insight and market intelligence. IRI's international data services now cover over 20 countries. They also offer InfoScan®, a store tracking service that provides firms with data available on electronic point-of-sale purchases of thousands of consumer brands sold all over the world. IRI also offers consumer behavior tracking through a proprietary panel of consumers in the United States and through an alliance with Europanel®, the leading European panel operator.

Market Opinion and Research International (MORI) (http://www.mori.com/) is the largest independently owned market research company in Great Britain, with 19 offices in 13 countries.

Roy Morgan Research (http://www.roymorgan.com.au/) specializes in researching and reporting on Australian consumption patterns. The company also provides updated polls

FIGURE 5.14
ACNielsen

Source:
http://www.acnielsen.com/

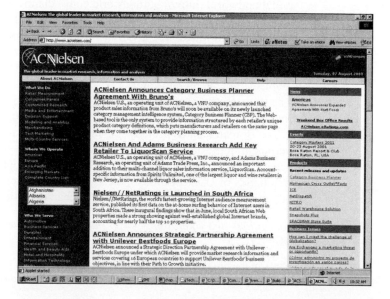

FIGURE 5.15
Information
Resources, Inc.

Source:
http://www.infores.com/

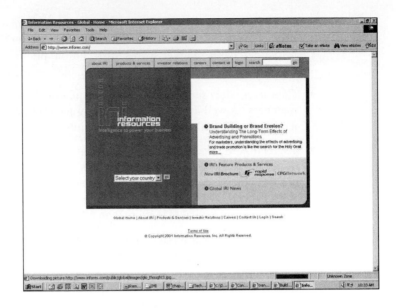

with regard to social, political, and economic issues. Roy Morgan conducts a wide range of surveys covering topics like the most popular brand choice, the most watched television programs, and the latest trends occurring throughout Australia. Users can even participate in surveys that are regularly updated and published online. In addition to utilizing demographic and psychographic market segmentation, Roy Morgan has developed its own Values Segments™ model for understanding consumer behavior. The model enables marketers to learn more about their target markets by analyzing consumers' thoughts, aspirations, self-image and behavior. The Values Segments™ model aims to answer important questions such as, "What would it take to change a *no* decision into a *yes*?" and "What factors influence and predict consumers' behavior?" Figure 5.16 is a diagrammatic representation of the Roy Morgan Values Segments™ model with detailed descriptions available by clicking on the appropriate segment name.

Operating in 40 markets around the world, NFO WorldGroup, Inc. (http://www.nfow.com/) is another global purveyor of market research.

NPDFoodworld (http://npdfoodworld.com/) claims to be the source of "essential market information." They are clearly a large, well-established organization whose website offers consumer information in a variety of industries from food to toys. The website has a member area with access to customized market information. There is a news and events section covering topics that affect the marketing business. Papers on leading edge trends are published in the research area.

The Bureau of Labor Statistics (BLS) (http://stats.bls.gov/) provides information on the buying habits of consumers, including data on their expenditures, income, and credit ratings. The Bureau regards itself as "the principal fact-finding agency for the [U.S.] Federal Government in the broad field of labor economics, and statistics." Most relevant to the researcher is the BLS's Consumer Expenditure Survey, which provides information on the buying habits of U.S. consumers, including data on their expenditures, income, and consumer unit (families and single consumers) characteristics.

Organizations and Operations—Who Participates in the Buying and How Does the Market Buy?

Users of the product may not necessarily be the ones who purchase it. Identifying such "gatekeepers" is an important issue that marketers must consider.

FIGURE 5.16
Roy Morgan Values
Segments™

Source:
http://www.roymorgan.com.au/
products/values/

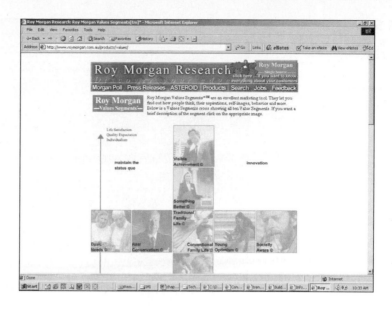

What kind of decision-making processes do consumers go through before making certain purchase decisions? Determining how consumers make a purchase decision is of prime importance to marketers. (Kotler, 1994)

Ascertaining who participates in any given consumer purchase and/or determining the dynamics of the consumer decision-making process requires that researchers either conduct primary research on the unique situation or review the academic/professional literature on the topic/s. If a researcher wants to employ the services of a professional research firm, a very useful metadex has been assembled by Aspy P. Palia, professor of marketing, University of Hawaii at Manoa (http://www.cba.hawaii.edu/aspy/aspymktr.htm/). This metadex has an excellent listing of marketing firms and services, not to mention scores of other websites of direct relevance to every marketing researcher and practitioner.

Databases such as ABI/INFORM GLOBAL (http://www.napier.ac.uk/depts/library/resources/ResourceGuides/ABIInform/ABIInform.htm) can be employed to help researchers quickly peruse relevant literature. ABI/INFORM GLOBAL is one of the largest business periodical databases providing full text articles and references on a wide range of business-related subjects, including accounting, advertising, economics, human resources, finance, marketing, law, management, information systems, and taxation as well as information on over 60,000 companies. The material is drawn from over 1,500 business, management, and trade journals. A search using the keywords *consumer decision making* returned 1,704 articles; using the keywords *decision makers* returned 398.

Online/Offline Consumer Media Attitudes and Use Patterns

Mediamark Research (http://www.mediamark.com/mri/docs/toplinereports.html/) provides demographic data on magazines, cable TV, and over 50 different product or service categories. It breaks down the viewers of U.S. cable TV networks according to age, sex, and income, while magazines are listed by total audience, circulation, readers per copy, median age, and income.

Burke Incorporated (http://www.burke.com/) provides a full service of custom marketing research, analysis, and consulting for consumer and business-to-business product and service companies. Their services include product testing, brand equity research, pricing

FIGURE 5.17
**Marketing
Resources/Tools**

Source:
http://www.cba.hawaii.edu/aspy
/aspymkto.htm/

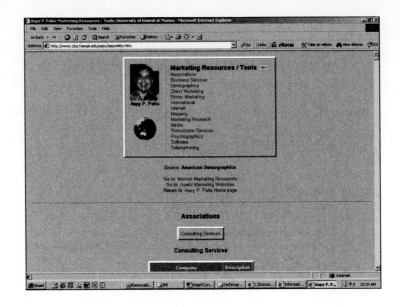

research, market segmentation, image and positioning studies, and a wide range of marketing research protocols targeted at both tactical and strategic business issues.

Arbitron Inc. (http://www.arbitron.com/home/content.stm) is an international media and marketing research firm serving radio and TV broadcasters, cable companies, advertisers, and advertising agencies, magazines, newspapers, and the online industry in the United States, and Europe. Since 1949, Arbitron has measured radio audiences in local markets across the United States and surveys the retail, media, and product patterns of local market consumers. The company is organized into three operational groups: U.S. Media Services, Portable People Meter Development, and Webcast Services; it has approximately 750 full-time employees worldwide.

Self-described as "a multimedia research company specializing in marketing information" Simmons Market Research (http://www.smrb.com/) is an established purveyor of marketing and media data covering over 8,000 brands and 400 product categories.

Online Media Attitudes and Use Patterns

CyberAtlas (http://www.cyberatlas.com/) collects a wide array of Internet-related statistics with a particular emphasis on Internet marketing, advertising, commerce, and technology. It is updated frequently and provides snapshots of how the Internet is being used and summaries of information from a variety of market research sources, supplemented by concise and thoughtful analyses. CyberAtlas is very robust and is considered one of the best websites to use when looking for Internet-consumer intelligence. The latest research is compiled from a wide variety of sources, including Media Metrix, Greenfield Online, Intelliquest, and Intern. The geography page provides information on surveys of online populations around the world. There is also a generous section on e-commerce that breaks down research into different areas, such as advertising, finance, and retail. The Stats Toolbox is a rich source of information, with lists on everything from weekly usage data to the top 10 banner advertisements.

Georgia Tech's Graphics, Visualization, and Useability (GVU) Center surveys (http://www.gvu.gatech.edu/user_surveys/) are among the most comprehensive efforts at data collection for identifying how and by whom the Internet is used. Recurring online surveys measure consumer demographics, psychographics, consumption patterns, and usage trends on the Internet. One of the features of this free service is that most of the data can be viewed in graph format that is easy to understand. The website's primary focus is to determine how and why consumers are using the Internet.

ACNielsen/NetRatings (http:// www.nielsen-netratings.com/) is another source of Internet-user information. Researchers can find data on Internet growth and user patterns.

eMarketer (http://www.emarketer.com/) describes itself as "the world's leading provider of Internet and e-business statistics." Indeed, the website does provide an overwhelming

FIGURE 5.18
CyberAtlas

Source:
http://www.cyberatlas.com/

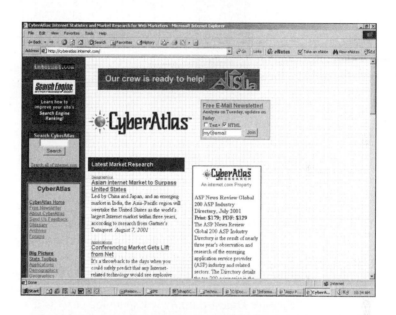

FIGURE 5.19
GVU Surveys

Source:
http://www.cc.gatech.edu/gvu/user_surveys/

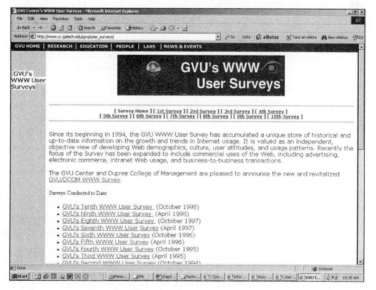

FIGURE 5.20
Hours Spent on the Internet—NUA Analysis

Source:
http://www.nua.ie/surveys/
analysis/graphs_charts/1996
graphs/hours.html/

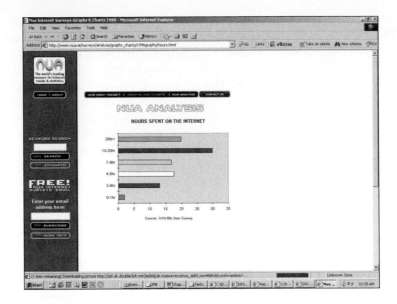

number and variety of reports, information, articles, and statistics covering e-business, marketing, and technologies.

Gartner (http://www.gartner4.com/) provides research on consumer online usage and interactive services and technology. Information is gathered from over 100,000 U.S. and European households and covers the financial, automotive, retail, and travel industries. The website provides users with decision support data and gives planning advice.

NUA (http://www.nua.ie) provides an extensive coverage of surveys and analyses. The company also offers updated information on Internet usage and a valuable weekly newsletter for free that summarizes many of the more interesting surveys pertaining to the Internet.

Sputnik Digest (http://www.sputnik.co.nz/) is a clearinghouse that provides Internet marketing news, campaigns, trends, breakthroughs, case studies, and analyses. The site says it offers "no dross, just the gems." Its website is broken into three sections: Reconnaissance, Intelligence, and Analysis. Sputnik Digest could be a good website from which to read bits of information from various other websites, assuming that it is updated regularly.

Survey-Net (http://www.survey.net/) claims to be "your source for dynamic, up-to-the-second information, opinions and demographics from the Net Community." Visitors can also participate in the various surveys at the website, ranging from business and politics to society and entertainment. The information accumulated online is available to everyone on the Internet. Users are free to republish or use any portion of their survey results as long as Survey-Net is acknowledged.

Summary

Consumer intelligence is the analysis followed by the synthesis of information on consumers. The emergence of the Internet and other interactive technologies has given companies a greater ability to gather information from and about consumers. Numerous resources are available on the Internet to market researchers in search of consumer intelligence data. General characteristics of consumer markcts can be obtained online from many government and private services throughout the world. This information can be used to answer the cornerstone questions as to what, when, why, where, and how consumers purchase, use, and evaluate products and services. Off-line and online media data are also readily accessible on the Internet. Such data can help marketers make decisions regarding appropriate media strategies.

With data online and in hand, marketers are better able to formulate and maintain relationships with their customers. Accordingly, relationship-marketing strategies have become increasingly necessary and effective as firms move to retain their customers in an environment of increased competition. As the world moves into the digital age, there will be an ever increasing need for and use of online consumer intelligence.

Your online learning center has a case study on *Consumer Intelligence* available now at www.mhhe.com/forrest.

Discussion Questions

1. Do you think consumer intelligence has become more important or less important with the emergence of the Internet? Justify your answer.
2. Name and describe the Seven Os.
3. Where does technographic segmentation fit within the Seven Os of consumer research?
4. Why do you think technographics are important in conducting effective one-to-one marketing?
5. What are some of the online tools and resources used by marketers to gather information about consumers?
6. Develop your own integrated consumer intelligence system. Describe what websites and/or services it would consist of.
7. Privacy is one of the major concerns of Internet users. How can market researchers gather consumer intelligence without making consumers feel that their privacy is being threatened?
8. What are the variables that market researchers need to consider when examining the general characteristics of the consumer market? How do you think such information can be used for one-to-one marketing?

Internet Project

Visit the following three websites and integrate the information presented within and across them into a single report on "Consumer Typologies and Trends."

- VALS™ (http://future.sri.com/VALS/types.shtml/).

- Faith Popcorn (http://www.faithpopcorn.com/trends/trends.htm/).

- Roy Morgan Values Segments (http://www.roymorgan.com.au/products/values/).

Further Reading

Barabba, Vincent P. and Zaltman, Gerald (1990). *Hearing the Voice of the Market: Competitive Advantage Through Creative Use of Market Information.* Cambridge, MA: Harvard Business School Press.

References

ACNielsen (1998). "Welcome to ACNielsen: The Global Leader in Market Research, Information, and Analysis," http://www.acnielsen.com/.
Anselmi, P. (1997). "Market Research in the Future." *Esomar Newsbrief*, vol. 5, no. 9, p. 5.
Asian Demographics (1998). Asian Demographics, http://www.asiandemographics.com/.
Australian Bureau of Statistics (1998). "Australian Bureau of Statistics World Wide Web Information Service," http://www.statistics.gov.au/.
Brady, R., Forrest, E., & Mizerski, R. (1997). *CyberMarketing: Your Interactive Marketing Consultant.* Chicago: NTC Publishing and the American Marketing Association.

Claritas (1998). "Welcome to Claritas," http://www.claritas.com/.

Cookie Central (1998). "Cookie Central," http://www.cookiecentral.com/.

Cookie Pal (1998). Milwaukee: Kookaburra Software, http://www.kburra.com/cpal.html/.

CyberAtlas (1998). "CyberAtlas: The Reference Desk for Web Marketing," http://www.cyberatlas.com/.

FIND/SVP (1998). FIND/SVP Home Page, http://www.findsvp.com/.

Forrest, E. (1985). Press Release, June 17, Tallahassee, Florida: Florida State University College of Communication Research Center.

Forrest, E., Kinney, L. and Chamberlain, M. (1996). "The Impact of Interactive Communication on Advertising and Marketing: And Now a Word from Our Consumer" in *Interactive Marketing: The Future Present,* Forrest, E. and Mizerski, R., Editors. Lincolnwood, Illinois: NTC Business Books.

Forrester Research (1998). "Technographics Segments," http://www.forrester.com/jump/tech01.htm.

GVU Center (1998). "GVU's Eighth WWW User Survey: Frequency of Use Graphs," http://www.gvu.gatech.edu/user_surveys/survey-1997-10/graphs/use/Frequency_of_Use.html/.

Kotler, P. (1994). *Marketing Management: Analysis, Planning and Control*, 8th ed. Englewood Cliffs, New Jersey: Prentice-Hall, Inc.

MIMEsweeper (1998). "Network Security through Content Control—MIMEsweeper," http://www.mimesweeper.com/.

NUA (1998). "NUA Internet Surveys: Graphs and Charts," http://www.nua.ie/surveys/analysis/graphs_charts/1996graphs/hours.html/.

Peppers, D., & Rogers, M. (1993) *One-to-One Media in the Interactive Future: Building Dialogues and Learning Relationships with Individual Customers*. New York: Currency/Doubleday.

Peppers, D., & Rogers, M. (1997). *The One-to-One Future: Building Relationships One Customer at a Time*. New York: Currency/Doubleday.

Popcorn, F. (1991). *The Popcorn Report: Faith Popcorn on the Future of Your Company, Your World, Your Life*. New York: Harper Business (http://www.faithpopcorn .com/).

Potter, W. J., Forrest, E., Sapolsky, B. S., & Ware, W. (1988). "Segmenting VCR Owners." *Journal of Advertising Research*, vol. 28, no. 2, pp. 29–39.

Roy Morgan Research (1998). "Roy Morgan Research: Roy Morgan Value Segments™," http://www.roymorgan.com.au/products/values/.

SRI (1998). "iVALS™ Segments Profiles," http://future.sri.com/vals/ivals.segs.html/.

Stat-USA (1998). Stat-USA Home Page, http://domino.stat-usa.gov/.

Survey.Net (1998). "Internet User Demographics," http://www.survey.net/.

TRUSTe (1998). TRUSTe Home Page, http://www.truste.org/.

U.S. Census Bureau (1998). U.S. Census Bureau Home Page, http://www.census.gov/.

USA Data (1998). "USA Data Local and National Demographic Marketing Information," http://www.usadata.com/.

Whalen, D. (1998). "The Unofficial Cookie FAQ: Version 2.02," http://www.cookiecentral.com/.

Yahoo! (1998). "Yahoo! Government: Statistics," http://www.yahoo.com/Government/Statistics/.

Chapter 6

Competitive Intelligence

Business moves fast. Product cycles are measured in months, not years. Partners become rivals quicker than you can say "breach of contract." So how can you possibly hope to keep up with your competitors if you can't keep an eye on them?

That's why competitive intelligence is so important. Forget James Bond. And forget the occasional racy headlines about industrial espionage. We're talking about new approaches to a good old-fashioned business dish: a heads-up on a new product, information on a rival's cost structure. . . . Thanks to the Web you can learn more about competitors faster than ever.

Imperato, 2000

Competitive intelligence has become an integral element in formulating business and marketing strategy. Competitive intelligence has, in the past, conjured up ideas of sifting through the competitor's rubbish, hacking into their computer systems, or obtaining information in an unethical and illegal manner. Today, 85 percent of the Fortune 500 companies have competitive intelligence departments or divisions, and such beliefs about its methodology have been rectified and its value has been proved.

> The payoff is measurable. Companies with well-established competitive intelligence programs show average earnings of $1.24 per share, while companies without it lose 7 cents a share. Competitive intelligence improves overall company performance, uncovers opportunities and problems, sheds light on competitor strategies, and improves the likelihood of a company's survival. (Norman, 1999)

Operating in the global economy means that companies will have to expand their monitoring activities if they want to stay competitive. Those who do not have a formal competitive intelligence system will find it increasingly hard to survive. By closely monitoring the competition, it is possible to anticipate future moves. Staying a step ahead through an information advantage turns into a competitive advantage.

Chapter objectives

This chapter aims to:

- Provide an understanding of what competitive intelligence is.

- Examine the practicalities of an effective competitive intelligence system.

- Explain why it is important to know the strategic direction that a company's present (and potential) competitors are taking.

- Outline the present and future ramifications of the Internet on competitive intelligence.

- Provide a program for conducting competitive intelligence online—by providing a stepwise procedure and relevant Internet resources.

What Is Competitive Intelligence?

Competitive intelligence is a systematic way of identifying and gathering timely, relevant information about a company's existing and potential competitors. Competitive intelligence necessarily involves an audit of a wide range of information about the structure, operations, personnel, and positions of companies, for example:

- Financial, market, product and price positions.

- Inbound and outbound logistics.

- Production and sales force processes.

- Trade relations.

- Advertising and promotions.

- Executive profiles.

Competitive intelligence is central to an organization's strategic planning and "serves as a catalyst in the decision-making process." According to Gross, "It is part of the value chain that takes data elements, converts these to actionable information, and results in strategic decisions. The keys to the successful utilization of competitive intelligence are analysis of data and synthesis of information" (Gross, 2000).

Leonard Fuld (president of Fuld & Company, a leading competitive intelligence research and consulting firm) is regarded by many as a long established expert in the field of competitive intelligence. His definition of what competitive intelligence is and is not is presented in Table 6.1.

The Practicalities of an Effective Competitive Intelligence System

For a competitive intelligence system to be effective, it must provide a constant flow of timely and accurate information that is disseminated to decision makers and transformed into actionable strategy and tactics. Without action, intelligence is useless. While competitive intelligence is derived from the collection of information on a firm's competitors, information alone is not intelligence. Intelligence is derived from information through analysis. According to Fuld and Company, "Competitive intelligence is information that has been analyzed to the point where you can make a decision." The collection of information is just the beginning of a successful competitive intelligence system. A case in point

TABLE 6.1
Defining Competitive Intelligence: A 10-Point Comparison

What Competitive Intelligence Is	What Competitive Intelligence Is Not
1. Information analyzed to the point that a decision can be made	1. A database search
2. Management tool providing early warning of threats and opportunities	2. A crystal ball
3. Approximations and best view of the market and competition	3. Spying
4. Takes many forms	4. Internet or rumor chasing
5. Way to improve the company bottom line	5. Slides, charts, and written reports
6. A process, a way of life within a corporation	6. A job for one smart person
7. An integral part of the best corporations	7. An invention of the twentieth century
8. Directed from the top executive	8. A piece of hardware
9. Seeing outside the corporate walls	9. A news story
10. Both short- and long-term	10. Just numbers or quantifiable results

Source: Adapted from Leonard Fuld, http://www.fuld.com/whatCI.html/.

is the German military in World War II. When the Allies invaded Normandy in June 1944, the Germans had a wealth of advance information on the date, scope, and general target of that invasion. Even though the information was available, ultimately what mattered was how it was used or, in this case, not used. The fact that the Germans failed to act on that intelligence is a management failure, not an intelligence failure (Fuld and Company, 1996).

An efficient intelligence system collects and analyzes information from a variety of sources, both primary and secondary. Primary sources consist of industry experts, suppliers who deal with competitors, the government, or any other source that would have first-hand knowledge of the competition. Secondary sources include news items, trade associations, industry reports, annual reports, share prices, and any other information that is generally available in the public domain regarding the competition.

After such information is gathered from all relevant sources, it is analyzed in order to discern an understanding of competitors' strategies and future directions. Competitive intelligence finds its ultimate utility in making informed marketing and strategic decisions that gain strategic advantage and reduce risks. If the intelligence is comprehensive, it will benefit the company by reducing costs, lowering risk, adding value, increasing productivity, and increasing reaction times (Simmons, 1997).

The process of gathering competitive intelligence is ongoing, with competitor profiles continually updated, ensuring that only timely information is disseminated to decision makers. By better understanding competitors a firm can place itself in a good position to anticipate and respond, whether it is an attack on the firm, a new product offering, a competitor's expansion or contraction, or the emergence of a new competitor. This idea is echoed in *The Art of War*, written around 500 B.C. by the military strategist Sun Tzu. This notable advice is still relevant to the business world today.

> If you are ignorant of both your enemy and yourself, then you are a fool and certain to be defeated in every battle. If you know yourself, but not your enemy, for every battle won you will suffer a loss. If you know your enemy and yourself, you will win every battle. (Sun Tzu, 500 B.C.)

A case in point: Xerox was involved in a fiercely competitive global market where monitoring competitors was important to effectively stay in the game. The American Productivity and Quality Center nominated Xerox as having one of the best competitive intelligence systems. "Xerox uses intelligence gathered on its competitors to better anticipate trends and develop counter strategies so its employees are better prepared to effectively develop and market Xerox products and services." Xerox's competitive intelligence system was able to identify issues with slow problem resolution. This information was then turned into actionable intelligence. The strategy implemented was to provide a total satisfaction guarantee, replacing machines within three years if customers were not satisfied. The result was a substantial increase in sales, and Xerox was distinguished from its competitors based on customer satisfaction, thus gaining a competitive advantage (Xerox, 1997).

The Impact of the Internet on Competitive Intelligence

The Internet has dramatically accelerated the speed with which anyone can track down useful material, or find other people who might have useful information. Before the Net, locating someone who used to work at a company—always a good source of information— was a huge chore. Today people post their resumes on the web; they participate in discussion groups and say where they work. It's a no-brainer. (Fuld in Imperato, 1998)

The Internet provides a new and powerful means that researchers can take advantage of when searching for information on competitors. Companies that know how to use the Internet's array of research tools will be able to transform an information advantage into a competitive advantage.

Before any information searches take place, it is necessary to define what information will be relevant to sufficiently address the research problem. If the information and research requirements are not correctly defined, then the research could go off on a tangent, proving both a waste of time and inaccurate.

The Internet provides a unique opportunity for companies to conduct their competitor information searches online and in-house. It also provides the opportunity and the means for companies that could not previously afford to conduct competitive intelligence to do so now.

There are a number of advantages to obtaining information online as compared with traditional means. As stated before, cost may act as a barrier for a number of companies wanting to conduct competitive intelligence; however, the Internet reduces costs. This is especially important for small companies. Another important advantage that the Internet brings is the ability to obtain new information quickly and from a wide array of sources. Searching for information on the Internet means that researchers can select certain keywords, searching as broad or as narrow as required. This makes the process of obtaining information relatively easy when compared with traditional means. Relevant information can also be located extremely quickly. Moreover, online information is revised more often, is distributed faster, and is more easily integrated into reports than printed material. By using the Internet to conduct competitive intelligence, companies can reduce costs, instantly obtain current information, access a wide variety of information, and track competitors around the world.

Twelve Steps for Conducting Competitive Intelligence on the Internet

The following are 12 steps that researchers can take when gathering competitive intelligence from the Internet.

1. Check Key Competitive Intelligence Research Sources

The first step, and the best website at which to begin the search for Internet competitive intelligence, is Bidigital.com (http://www.BIDIGITAL.COM/ci/). This website has a (if not *the*) most comprehensive metadex covering competitive intelligence: The Competitive Intelligence Resource Index. This is a search engine and listing of websites by category used for finding competitive intelligence resources such as information sources and the vendors of competitive intelligence services and products. The categories include Associations, Books, Companies—Consulting, Market Research, Online Information and Databases, Documentation, Education, Jobs, Publications, and Software.

Peppers and Rogers Group Consulting (http://www.1to1.com/) has free registration to its website, which may be the *only* place a researcher will need to go to gather the majority of their competitor intelligence. Simply put, it provides access to virtually every competitive intelligence resource available on the Internet, including the following:

- Search news sources—business, technology, and new economy news—or search the entire Internet.

- Get a public company report. The Public Company Report section provides convenient access to key information on public companies, including detailed financial data, company profiles, quotes, U.S. Securities and Exchange Commission (SEC) filings, and analyst recommendations.

- Examine financial data. Check out up-to-date information on earnings, split schedules, insider trading, and company financials.

- Get company profiles. One click to an overview of business news, company contacts, competitor information, and recent news.

- Get the latest developments. Find the most recent press releases and the latest trademark or patent filings. This section also shows information on technical company profiles, press releases, summarized financial data, quotes and charts, SEC filings, earnings, competitors' analyst recommendations, and insider trading.

FIGURE 6.1
Report Gallery

Source:
http://www.reportgallery.com/

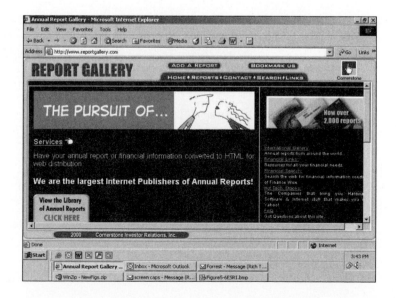

A search by company name or ticker symbol (the company abbreviation used in stock market listings) reveals the following information:

- Company background.

- Company press releases.

- Company profiles.

- Company financials.

- SEC filings.

- Summarized financial data.

- Insider trading information.

- Analyst reports and comments.

The electronic data gathering, analysis and retrieval system known as EDGAR (http://www.sec.gov/edgar.shtml) is a comprehensive U.S. government website that performs the collection, validation, indexing, acceptance, and forwarding of submissions by companies and those who are required to file financial details with the SEC. The system is able to retrieve publicly available information from January 1994 to the present.

2. Search for Company Information

For the past decade, information on the Internet about companies has grown tremendously (Scholz-Crane, 1997). The timeliness and accuracy of this company information must always be taken into account when considering its usability. This is extremely important because a number of problems may arise if outdated information is used for decision-making purposes.

Company information can take the form of annual reports, financial statements, stock information, or company profiles compiled by independent sources. Among these independent sources are the following websites:

FIGURE 6.2
Hemmingway Scott

Source:
http://www.hemscott.net/

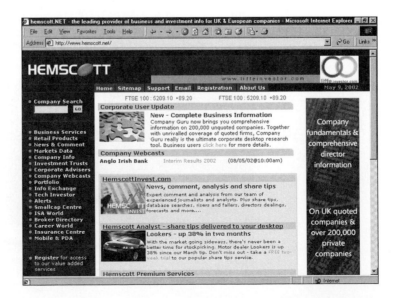

OneSource Information Services, Inc. (http://www.onesource.com/company/company. htm/) provides Web-based business information for a fixed annual subscription rate. OneSource will provide the competitive intelligence researcher with "corporate, industry and market intelligence . . . on over 1 million public and private companies from more than 25 information providers drawing upon over 2,500 sources of content."

The Report Gallery (http://www.reportgallery.com/) provides access to an extensive range of annual reports online and also has links to company home pages. It currently lists over 2,200 annual reports and covers the majority of the Fortune 500 companies. The website also has an International Gallery that provides annual reports on companies in Japan, the United Kingdom, South Africa, and other countries in Europe and Asia.

FIGURE 6.3
EDGAR (U.S. Securities and Exchange Commission)

Source:
http://www.sec.gov/edgar.shtml/

FIGURE 6.4
OneSource Information Services, Inc

Source:
http://www.onesource.com/company/company.htm/

American Business Information (ABI) can be found at http://www.abii.com. Their variety of products and services makes this website a good choice for constructing a mailing list or doing basic research on a company.

Harris InfoSource (http://www.harrisinfo.com/) researches, compiles, and provides business information for sales and marketing professionals. "The Harris core database features more than 700,000 manufacturing and service establishments with multiple decision makers for each company. This database is then segmented into an array of information products available on CD-ROM, online and in print by geography and employment size."

Connect 4 (http://www.connect4.com.au) provides reports for the top 500 Australian companies, with some going back to 1992. Prospectuses and details on mergers and acquisitions can also be obtained. Documents are available through a yearly subscription or by paying per download.

Hemmingway Scott (http://www.hemscott.net/) provides an alphabetical collection of all listed companies in the United Kingdom, removed companies, name changes, and details of mergers and acquisitions. The following details are provided for each company: summary details, five-year summary profit and loss statement with balance sheet, daily share price, brokers' consensus, share price graph, advisers, directors, major shareholders, registrars, contact details, and key dates.

The Streetlink (http://www.streetlink.com/) website provides direct access to scores of corporations' financial reports, newsworthy items, corporate profiles, and quarterly and annual reports.

3. Search the Websites and Personal Pages of Competitors

Competitors' websites can provide information and insight on present as well as future marketing strategies. Researchers can scrutinize a competitor's website for style, substance, and key features. Note particularly what product information is provided and what promotional strategies and tactics are being employed. Competitor websites may feature relevant details about the company such as annual reports, press releases, special-product information, and job openings. If there is a discussion or chat facility, researchers can read what customers are saying about them. Although users will probably not find any insider

FIGURE 6.5
Connect 4

Source:
http://www.connect4.com.au

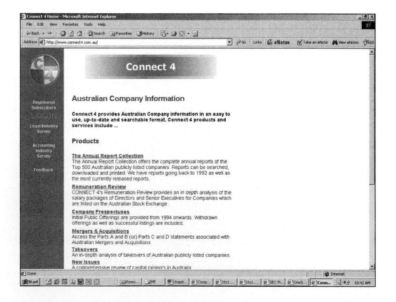

information on these websites, they provide a good starting base for amassing competitive intelligence.

The following observations that there are "no places like home pages" were made by competitive intelligence professionals in an interview with *FastCompany Magazine.*

> **Leonard Fuld**: It's so obvious that I'm reluctant to say it: if you want to find out about your competitors, spend time with their home pages. Home pages are such an obvious resource that people often don't take them seriously. . . . It's a great place to gather intelligence on that company. It includes all kinds of data about R&D operations: where they are, what they specialize in. You can take that information and go to the IBM Patent Server http://www.patents.ibm.com/ [now http://www.delphion.com], which archives 2 million patent citations. You'll make some interesting connections . . . when a company lets people post personal home pages; you really get a feel for their personalities and intentions. These pages can be extremely valuable. They're also a head-hunter's dream! (Imperato, 2000)

> **Marc Freidman:** Our competitors' home pages are among my first stops. I'm really thorough about going through them. If you really push on them—if you focus on the minutiae and make interesting connections—you can generate valuable insights. We do business in 170 countries. Home pages can give you a quick take on what your competitor is selling in Argentina or who its partners are in Belgium. (Imperato, 2000)

While much can be learned from home pages, researchers must—as always—be cautious and critical of what gets posted and reported on corporate sites.

> **Tracey Scott:** Home pages are valuable. But they also contain lots of misleading information. . . . Companies tend to post only their most optimistic messages. If you're worried about when a competitor is going to release a new product, and all you do is track press releases on its home page—well, don't be surprised when the product launches much later than those releases suggested it would. All the detail on the web can be deceiving. Once, on a company's site, I read specs for a new product, complete with engineering drawings, and then I called someone at the company, who said, "We haven't started building it yet." (Imperato, 2000)

4. Search for Trade Associations and Conferences

Trade associations can provide useful and unbiased information about competitors. This information can be a good complement to that obtained from competitors' websites. Researchers can obtain an alphabetical listing of trade associations, which are also grouped by industry, by searching in Yahoo! (http://www.yahoo.com/Business_and_Economy/Organizations/Trade_Associations/).

Often, trade association websites will list their industry's conferences. And conferences can be a rich source of information on the business and marketing positions of competitors. As one competitive intelligence practitioner, Tracey Scott, noted, "I love conference proceedings. Most companies send their best people to speak at conferences. It's a great way to track talent and to track down people who might have useful information and insights" (Imperato, 2000).

5. Peruse Job and Career Websites

There are many ways that useful competitive intelligence can be obtained from publicly available information. For example, a competitor's job recruitment program can be monitored in order to gain an insight into their strategic direction. The competitor could advertise for a large number of employees in a variety of areas, some of which are in other geographical locations. This information could indicate that the competitor is expanding and looking to other markets. From this information an insight of the competitor's strategic direction can be determined and strategic decisions can be made based on how the competitor's activities will affect the researcher's organization. Strategic decisions can then be formulated if necessary. Again, the observations of competitive intelligence practitioners explain the importance of gathering competitive intelligence in this manner.

> **Leonard Fuld**: Help-wanted ads are a very underrated source of business intelligence. They offer great clues about where a company is heading in its pursuit of markets and technologies. CareerPath.com and the Monster Board are two websites (http://www.careerpath.com/ and http://www.monsterboard.com/) that our analysts use all the time. Companies are between a rock and a hard place here. Most of them desperately need talented people, so they have to advertise their openings aggressively. But the more jobs they post, the more they expose themselves to people like us, who know how to analyze the postings. If you examine the kinds of backgrounds that a company looks for in its systems people, you can get a good sense of its technical infrastructure. (Imperato, 2000)

> **Tracey Scott**: Human-source information is more interesting and more accurate than secondary information. That's why I spend a lot of my time tracking people. I always look for "star talent" and think about what the comings and goings of those people mean. (Imperato, 2000)

6. Survey Competitor's Customers Online

If researchers need or want firsthand information on their competitor's strengths and weaknesses, it may be useful to survey the competitor's customers. Direct measurement of brand image, attributes, brand equity, advertising, and promotional effects can readily be obtained online. Finding competitor brand users who are online will, of course, prove more or less difficult depending on the product class. The target market must be identified along with relevant questions. Newsgroups provide one means of identifying competitors' customers. See also Chapter 7 for a detailed analysis on how to conduct online surveys.

As noted in Chapter 5, one unique development on the Internet has been the emergence of customer sound-off websites, which allow consumers to register their opinions and experiences regarding any given product or service. Obviously, these websites can provide information on how consumers evaluate the products and services of competitors.

7. Utilize Comparative-Shopping Services

Shopping websites can also serve a dual purpose. In addition to helping users buy a product over the Internet, these websites can instantly demonstrate how a company's product is being compared and evaluated with respect to those of their competitors. Some of these websites are:

- mySimon (http://www.mysimon.com/).

- DealTime (http://dealtime.com/).

- RoboShopper (http://www.roboshopper.com/).

8. Search Newsgroups and Read Mailing Lists

By joining a newsgroup, firms can obtain valuable information about what their customers think about them as well as their competitors. Google Groups (http://groups.google.com) allows researchers to find over 80,000 special interest groups. The service gives access to a vast array of Internet discussion groups that researchers can join or just read to see what people and experts in various areas are talking about. For detailed explanations of newsgroups, see Chapters 8 and 9.

9. Find News That Can Be Used

Information gleaned from newspapers can provide some unique insights into a competitor's business directions. Ultimately, people formulate the strategies and make the decisions that determine every company's competitive position.

> That is why the people factor is so important . . . you can't reduce competitive intelligence to a spreadsheet. One exercise we like to do is to profile the top managers in a company or business unit. What's their background? Their style? Are they marketers? Are they cost-cutters? The more articles you collect, the more bios you download, the better you get at creating these profiles. All this material is on the web. (Fuld in Imperato, 2000)

Hence, the mantra for gathering personnel information on the Internet is "Think Global, Snoop Local" (Fuld in Imperato, 2000):

> **Leonard Fuld:** One of the great things about the Web is that it's a window on the world. But often the best sources of information on a competitor are the most local—the community newspaper in the town where a company is headquartered or has a big plant. . . . Even the smallest papers have websites these days. NewsLink (http://www.newslink.org/) connects you to more than 3,600 newspapers and magazines from around the world—even college newspapers—and it's searchable by state.
>
> One client hired us to help figure out whether a competitor was going to start competing more aggressively on cost. Our analysts tracked down all kinds of articles, including a profile in a local newspaper of the competitor's CEO. The profile said, very matter-of-factly, that this guy took the bus to a nearby town to visit one of the company plants. Those few words were a small but important sign to me that this company was going to be incredibly cost conscious. . . . [Also the] local paper did an in-depth piece on life at one of his company's factories, complete with great data on how many people worked there, what the average salary was—remarkable stuff. We put that information together with other data and developed a pretty reliable estimate of manufacturing costs at this plant. Hometown papers are one of the few places where you can get that kind of information. Always look locally. (Fuld in Imperato, 2000)

> **Tracey Scott**: Be sure to look beyond traditional business sources too. I'm a big believer in preferring soft information to hard information—and in reading between the lines. Two of my favorite local sources are the wedding announcements page and the lifestyle section. Remember *Working Girl*? Melanie Griffith is working on a deal and reads that the daughter of one of the big players is getting married—so she shows up at the wedding reception and makes her pitch. I've never done that. But you can make interesting connections if you combine business news with "social" news. (Scott in Imperato, 2000)

Other Internet tools that can assist in the search for personnel and company news are the following:

OnlineNewspapers.com (http://www.onlinenewspapers.com/) is purported to be the world's largest listing of online newspapers, listing over 10,000 newspapers from around the world, with links to more than 5,000 newspapers on the Internet, searchable by country and then by publication.

DataTimes (http://www.datatimes.com/) features low connect charges and transactional charging, making it a good choice for the novice business researcher. It also has one of the best collections of online newspapers.

eLibrary (http://www.elibrary.com/) has 900 magazines in full text as well as newspapers, news wires, books, and reports that can be searched by topic, thus providing a useful research tool.

PR Newswire (http://www.prnewswire.com/) provides full text company news, allowing researchers to search for news by company name. PR Newswire also provides some links to the companies' websites, financial and summary information, annual reports, stock quotes and other information.

10. Personalize Information Searches

By setting up their own personalized news page, researchers can collect information on a regular basis. This is an extremely efficient and easy means in which to collect competitive data. Companies and topic areas need to be specified. Refer to Chapter 3 for a more detailed analysis of customizing information for personal intelligence. Again, two of the most robust personalized information retrieval services are IntelBrief and Market Guard 24/7.

IntelBrief (http://www.intelbrief.com/) provides a wide range of intelligence services (that is, world, regional, military, government, technology, and the like) including competitive intelligence. As stated at IntelBrief's website, their mission is to "mine the wonders of the net to provide you with the information you need, when you need it, how you want it." In this quest, IntelBrief integrates newsfeeds and information from over 2,000 sources.

Market Guard 24/7 (http://www.marketguard247.com/) is a scheduled retrieval service of relevant competitor and Internet news. The Market Guard 24/7 reporting service monitors competitors' websites and the Internet for recent news articles, bulletin postings, press releases, search engine listings, and news wire updates for stories about any given company's products and events.

11. Outsource the Competitive Intelligence Function

> One of the dangers of pay-as-you-go information services is that you can ring up serious bills pretty quickly. But competitive intelligence is like any other part of business: usually, you get what you pay for. (Marc Friedman in Imperato, 2000)

Contracting the competitive intelligence task is another option if a company does not have the resources and skills to conduct the operation in-house. One of the advantages of contracting out this work is the objectivity of the consultant, as they are not directly involved in the business. They can offer an expertise that few firms will be able to supply inside their organization. The consultant can also prepare the report relatively quickly, and it can be updated on a regular basis. The disadvantages include cost and the regularity of the

FIGURE 6.6
PR Newswire

Source:
http://www.prnewswire.com/

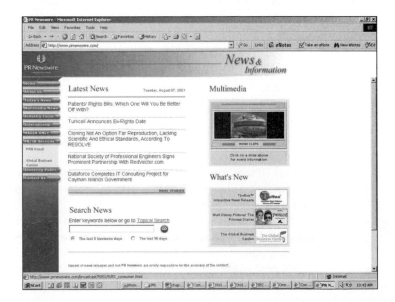

FIGURE 6.7
IntelBrief

Source:
http://www.intelbrief.com/

information. The more regularly intelligence updates are required, the more costly the competitive intelligence system becomes. There are a number of companies on the Internet that offer a variety of competitive intelligence services, including the following:

Fuld and Company (http://www.fuld.com/) is a key research source of competitive intelligence. The website provides indexed competitive intelligence information, making searching extremely organized and easy. Not only does Fuld and Company provide a great website for a firm to start their own competitive intelligence, but researchers can also employ the company to undertake competitive intelligence on their behalf or to organize seminars, training, and consulting.

The website provides a vast array of information, from tips on how to conduct competitive intelligence to the resources needed to set up a competitive intelligence system. The resources are categorized accordingly:

- Associations, business/economic, company information.

- Competitor intelligence sites.

- Custom/news clippings.

- Financial/markets, government.

- Information services, job listings.

- Law and legal resources.

- Libraries, Internet search tools/locators.

- News, patent information.

- Phone directories.

- Trade shows and conferences.

- Usenet/discussion group search engines.

- Industry specific information and international.

FIGURE 6.8
Fuld and Company

Source: http://www.fuld.com/

Researchers can also find competitive intelligence success stories and excerpts from the book *New Competitor Intelligence* by Leonard Fuld on this website.

Hoovers (http://www.hoovers.com/) describes itself as the ultimate source for company information. The website provides information on more than 12 million private and public companies worldwide. Company information is readily available in summary form for nonsubscribers and in detail for those who pay a fee. Licenses are also available for multiple users, although the cost depends on a number of factors. Using company names, users can search for company information; or with keywords, users can search by industry, location, annual sales, and company type. Detailed information about companies in a variety of industries is also available. Industry snapshots are provided outlining the major companies and providing relevant news items about the industry. Hoovers also provides company listings further categorized. For example, the software Industry Snapshot categorizes the industry into business, communication, engineering, and design. A user can obtain a variety of information about a company that has been selected. The Company Capsule provides:

- Background information about the company.

- Stock chart.

- Company profile including employees.

- Sales, growth, and company rankings by industry.

The Financials link provides all the relevant financial information including annual and quarterly financials, comparison and market data, and historical financials. News provides all relevant online news about the company of interest, supplying a variety of tools in order to obtain the information.

Dun & Bradstreet (http://www.dnb.com/) is recognized around the world as the leader in providing global business expertise and information to customers. They are also the only global information provider that collects financial statements on both publicly and privately held companies. Their website provides information on more than 47 million companies representing more than 200 countries.

FIGURE 6.9

Hoovers

Source:
http://www.hoovers.com/

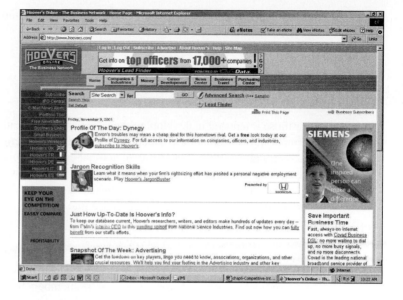

FIGURE 6.10

Productscan

Source:
http://www.productscan.com/
home.htm

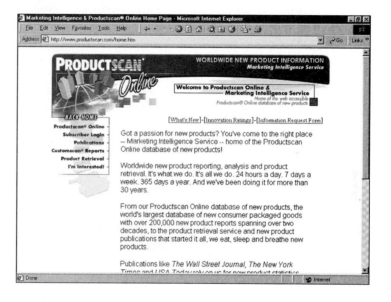

Aware (http://dialspace.dial.pipex.com/aware/aware.shtml#About/) is a competitive in-telligence research company that specializes in the United Kingdom and Europe. EMA In-ternational (http://www.emainternational.com/) is an internationally focused company concentrating on U.S. and international acquisitions and competitive intelligence.

Productscan (http://www.productscan.com/home.htm) is an online database of new products that is touted as the world's largest database of new consumer packaged goods. Their website contains over 20,000 new product reports, spanning nearly two decades.

12. Start Your Search Engines

If by now these tools have not helped uncover everything a researcher needs to know about their competitors, they can always conduct a series of Internet searches using their favorite search engines. Oddly, this often is the first and only step many individuals take in their quest for competitive intelligence.

Professional and Educational Sources—Lifelong Learning about Competitive Intelligence

For those interested in developing their "expertise in creating, collecting and analyzing information; disseminating competitive intelligence; and engaging decision makers in a productive dialogue that creates organizational competitive advantage," researchers can join the Society of Competitive Intelligence Professionals (SCIP) at http://www.scip.org/.

The society is designed to help individuals obtain the competitive intelligence skills necessary to turn competitive intelligence into a competitive advantage for their company. SCIP provides a wide array of valuable information for researchers to browse. SCIP conducts surveys about competitive intelligence that you can participate in and/or review results of past studies. The publication section has newsletters and journals that detail the topic of competitive intelligence. Peer assistance provides the opportunity to contact competitive intelligence professionals and SCIP members from around the world, allowing researchers to discuss competitive intelligence issues with the experts. SCIP also provides details of upcoming competitive intelligence events such as conferences, seminars, and programs. Indeed, if there is anything a researcher would like to know about competitive intelligence, the SCIP website is the place to visit.

Another source of professional competitive intelligence development can be found at the Montague Institute (http://montague.montague.com/review/buslibbest.html). The Montague Institute has an excellent website that provides a wide range of information resources on competitive intelligence. The Montague Institute sponsors events and educational programs and also provides off-line and online information services.

Competia (http://www.competia.com/home/) claims to be "the world's largest community, portal and magazine for professionals in competitive intelligence." Indeed, the website does provide access to many worthwhile and relevant competitive intelligence

FIGURE 6.11
Society of Competitive Intelligence Professionals

Source: http://www.scip.org/

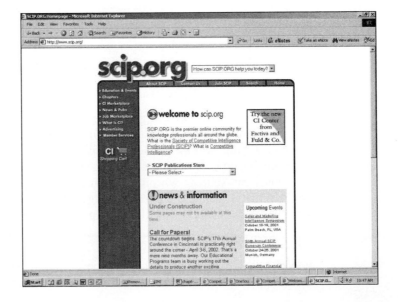

resources including news, educational modules, and a database of links to over a thousand online articles regarding competitive intelligence and strategy.

Join a Discussion Group

Aurora (http://www.aurorawdc.com/) and SCIP (http://www.scip.org/) also offer forums to discuss items of interest with other competitive intelligence professionals and researchers. Subscribe to "the ultimate company and business information tool," 1Jump (http://www.1jump.com/). For US$19.95 per month, users can search for company information directly from their desktop. As mentioned on their website, 1Jump is "a stand-alone

FIGURE 6.12
Montague Institute Competitive Intelligence Archives

Source:
http://montague.montague.com/review/buslibbest.html

FIGURE 6.13
1Jump

Source:
http://www.1jump.com/

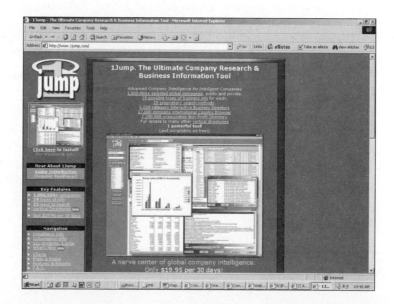

software program designed specifically to help business professionals conduct research on companies . . . with over 1 million individually-selected companies worldwide, up to 29 types of business information on each company, 25 proprietary ways to pinpoint this information, and an integrated interactive Business Directory with 6,000 categories . . . 1Jump is a powerful professional resource. Locate, compare and contrast companies; instantly copy your findings to your spreadsheet or word processor; create instant customized graphs."

Summary

Competitive intelligence is the continuous monitoring of the activities of competitors. This information is turned into actionable intelligence whereby strategic and marketing decisions can be made. Competitive intelligence is important because in order to be smarter than one's competitors, a firm must be able to anticipate the next moves of others and react accordingly. Competitive intelligence should be gathered through legal and ethical means.

The Internet has opened up a unique opportunity for organizations to set up a competitive intelligence system in-house that is both cost-effective and timely. There are a vast number of research tools that can be utilized on the Internet. The abundance of information may create problems for those researchers who do not have the skills to cope with and filter relevant information. For those who follow the 12-step process outlined in this chapter, the Internet will provide an information advantage that can be turned into a competitive advantage in the marketplace.

 Your online learning center has a case study on *Competitive Intelligence* available now at www.mhhe.com/forrest.

Discussion Questions

1. What is competitive intelligence and how can it be used effectively in the decision-making process?
2. What are some of the ethical and legal considerations that need to be addressed when monitoring the competition?
3. What impact has the Internet had on competitive intelligence? How is it likely to continue?
4. What are some of the advantages and disadvantages when using the Internet for competitive intelligence?
5. What are the advantages of conducting competitive intelligence in-house versus contracting the function out?
6. What information can you expect to find on your competitor's website? What information do you not expect to find? How can this information be used?
7. Choose a company and conduct a competitive intelligence search on the Internet using the steps outlined in the chapter.

Internet Project

Go to the Pepper and Rogers Group Consulting website (http://www.1to1.com/). Register (this is free) and pick one company/corporation. Prepare a competitive intelligence report on that company/corporation using the one-to-one research resources.

Further Reading

Hussey, David, & Jenster, Per (1999). *Competitor Intelligence: Turning Analysis into Success* (Wiley Series in Practical Strategy). Canada: John Wiley & Son Ltd.

References

Aaker, D. (1995). *Strategic Market Management,* 4th ed. Canada: John Wiley & Sons.

Anonymous (1996). "Survey Examines Market Researchers' Needs and Methods." *Information Today*, November, vol. 13, no. 10, p. 18.

Boucher, J. (1996). "Using Information Services to Sneak a Peek at the Competition." *Bank Marketing*, March, vol. 28, no. 3, pp. 32–5.

Fuld, L. (1998). *The New Competitor Intelligence*. Cambridge, Massachusetts: Fuld and Company, Inc. (http://www.fuld.com/chapt1.html/).

Gross, Margaret (2000). "Competitive Intelligence: A Librarian's Empirical Approach." *Technology Information* (Tutorial), September (http://www.findarticles.com/mODPC/8-8/65575483/pl/article.jhtml/).

Gulliford, J. (1998). "The Challenge of Competitor Intelligence." *Management Services*, January, vol. 42, no. 1, pp. 20–2.

Imperato, Gina (2000). "Competitive Intelligence—Get Smart," *FastCompany*, Issue 14, p. 269 (http://www.fastcompany.com/online/14/intelligence.html).

Jurek, R. (1996). "The Business Unit's Information Professional," *Marketing Research*, Winter, vol. 8, no. 4, pp. 41–3.

Kassler, H. (1997). "Mining the Internet for Competitor Intelligence," Online, September/October, vol. 21, no. 5, pp. 34–45.

Kotler, P., Armstrong, G., Brown, L., & Adam, S. (1998). *Marketing*, Sydney: Prentice Hall.

McCure, J. (1997). "Snooping on the Net," *Management Review*, July/August, vol. 86 no. 7, pp. 58–9.

Malhotra, Y. (1993). "Competitive Intelligence Programs: An Overview" (http://www.brint.com/papers/ciover.htm).

Miesing, P. (1997). *Industry Analysis and Competitive Dynamics*, Albany University (http://www.albany.edu/~pm157/teaching/topics/companal.html/).

Monroe, A., & Harris, R. (1996). "Turning into Competitive Intelligence," *The Magazine for Senior Financial Executives*, June, vol. 12, no. 6, pp. 46–52.

News from Xerox (1997). March (http://www.xerox.com/PR/NR970317-benchmark.html/).

Norman, Jan (1999). "Knowledge Is Power—Competitive Intelligence or Legal Information Gathering Gives Companies a Strategic Edge over Rivals," *The Orange County Register*, June 14 (http://www.otterbein.edu/home/fac/brccbly/general/bitsnbytes/comintel.htm).

Scholz-Crane, A. (1997). "Evaluating World Wide Web information." The State University of New Jersey Rutgers (http://crab.rutgers.edu/~scholzcr/eval.html/).

Simmons, D. (1997). "Competitor Intelligence Can You Manage without It?" *Business Information Review*, December, vol. 14, no. 4, pp. 173–7.

Stuart, A. (1996). "Click and Dagger," CIO Web Business, July (http://www.cio.com/archive/webbusiness/0796_click_1.html/).

Westervelt, R. (1996). "Gaining an Edge." *Chemical Week*, June, vol. 158, no. 25, pp. 29–31.

Chapter  7

Internet Surveys

As a survey research tool, the Internet is coming of age. As Internet usage increases around the world, Internet survey research continues its transition from an alternative to a mainstream primary data collection method. This transition is being accelerated by the growth in problems experienced with phone and mail surveys. Today, 6 out of 10 people refuse to respond to telephone surveys. As many as 4 in 10 receiving a legally mandated census form refuse to fill it out (Edmondson, 1997). Consequently, Internet surveys are becoming an integral component in marketing research. Over the past four years, companies and researchers have experienced the unique advantages of using the Internet to survey individuals. Indeed, it has been demonstrated that "the use of electronic survey methods can cut costs by 25 to 40 percent and provide results in half the time it takes to do traditional telephone surveys." Consequently, the profit margins of a research firm can increase significantly (McDaniel & Gates, 2002).

Such demonstrable benefits, coupled with the continued rapid adaptation to the Internet by the general public, make it a crucial component of every market researcher's cache of tools for gathering primary data. As the effectiveness and response rates of traditional mail and phone survey methods continue to decline, the Internet's future as a primary method of survey research seems assured.

Already, there are instances where Internet surveys are the most appropriate (Watt, 1997):

- For studies on computer-related products.

- For consumers who purchase products over the Internet.

- For Internet populations and users of Internet services.

- For business and professional users of Internet services since, for example, over 80 percent of businesses in the United States have Internet connections.

- For business-to-business primary research, where the audio and graphic abilities of the Internet can enhance the quality of the Internet survey.

Chapter objectives

This chapter aims to:

- Give an overview of the advantages and disadvantages of Internet surveying compared with traditional methods such as mail and phone surveys.

- Look at the various methods of online sampling and recruitment that can be employed.

- Outline the aesthetic and psychological factors that should be considered when designing and constructing Internet surveys.

- Provide a guide to alternative methods of Internet survey distribution for those wishing to conduct an Internet survey on their own.

- Supply guidelines on selecting a commercial service should a researcher decide to commission an Internet survey research project.

- List notable software and survey support services on the Internet. The websites are exemplary of the many types of programs and services available to assist in designing, sampling, and executing online surveys.

Comparative Advantages of Internet Surveys

The way survey research is conducted has changed forever because of the Internet. It is projected that by 2005 online research will account for 50 percent of all marketing revenue—over US$3 billion. The reason for this phenomenal growth is straightforward: The advantages outweigh the disadvantages. (McDaniel & Gates, 2002)

The Internet provides market researchers with a new and (in many respects) inherently superior survey research vehicle. To date, it has been demonstrated that when compared with traditional survey methods (that is, mail surveys and personal or telephone interviews) Internet surveys prove advantageous in numerous ways (as delineated in Table 7.1).

The following benefits can be derived by examining the Internet across the entire survey research sequence—from *design* to *distribution* through *completion* and *return*.

Design

In terms of design, the Internet offers greater versatility and customization of both the survey instrument and the sample frame.

TABLE 7.1

Comparative Attributes of Internet, Personal, Telephone, and Mail Surveys

Attributes	Internet Surveying	Personal Interviews	Telephone Interviews	Mail Surveys
Cost	Very low	Very high	Medium	Low
Speed of response	Fast	Instant	Instant	Slow
Response rate	High	Very high	Medium	Low
Population segments accessible	Many	All possible to be accessed	In between mail and Internet	Many
Geographic reach of survey conducted	Very high	Very low	Medium	High
Accessibility of medium to respondents	Varies	Varies	Medium	Very high
Time taken for survey distribution	Fast	Long	Medium	Long

Source: Adapted from Pope et al. (1997).

Survey Instrument

More Aesthetic   Internet surveys have the capability of being enhanced through the use of animated graphics, audio, and video. This is especially helpful for conducting research that requires visual and/or audio aids, such as surveys on new products or business-to-business surveys.

Customized Surveys   Internet surveys can be highly personalized in that respondents can be "asked only pertinent questions, being able to pause and then resume the survey as needed, and having the ability to see previous responses and correct inconsistencies" (McDaniel & Gates, 2002). By tracking the usage patterns and geographical location of respondents, it is possible for researchers to program customized surveys that are suitable to the respondent. For example, a Japanese respondent may receive a survey written in Japanese; an Australian may receive a survey that does not contain a section that is relevant only to a U.S. respondent. Follow-up questions that are tailor-made according to respondents' previous responses are especially helpful when conducting longer surveys (Weissbach, 1997).

Sample Frame

Reaching the Hard-to-Find   Searching by telephone, a company spent six months and thousands of dollars looking for specific respondents who had purchased a certain home-office product. The company found only a few respondents. Searching online, the company managed to find several hundred respondents in just a few weeks at a fraction of the cost (Edmondson, 1997).

Finding the Hard-to-Reach   Some segments of the population that are "among the most surveyed on the planet" are "the most difficult to reach (doctors, high-income professionals, CEOs in global firms) and are well represented on the Internet" (McDaniel & Gates, 2002).

Finding Highly Specific Research Targets   **Trend leaders** populate the Internet. These are the individuals who are the first to try out new ideas, products, services, and technologies, and are regularly targeted by marketers, advertisers, and manufacturers (Solomon, 1996).

Distribution

In terms of distribution, the advantages of Internet surveys are twofold, with instantaneous global reach and improved panel management.

Instantaneous Global Reach

Distribution of a survey to tens of thousands of people around the world is completed with a click of a mouse button and without postal fees, long-distance telephone call charges, or labor costs. Again, in comparison with other forms of survey distribution where the costs and time can be considerable, the Internet is unparalleled.

Improved Panel Management

Creation and maintenance of preaggregated clusters of respondents can be accomplished with less cost and more precision. The profiles and responses of panel members can be instantly solicited, retrieved, and analyzed.

Completion

With respect to completion rates, accuracy, and enjoyment, Internet surveys are the most successful.

Higher Response Rates

Internet surveys are completed at the respondent's—not the researcher's—convenience. The keyboard and mouse replace the tedium of filling out printed questionnaires by hand (CustomerSat, Inc., 1997). Even a well-designed mail survey distributed according to an exact sampling frame will often register a low response rate, as many survey forms are relegated to the trash can (Costes 1997). "Busy respondents may be growing increasingly intolerant of 'snail-mail' or telephone-based surveys. Online surveys take half the time [when compared with phone interviews] . . . and are much more stimulating and engaging . . . the result: much higher response rates" (McDaniel & Gates, 2002).

Moreover, it is argued that the confidentiality assurance of Internet surveying, especially on sensitive issues, may well increase the level of response in comparison with telephone and face-to-face interviews. Sproull and Kiesler (1986) found that computer-interviewed respondents answered more questions than those respondents who filled in a paper survey. The one-to-one interactivity of the Internet enables the researcher to remedy the problem of survey sponsor anonymity (Costes, 1997), as the ability to directly communicate with the survey sponsor and to clarify the study's purpose increases the response rate.

Greater Response Accuracy

Internet surveys, whether conducted through a website or via e-mail, generate greater response accuracy by reducing response error, interviewer bias, information processing mistakes, and sampling-distribution problems. Respondents of the survey have the opportunity to ask about the purpose, ask about the meaning of questions, and pose any other questions they might have with regard to the survey (Oppermann, 1995). This is useful as feedback to the researcher and also to generate more accurate responses. In addition, automatic scanning of surveys can identify questions that were unanswered or incorrectly responded to and alert the respondent before allowing the survey to be submitted.

Reduced Human Error

As collected data do not need to be retyped or tabulated, results can be transferred directly from the survey to the database in electronic form. Thus, human error in data entry is reduced, if not eliminated.

Reduced Interviewer Bias

Golden, Beauclair, and Sussman (1992) found that e-mail remains void of "the nonverbal cues and nuances conveyed in face-to-face communications." This would suggest that e-mail surveys are more reliable due to the absence of interviewer-introduced biases that are found in telephone and face-to-face interviews.

Reduced Sampling Distribution Problems

Undeliverable e-mails are returned almost immediately, allowing researchers using e-mail surveys to ascertain quite quickly whether the respecified total number of respondents is actually reached. Adjustments to include more respondents in the sample can then be made accordingly (Oppermann, 1995). This is unlike mail surveys, when several days or weeks may pass before the undeliverable mail is returned.

More Enjoyable

SurveyOnline, an Internet survey research company, found that "people who answer questions via the Internet seem to enjoy the process, especially when compared with traditional pencil and paper formats." In addition to the positive effect occasioned by the ability to complete a survey at the respondent's convenience, it is suggested that such elements as "graphics, interactivity, links to incentive sites, and real-time summary reports make Internet surveys more enjoyable" (McDaniel & Gates, 2002). Follow-up is also faster and cheaper, which could contribute to an overall positive feeling about online surveying (CustomerSat, Inc., 1997).

Return

Surveys conducted over the Internet can be undertaken in less time and at lower cost them traditional survey methods.

Quicker Turnaround

In a study conducted by Bachmann, Elfrink, and Vazzana (1996), the results clearly show the superiority in response time of e-mail surveys. They found that e-mail surveys were returned, on average, 6.5 days faster than paper-based mail. Moreover, the study showed a rapid rise in the cumulative percentage of e-mail responses received, with more than 50 percent of the total responses in the e-mail group arriving within two days and more than 80 percent within one week.

Reductions in Tabulation

Internet surveys reduce the time needed for result tabulation. Since there is no need for manual entry of data, results can be downloaded directly into databases and analytical software (Iyer, 1996). Consequently, the average delivery time of a report can be reduced by more than five times, that of standard mail and telephone methods (Media Marketing Consultants, 1998). Ongoing surveys can be monitored and information gained instantly. Coupled with direct downloading and data processing, it is possible for researchers and decision makers to access survey results in real time.

Internet Survey Shortfalls

There are several factors researchers should be cognizant of when employing the Internet as a data-gathering tool. Among the notable shortfalls unique to Internet surveys are the problems of the demography and psychology of Internet users.

FIGURE 7.1
WWW User Survey

Source:
http://studio.cloudnet.com/
survey.html/

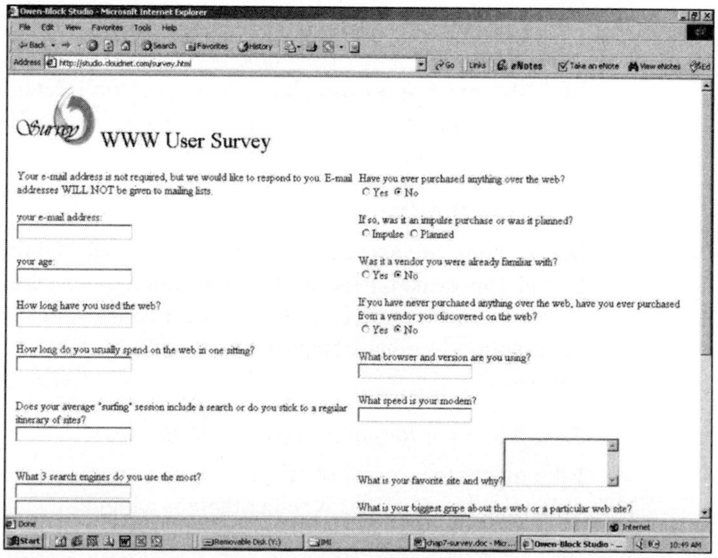

Demography of Users

While the Internet-user population does not statistically represent the general population as a whole, it is reflective of a multinational constituency.

Representational Considerations

While there are over 6 billion people on the earth, there are only between 350 and 380 million using the Internet. Even in the United States, where the Internet is widely used, only 29 percent of the population are estimated to access the Internet at least once a month (Waller, 2001). As such, the Internet-user population is clearly not representative of the population at large. Researchers need to take this into account when contemplating the use of the Internet as a survey tool.

Multicultural Considerations

The Internet is global; hence, differences in language, slang, and culture may lead respondents to misinterpret or even be offended by the questions. Researchers need to be wary of these considerations when wording surveys.

Psychology of Users

As with any survey, *who* decides to respond and *how* they decide to respond have a direct bearing on the validity of the results. The Internet is especially vulnerable to misrepresentative, suspicious, and/or deceitful respondents.

Self-Selection

One of the most serious disadvantages to surveying on the Internet is the problem of self-selection. It is difficult to verify the sample within Internet surveys. A sample of any online population taken only from those willing to respond or give their personal contact information over the Internet can easily prove biased. As Kully (1997) notes, "It is the equivalent to sampling only the top of the pyramid and trying to draw conclusions of the entire pyramid." If incentives are offered in order to increase response rates (especially for surveys conducted on the company's own website), volunteer respondents are often the only ones who reply. As a result, the findings are most probably skewed as the randomness of a survey is reduced (Eaton, 1997).

Anonymity of Internet Users

It is a well-known fact that some people take on a different personality when they are online. Moreover, it is difficult to verify a person's details when they are online unless a preselected panel of respondents is used (Krasilovsky, 1996). This issue could present some data validity problems for researchers.

Anxiety in Divulging Information

Many people are apprehensive about giving information about themselves online due to the fear of abuse and misuse of the information given (Weissbach, 1997). In addition to cyberstalkers and con artists, users are aware of irresponsible companies that have sold survey information to other companies who, in turn, have used such information for spamming purposes.

Truthfulness of Respondents/Multiple Entries

Like most other forms of surveys, there is no guarantee that the respondent does not provide false information. Whether there is a higher tendency to do so on the Internet is yet to be ascertained. In most Internet surveys, there is no control over people answering more than once. In one case, a well-known software publisher rigged multiple votes in favor of its product against a competitor in an Internet survey. Only the sheer volume of duplicate questionnaires created suspicion, and the scam was eventually uncovered (Eaton, 1997). However according to Scott Spain (of W3Survey.net), there are several methods to help overcome the problem of multiple entries, including the following.

- *Cookies.* This will work only if the user does not turn off the function and if the person completes the survey from the same computer.

- *Internet protocol* (IP). A researcher can set the **Common Gateway Interface** (CGI) to prevent multiple entries from the same IP address. However, if the person logs off their connection and them comes back again, they would probably have a different IP address.

- *Unique URL.* If a user is sending invitations (by e-mail), a unique URL system can be set up so that each participant gets a unique address for participation. It would look something like this: http://www.domain.com/cgi-bin/survey.pl?12345/, where "12345" is a unique, nonsequential identification number that must be used if accessed. If a user leaves that off, it won't allow them into the survey; if a user tries to change a number, it could take them hours to guess another available one.

- *Unique passwords.* A username/password combination system can be set up to allow each username/password to participate only once. Researchers can also allow multiple entries, but capture the username and password in the data so they can eliminate the duplicates later.

- *Clean it out.* It is probably easiest to allow duplicate entries that are cleaned out later. It is not hard to track down multiple entries by analyzing several criteria such as IP, browser type, personal information given, and typing patterns.

Designing Internet Surveys

In addition to adhering to all the principles of questionnaire design (delineated in any market research text), there are a number of tenets that researchers should observe when constructing a data collection instrument for use on the Internet. Specifically, they should keep in mind the following aesthetic and psychological considerations.

Aesthetic Considerations

Keep It Short and Simple

Paper surveys are typically short, in order to improve response rates. The same can be said of Internet surveys, which should be kept short (one or two screens) in order to generate high response levels. Respondents to online surveys typically have a shorter span of attention than respondents to mail and personal surveys; they will often lose interest after 25 to 30 questions. This compares unfavorably to telephone interviews, which can last for 30 minutes at a time (Krasilovsky, 1996). Additionally, it should be remembered by the researcher that many people still pay for each e-mail message they receive and some pay according to the length of the message; thus short surveys are both wise and kind. If the survey is very lengthy, it is best to break it up into several smaller pages rather than having one long page (Buchwald and Applied Business Intelligence, Inc., 1998).

Have Form Follow Function

The response-entry module should match the nature of the question. One set of guidelines states that researchers should use "buttons or drop-down menus for a single response, check boxes for multiple answers. . . . Buttons are best when there are five or fewer answers to choose from; a drop-down menu is easier to use with more than five answers. For really lengthy lists with short identifiers, such as the 50 U.S. states, it's wise to allow respondents the option of typing in the two-letter abbreviation rather than forcing them to scroll through the list" (McDaniel & Gates, 2002).

Take Care of the Eyes of Respondents

Eyestrain is a major reason that respondents may be dissatisfied, and it contributes to increased break-off rates. As a general rule, use cool colors while avoiding bright backgrounds (Buchwald & Applied Business Intelligence Inc., 1998).

Liven It Up (within Reasonable "Downloadable" Limits)

Researchers should make their surveys as interesting as possible by using graphics and color, and by using language that is as exciting and interesting as possible. It is also important to ensure that the language used will be understood by the targeted sample, whether formal or colloquial. Keeping the survey instrument lively can maintain the novelty of taking surveys on and through the Internet and can lessen the possibility of lower response rates in the long run. It is conceivable that over time the novelty of completing Internet surveys will wane. Users need only to delete the request for participating in surveys from their e-mail box. This would result in a drop in response rates. As predicted by Parker (1992), "sooner or later, e-mail subscribers may become pressers of the delete key, who pitch your questionnaire, unread, into the electronic world's equivalent of the circular file."

Also, it is important to keep in mind the technical capabilities of a respondent's computer and Internet connection. A survey should not be so fancy in its use of color and graphics that it burdens survey participants with colossal download times (Iyer, 1996).

Psychological Considerations

Exercising Proper Netiquette

First and foremost, proper netiquette means being forthright, nonintrusive, and respectful of the Internet user. As with other forms of survey research, *the identity of the researcher and the purpose should be made clear*. By being aboveboard the researcher can add credibility to the survey and make respondents feel that their opinions are valuable (Woodall, 1996). If revealing the name of the survey sponsor may result in response bias and/or sponsor confidentiality is absolutely essential, expect a much lower response rate. Keep in mind that a substantial percentage of Internet users are concerned about the confidentiality of personal information and believe privacy is the most important issue facing the Internet today. Confidentiality assurance, especially on sensitive issues, may well increase the level of response. This is especially the case with e-mail surveys and e-mails soliciting respondents to visit websites that contain surveys. Just as a headline in an advertisement can determine whether or not the consumer goes on to read the copy, a suitable e-mail heading is necessary to elicit participation in an online survey. The heading should identify the sponsor and purpose of the survey. Suitable and meaningful incentives to participate should be given. In addition, researchers should always provide clear instructions for survey participation, as well as for removal from the mailing list used to contact the individual.

Minimizing Respondent Bias

Respondent bias can be minimized if *a third party is employed to conduct the survey*. This could be a university or someone not directly connected or involved with the project. Apart from having more experience with online surveys and better systems, a nonbiased third party conducting the survey will generally obtain nonbiased answers.

Conducting Nonintrusive Surveys

Using bulk e-mail lists that send surveys or invitations to complete surveys is frowned upon. Respondents should always be given a way to vacate a mailing list. When compiling a survey sample it is necessary to cross-check lists to avoid double mailings to the same e-mail account.

Respecting the Privacy of Individuals

Using the Privacy Principles that were set by the U.S. Information Infrastructure Task Force, Bowers (1997) recommends the following as responsible practices in gathering and using private information online.

- Disclose the purpose of collecting information.

- Explain what steps will be taken to protect the confidentiality, quality, and integrity of the information collected.

- Explain to the respondent the consequences of providing or withholding information.

- Make the rights of redress available to individuals for wrongful or inaccurate disclosure of their personal information.

These guidelines should be adhered to in order to gain higher response rates and prevent mistrust. An explicit privacy policy listing the information set in the guidelines above should be made available to respondents. In addition, the Australian government's Privacy Amendment (Private Sector) Act 2000 is one of the world's most encompassing pieces of legislation on the matter of personal privacy.

FIGURE 7.2
Example of a Privacy Policy Statement

Source: Excite Customer Information Privacy Policy (http://www.excite.com/companyinfo_excite/excite_privacy/0,2 0398,,00.html/)

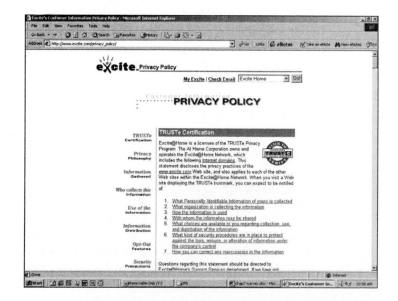

Personalizing Surveys

Respect for the respondent can also be demonstrated through surveys that are personalized. Most people like to have their names used. However, there remain some who regard this as bad netiquette, and thus personalization could in some instances reduce response rates.

Providing Incentives

Respondents are the ones who have to take the step (or click) to gain access to the survey. Accordingly, providing incentives to participate in the survey can heighten response rates. Incentives can be either material or nonmaterial and can be used to heighten participation as well as survey completion.

Material Incentives   Cash and prizes can be used as incentives to stimulate participation in almost any survey. Free screen savers and software are often used as incentives for those who are more computer literate and for people who work in the computer industry. Broadly speaking, using products from a company as a prize for participants would be a greater incentive for customers of that company. Company giveaways are best used in situations where a company wants to find out more about its customers. Keep in mind that in some countries giveaways are illegal; a contest or nonmaterial incentives may hence be more appropriate.

Nonmaterial Incentives   These are also a powerful way to get respondents to participate in a survey. Nonmaterial incentives usually appeal to the more noble side of people. For example, the GVU surveys of the Internet population did not introduce cash incentives until the eighth survey. For the most part, individual participation was seen as a means of contributing to the knowledge and understanding of the online world. The subsequent introduction of a cash prize incentive did not increase the number of people participating in the survey. This would suggest that nonmaterial incentives could be an equally powerful way to solicit respondents.

Another, perhaps more commonly used, form of nonmaterial incentive is to promise better, more *customized services* to the customer who fills in a survey form. These short surveys are usually conducted when customers make a purchase online or when they request some additional information. Allowing access to information—only after completing surveys—is another form of nonmaterial incentive that has proved to be effective.

Setting Time Limits

While transmission of the survey is almost instantaneous, researchers must remember that respondents do not check their e-mail or visit websites daily (Woodall, 1996). Hence, it may be wise to set a deadline in which respondents need to reply in order to obtain the rewards that are given as an incentive for participating in the survey.

Sampling Methodologies for Internet Surveys

As originally delineated by Watt (1997), there are several sampling techniques that may be used when conducting surveys on the Internet. Unrestricted samples allow everyone to participate. Such sampling is simple to administer but may not be appropriate for most surveys as it is a poor representation of the population. Screened samples allow only certain respondents who qualify to participate in the survey. Recruited samples are respondents who have already been recruited and are willing to participate in surveys. Recruited samples can be obtained through advertising/postings, opt-in lists, loyalty marketing and incentive programs, random intercepts with banner ads, as well as intercepting visitors to the company website.

Necessarily, the researcher must determine what sampling method is best suited for any given survey research project. Factors of time and money invariably come into play when deciding on the most appropriate sampling method. Bigger, better, and more representative samples usually come with bigger price tags that reflect the additional time and expertise that must be expended. Table 7.2 overviews the three methods of Internet sampling, while Table 7.3 outlines the advantages and disadvantages of using Internet samples recruited by five different methods.

Internet Survey Distribution Options

In sum, the various methods of conducting surveys on the Internet all have their advantages and disadvantages. Depending on a researcher's task, budget, and programming expertise, there are compatible survey research services and software. Once the survey platform is

TABLE 7.2
Types of Internet Population Samples

Unrestricted samples	This occurs where there is no control whatsoever on the individuals who participate in the survey. Anyone who so wishes may participate, resulting in poor representation due to the self-selection of respondents. Unrestricted samples are best used in point-of-sale surveys, website user profiles, and the recruitment of focus group members.
Screened samples	Screened samples represent better samples as quotas of desired sample characteristics are imposed. Demographic characteristics are most often the screening criteria used to filter out the respondents. Sometimes product-related criteria such as product use and past purchase behavior are used. Samples are usually screened by employing a branching or skip pattern, wherein screening questions are asked before a qualified respondent is shown the full questionnaire. Some survey systems are even able to assign respondents to the various predivided segments, with the appropriate questionnaire presented to the respondent according to the segment to which they are allocated.
	Many current online survey companies use this type of sample by maintaining what Watt (1997) calls a "panel house." A group of willing, qualified respondents are pooled into a database, which classifies respondents into different demographic segments according to a screening questionnaire that is filled in prior to being entered into the panel house. Respondents are usually offered a financial incentive to participate.
	It is noteworthy that newsgroups and discussion lists can assist the researcher in generating a screened sample. Internet users who participate in newsgroups and discussion mailing lists do have similar interests that create a variation of psychographic screening.
Recruited samples	The makeup of respondents is known as they are already in a database, and hence respondents can be prescreened and selected according to criteria laid out by researchers. Potential respondents from an existing database are approached and recruited through their websites and e-mail as well as through various traditional samples such as the telephone, mail, or in person (Watt, 1997). In most cases, respondents who are selected are notified by e-mail and directed to a website where the online survey is completed.

Source: Adapted from Watt (1997)

FIGURE 7.3

Focusline.com
Conducts Internet
Surveys by Building
a Pool of Willing
Respondents with
Screened Samples

Source: http://focusline.com/

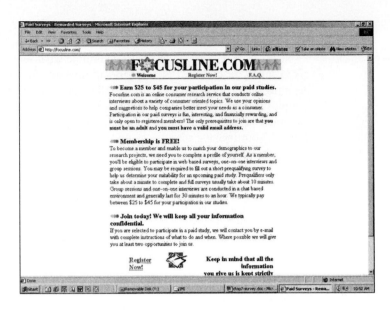

TABLE 7.3

Advantages and Disadvantages of Using Samples Recruited by Different Methods

Source	Advantages	Disadvantages
Recruited panel. Created through Internet-based advertising or postings, and offering compensation.	Can build large pools of individuals who can respond quickly.	High advertising costs, and without constant motivation and compensation have high dropout rates; also have the problem of attracting professional survey takers.
Opt-in list rentals. Created from lists of e-mail users who agree to receive "other services" e-mail.	A number of highly targeted opt-in lists of individuals willing to participate in surveys are available.	High costs of list rental; strict limitations on usage; and restricted access to personal information.
Opt-in panels. Created from Internet-based loyalty marketing or incentive programs.	These rapidly growing, self-sustaining programs, featuring built-in incentives, are potential sources of highly targeted online users.	Time and effort are needed to establish a relationship with a list provider and negotiate terms. Unless a researcher is able to capture personal data, conducting longitudinal studies is complicated.
Random website intercepts. Web users solicited through random banner ads.	This can provide for a more random sampling of the Internet population.	High cost and ineffectiveness of banner ads; with click through rates of less than 1 percent, the amount of time to obtain the desired sample size is unpredictable.
Company website visitors. A sample or panel comprised of visitors to the firm's site.	These samples/panels are essential for developing relationship and one-to-one marketing strategies.	As with any survey, the opinions of those who agree to participate may differ from the opinions of the noncooperative visitors to a website.

Source: McDaniel & Gates (2002)

selected, the question is how best to construct and implement an online survey. This is the next topic of concern.

E-Mail Surveys

In order to command instant attention online, researchers may want to combine their Web surveys with e-mail. This can be done by posting the URL of the website containing the survey in the e-mail message so that respondents can just click on the URL link and open the website containing the survey. This combines the flexibility and more advanced features of the other methods with the attention-demanding power of the e-mail.

E-mail surveys use pure text (**ASCII**) or attachments. Pure text e-mail surveys are akin to paper surveys, wherein the respondent types the answers in the appropriate places in the survey. The advantage of this type of survey is that it demands instant attention, as it is not likely that the respondent will totally ignore an e-mail that is left in their mailbox. It is also relatively easy to conduct without much programming expertise. In addition, multiple surveys are eliminated using this method, unless the respondent has several different e-mail accounts.

The shortcomings of this method are that the survey is limited to plain text, and visual graphics for grids and scale responses cannot usually be included unless the e-mail program accepts **html**. There is also no way to check for response errors until the questionnaire is returned. Thus, there is no opportunity for requesting that the data be reentered, unless the respondent is sent another e-mail and asked to complete the questionnaire again. Questions that are skipped, along with damaged text, may require costly hand-coding, using specialized software that allows data to be entered directly into a database. Otherwise, it will be necessary to print every survey and hand-code all the results.

Internet users can choose from a multitude of different e-mail programs, hence creating another problem with ASCII text surveys. What is sent is not necessarily what is seen when it is opened by respondents. Often formatting, spacing, and alignment become contorted. This may result in difficulties completing the survey.

Finally, it must be pointed out that e-mail survey questions and responses are very susceptible to modification or deletion by respondents (Krasilovsky, 1996). If constraints only permit text-based e-mail surveys, the researcher should send out a preceding message seeking permission to send the survey; Internet users do not look fondly upon unsolicited e-mail surveys (spamming) and are likely to return abusive **flame messages** (Krasilovsky, 1996).

On-Site Intercept Surveys

Another often used method is to conduct surveys on those customers, prospects, and visitors who come to a firm's website without invitation. Often companies ask customers to fill in a short survey when they are purchasing an item. In other instances, contests are conducted on the site or free e-zines are offered to encourage participation. It is also possible to have pop-up surveys that appear randomly once the website downloads, inviting the visitor to participate in the survey. This can contribute to a more random sample and higher response rates.

Newsgroups and Discussion/Mailing Lists

There are times when a researcher will want information from people who have a strong interest in a specific topic. In this instance, newsgroup and discussion/mailing list surveys may be the way to go. One very convincing argument for using newsgroups and discussion/mailing lists is that they represent a well-segmented market of the population according to interest and/or geography, which would be an ideal sample for the market researcher in many cases. However, of all the ways to conduct surveys on the Internet, newsgroups and discussion/mailing lists are by far the most potentially explosive. Mistakes here can generate hate mail, resulting in the loss of goodwill, and can get the researcher's entire company banned from newsgroups and discussion/mailing lists—not to mention ruining the survey.

For newsgroup surveys, it is important to become familiar with the style and substance of the newsgroup by observing for at least two weeks, and always read the **FAQ**s. Do not ever judge a newsgroup by its name. Researchers should check out http://www.tile.net/ to find a suitable newsgroup related to the research topic. Reading Chapter 8 (which addresses newsgroup research techniques) is recommended before sending out survey invitations to any newsgroup. Predicably, it has been found that topics of relevance to respondents usually command much higher response rates and faster responses (Gjestland, 1996). Often newsgroups and discussion/mailing lists can assist the researcher in finding a sample that is likely to have an interest in the survey topic.

Mailing lists can be categorized into two types: *one-to-many* e-zine type mailing lists, where no discussions are conducted, and *many-to-many* type discussion lists, where everyone in the list can participate in discussions of the given topic. For a directory of publicly accessible mailing lists, List-Universe.com, the E-mail List Publisher Resource Network (http://list-universe.com/), provides a large collection of resources, directories, communities, tools, tips, tricks, suggestions, ideas, and strategies for researchers seeking the most suitable mailing tactics and lists (whether it is a discussion list, newsletter, or e-mail list). Researchers should keep in mind that mailing lists are probably even more sensitive to improper netiquette, so they should make sure invitations to participate in surveys are courteous. It is also important to allow members to see that the survey will somewhat benefit the members of the mailing list as a whole. Again, the following guidelines should be heeded.

- Make sure a survey is strongly topic-related, and that its results will contribute to the knowledge of the mailing list.

- Being a regular contributor to the mailing list and regularly helping other members on the mailing list with problems will earn a researcher a good reputation, resulting in greater participation.

- Malcolm Weir (1998) suggests taking time to write a discussion of various approaches, pros and cons, and so forth, before seeking opinions or comments using a survey. In other words, create a discussion that leads into the survey.

- Allow the members of the mailing list access to the results of the survey (or at least part of a summary on the major findings).

In-House or Outsource? Internet Survey Research Firms and Services

With a good grounding in the basics of constructing and conducting surveys online, the user faces one more crucial decision. Who should do the actual survey research? Should it be conducted in-house or outsourced to a commercial service? Should a firm have neither the time nor the inclination to conduct their own survey, there is an ever growing group of online consultants and Internet commercial services from which to choose. It is worth mentioning that the number of companies conducting online survey research has been increasing at a dramatic pace. Since mid-1996, the number of websites that are listed on the Internet for *market survey research* services increased from a few hundred to nearly a million (965,000 results were returned using Google on July 24, 2001). Of course all these hits are not research companies, but rather Web pages that contain the phrase market survey research. Fortunately, there are several excellent online directories with comprehensive lists of companies that can be commissioned to conduct Internet surveys.

Online Directories of Internet Survey Research Firms and Services

In addition to providing a host of resources and tools for market researchers, @Research-Info.com (http://www.researchinfo.com/) provides a Research Company Directory of market research firms that can be explored by type of research conducted, geographical area (mainly U.S.), and/or type of industry.

Quirk's Marketing Research Review (http://www.quirks.com/) contains the Researcher SourceBook™, which has listings of more than 7,300 firms providing marketing research products and services. This website has a directory that is searchable by company, contact name, geography, and specialty.

Zarden Market Research Direct-A-Net (http://www.zarden.com/) provides an excellent directory for finding market research companies. Zarden allows searching through its directory by type of service provided, by alphabetical order, and by state/country.

At Volition.com (http://www.volition.com/opinions.html), researchers can find a list of over 30 online market research firms that will pay for users' opinions, with cash, prizes, and/or points given for participating in their surveys and related research activities.

Internet Survey Firm Selection Criteria

Researchers will need to sift through all the possible contenders for their Internet survey business. A reliable survey research firm should use the following suggested selection criteria.

Have Experience with Various Clients

Obviously the more experience that the company has with online surveys, the more reliable in general they should be. Researchers should check a potential company's website for other clientele; note how long they have been in the online market research business and whether their clientele includes any big firms.

FIGURE 7.4

@ResearchInfo.com

Source:
http://www.researchinfo.com/

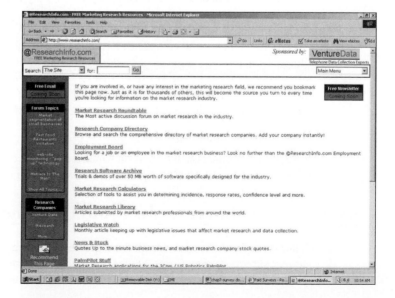

FIGURE 7.5
**Volition.com's List of
Companies That Pay
for Survey
Participation**

Source:
http://www.volition.com/
opinions.html/

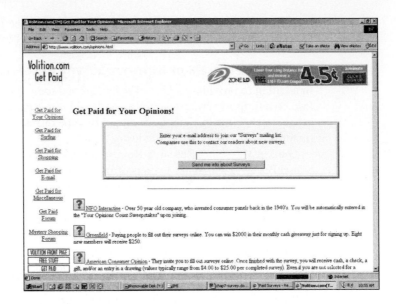

Have Advanced Real-Time Data Processing Services and Access to the Latest Data

One of the benefits of the Internet is the ability to process data that is gathered in real time. As a decision maker, a researcher would desire to have easy access to real-time information in order to make timely decisions. Therefore, researchers should look for companies that provide this capability.

Are Up to Date in the Technical Area

It is important to be able to get information in the lowest-priced and fastest way possible. Software and technical advances in this area are making it to gather data easier from the respondents. Researchers should find a company that is always on the move and that is continually updating itself. This is especially true in a situation where a researcher intends to utilize the services of a research company over a long period of time.

Have Capabilities That Match the Needs of the Research Project

Keep in mind that not all companies have the same capabilities; some companies have multilingual capabilities, some have random sampling abilities, and others focus solely on Internet surveying. Yet there are some that have experience in gathering data through other media as well. Researchers should identify what capabilities and data the research project requires, and make sure that the company chosen has those capabilities.

Have Industry/Area Focus

Researchers should note the areas on which a research company focuses. Most likely, firms have had experience conducting online survey research in a particular industry.

Do-It-Yourself Internet Surveys: Just Add Questions

A number of websites provide all the ingredients a researcher needs to conduct an Internet survey: servers, survey forms, advice on design and distribution, editing, publishing, even tabulation and analysis packages. All researchers need to do is supply the questions.

FIGURE 7.6
WebSurveyor's
"Conduct a Web
Survey Right Now"

Source:
http://www.websurveyor.com/
home_now.asp/

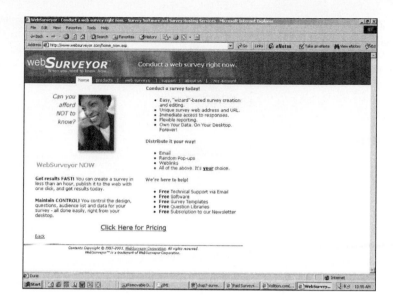

One such website is WebSurveyor (http://www.websurveyor.com/). As self-professed on their website, with WebSurveyor researchers can indeed create and conduct their own survey. "You control the design, questions, audience list and data. You can publish it to the Web and get the results back as well."

Online Surveying Software and Support

The following are some of the more notable software, reference, and survey support services on the Internet. The websites are exemplary of the many types of programs and services that are available to assist researchers in designing, sampling, and executing online surveys.

Interactive Marketing Research Organization (IMRO) (http://www.imro.org/), was formed in 2000 and defines itself as "a confederation of world leaders among firms involved in new technology marketing research, to lead in the development, dissemination, and implementation of interactive marketing research concepts, practice and information."

Covering 18 countries, Survey Sampling, Inc. (http://www.surveysampling.com/ssi_home.html) is touted to be the "word's largest and most reliable sample source for telephone and Internet surveys."

The Guide to Available Math Software (http://gams.nist.gov/) is "a cross-index and virtual repository of mathematical and statistical software components of use in computational science and engineering."

CustomerSat, Inc. (http://www.customersat.com/index.html/) provides samples of online surveys and allows users to post their own surveys. Researchers can visit Customer-Sat.com University and learn how to compose a survey or analyze the results, get an executive perspective on measuring and enhancing customer satisfaction and loyalty, and find information on more advanced topics, as well as the latest in Internet customer research. Check out their Executive White Paper, which covers the following topics:

- Introduction.

- Internet advantages.

FIGURE 7.7
Interactive
Marketing Research
Organization

Source: http://www.imro.org/

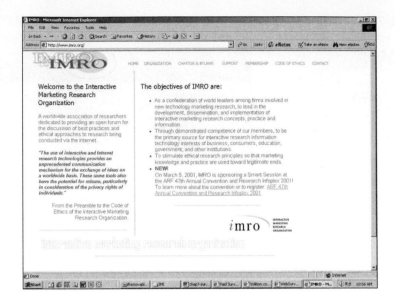

- Customer access to the Internet.

- Types of survey questionnaires and their design.

- E-mail survey or Web survey.

- Web surveys.

- Positively identifying respondents.

- Customer confidentiality and anonymity.

- Survey response rates.

- Measuring response rate differences.

- Respondent incentives.

- Rules of thumb for decision makers.

- Disseminating survey results in real time via the Internet.

- Customer relationship systems trigger surveys.

- Combining Internet-based data collection with conventional techniques.

- Case study: first worldwide customer satisfaction survey on the Internet.

CustomerSat, Inc. also includes 2,000 sample questions that suggest attributes for inclusion in a researcher's next survey of customer satisfaction and loyalty, employee satisfaction and commitment, or management effectiveness.

Virtually any and all the Internet survey software programs available are listed and evaluated at @ResearchInfo.com (http://www.researchinfo.com/), and many can be directly downloaded for trial.

Infopoll, Inc. (http://infopoll.com/) is a highly recommended website for those interested in designing and conducting survey research off-line or online. As advertised on its website, Infopoll, Inc. "offers online survey software and services enabling everyone to

FIGURE 7.8
CustomerSat, Inc.

Source:
http://www.customersat.com/
index.html/

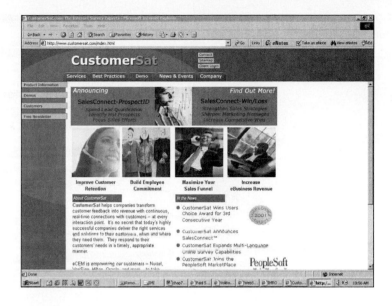

FIGURE 7.9
@ResearchInfo.com's
List of Available
Survey Software

Source:
http://www.researchinfo.com/
docs/software/index.cfm/

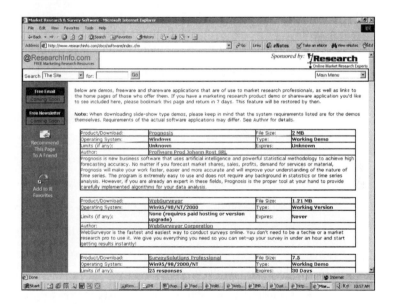

easily create professionally looking questionnaires, collect instant feedback and business intelligence from customers, partners and employees, and deliver real-time customized reports anywhere and anytime." They indeed provide "everything one needs to conduct a survey or poll successfully." Their free program called Infopoll Designer Version 7 is a well-designed questionnaire authoring tool that allows researchers to create their own data collection instruments.

The selection of software that can best serve a researcher's needs can be assisted by the following checklist compiled by Scott W. Spain (1998). Spain is an experienced veteran and recognized expert in Internet survey research, and the checklist is based on his own and his clients' requirements.

FIGURE 7.10
Infopoll, Inc.

Source: http://infopoll.com/

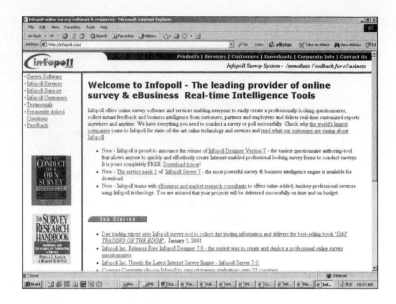

- Complete customization of HTML, not just backgrounds and fonts.

- Choice of multipage or single-page format.

- Choices of how many questions appear on each page.

- Results saved to a database, not a POP3 e-mail box.

- True skip patterns (where users can skip through a list of items by looking at every nth item).

- Skip patterns based on multiple criteria from any page.

- True branching (multiple questionnaire versions based on answers given).

- Response piping (including a response in a later question).

- Backup capability for respondents using their browser's "back" button without losing data.

- Quota and duplicate control options.

- Security/password protection options.

- Data validation choices (client side, server side, or both working together) and advanced data validation.

- Randomization of response choices (must also be able to choose to leave certain response choices "in order"), questions, and blocks of questions.

- Real-time display of survey results.

- Grid questions with the ability to color every other line.

- Most importantly, 100 percent compatibility with all form-capable browsers.

Note that everything above is completely useless if the software requires cookies or other newer versions of Web browsers to run.

Summary

The Internet presents researchers with a distinctly unique vehicle for conducting market survey research. Internet surveying has many advantages over traditional surveying methods, most notably significant savings in time and money. However, the Internet still continues to face the problems associated with being able to generalize, although researchers are finding that Internet surveys are yielding similar results to those of surveys using traditional methods.

Apart from surveys on the Internet population regarding computer products and online companies (which conduct their business on the Internet), Internet surveys may still need to be supplemented with traditional forms of surveying. This is especially true in countries with significantly smaller percentages of populations with Internet access. However, the future looks bright for Internet surveying with the continued rapid and widespread adoption of Internet use. Combined with greater **bandwidth** and the trend toward media convergence, Internet surveys will, in the future, become mainstream and generalizable.

There are several methods of Internet surveying that employ different types of distribution—e-mail, on-site, newsgroups, and discussion/mailing lists. E-mail surveys are perhaps the easiest to program but often require hand-coding as respondents can easily alter the questionnaires. E-mail surveys are perhaps best suited for low-budget research with few respondents.

There are basic guidelines that researchers can follow when conducting surveys online, many of which can be summed up in one word: netiquette. Researchers should always remember to be forthright, nonintrusive, and respectful of the Internet user. This will ensure they get past the first hurdle: the respondent's delete button. It is vital to respect Internet users' privacy, to not spam them, and to try to offer some form of incentive that is relevant and useful to them.

Newsgroups and discussion lists are excellent populations from which to draw samples, as they are predefined interest groups. An effective researcher makes an effort to be a regular contributor to the community and to stimulate discussion before inviting people to participate in a survey (rather than just using a cold, hard "please participate in this survey" approach). Surveys conducted on an organization's website are most successful when there is substantial traffic on the website and there are sufficient incentives to motivate the respondent to participate.

When choosing an online survey research firm, companies should select one that is experienced, is technically up to date, and has capabilities that matches their research needs. It would also be preferable to find a firm that allows the real-time processing of and access to survey data. Since a substantial proportion of the population does not have Internet access as yet, it would be appropriate in most cases to find a firm with multiple survey delivery methods.

Your online learning center has a case study on *Internet Surveys* available now at www.mhhe.com/forrest.

Discussion Questions

1. What do you believe to be the most important advantage that Internet surveys have over traditional forms of surveying methods? Why?

2. It is conceivable that, in the future, e-mail invitations to participate in online surveys could be regarded as junk as the novelty factor wears off and as consumers continue to receive such invitations from spammers. As a market researcher who recognizes the value of the Internet as a survey tool, what are some of the ways that you can circumvent such a scenario?

3. What future events and/or trends do you foresee with respect to Internet survey research?

4. How would you design and conduct an Internet survey with 25 questions and a sample of 100 students?

5. Would you complete a survey on the Internet if there were no incentive (either material or nonmaterial)? Explain your answer.

6. Think of one material and one nonmaterial incentive you believe appropriate for an academic survey of Internet-user attitudes regarding spamming on the Internet.

7. What do you believe are the two most important criteria in selecting a commercial research service?

8. You conduct research regularly on several newsgroups and discussion lists. You need to keep up your reputation and image in the community in order to receive good response rates consistently. What are some of the things you can do to build and maintain your reputation in the virtual community and keep community members happy before, during, and after the research?

9. What impact will media convergence have on Internet survey research? Give some possible scenarios of how researchers may conduct surveys over the Internet in the year 2012.

Internet Project

Go to Infopoll, Inc. (http://www.infopoll.com/).
1. Design your own survey using Infopoll Designer.
2. Publish your survey online.
3. Solicit your friends/colleagues/customers to go to the website and complete the questionnaire.
4. Write a report summarizing the results.

Further Reading

Dillman, Don A. (1999), *Mail and Internet Surveys: The Tailored Design Method*, 2nd ed. Canada: John Wiley & Sons.
Nesbary, Dale *Survey Research and the World Wide Web* Boston, Massachusetts: Allyn & Bacon. 0205289940.

References

Alreck, P. L., & Settle, R. B. (1995). *The Survey Research Handbook*, 2nd ed. Chicago: Irwin.
Bachmann, D., Elfrink, J., & Vazzana, G. (1996). "Tracking the Progress of E-mail vs. Snail-Mail." *Marketing Research*, Summer, vol. 8, no. 2, pp. 31–5.
Bowers, D. K. (1997). "Privacy Online." *Marketing Research*, vol. 9, no. 3, pp. 37–8.
Buchwald, J., & Applied Business Intelligence, Inc. (1998). *The Ten Commandments of Internet Surveying*. California: Applied Business Intelligence, Inc.
Chisholm, J. (1995). "Surveys by E-mail and Internet." *UNIX Review*, vol. 13, no. 13, pp. 11–16.
Colby, C. (1996). *Spam and Research on the Internet*. Great Falls, Virginia: Rockbridge Associates, Inc.
Costes, Y. (1997). *Effectiveness of E-mail vs. Paper-Mail as a Survey Media*. Universite Paris Dauphine.
CustomerSat.com (1997). Company brochure, http://www.CustomerSat.com/.
CustomerSat.com (1997–8). "An Introduction to Internet Surveys" (http://www.customersat.com/intro.htm#WhySurvey/).

CustomerSat.com (1997–8). "Advantages of Using the Internet for Surveying" (http://www.customersat.com/usinginternet.htm/).

CustomerSat.com (1997–8), "Deploying Surveys" (http://www.customersat.com/deploy.htm/).

Davis, G., (1997). "Are Internet Surveys Ready for Prime Time?" *Marketing News*, vol. 31, no. 8, p. 31.

Eaton, B., (1997). *The Problems and Pitfalls of Net Survey Methodologies* Petaluma, California: Creative Research Systems, Inc.

Edmondson, B., (1997). "The Wired Bunch." *American Demographics*, vol. 19, no. 6, pp. 10–15.

Ellsworth, J. H., and Ellsworth, M. V., (1997). *Marketing on the Internet.* New York: John Wiley & Sons.

Georgia Tech Research Corporation (1997). "Most Important Issue Facing the Internet" (http://www.gvu.gatech.edu/user_surveys/survey-1997.10/graphs/general/Most_Import_Issue_Facing_the_Internet.html/).

Gjestland, L., (1996). "Net? Not Yet." *Marketing Research*, vol. 8, no. 1, pp. 26–9.

Golden, P. A., Beauclair, R., and Sussman, L. (1992). "Factors Affecting Electronic Mail Use." *Computers in Human Behavior*, no. 8, pp. 297–311.

Hair, J. F., Anderson, R. E., Tatham, R. L., and Black, W. C. (1995). *Multivariate Data Analysis*, 4th ed. Englewood Cliffs, New Jersey: Prentice Hall.

Hodges, J., (1996). "It's Becoming a Small World Wide Web after All: Publishers, Advertisers Regionalize Content Services." *Advertising Age* [Online], February 12 (http://www.adage.com/).

Iyer, R., (1996). "The Internet: A New Opportunity for Marketing Research Firms," *Quirk's Marketing Research Review*, May.

Krasilovsky, P., (1996). "Surveys in Cyberspace," *American Demographics*, November–December, pp. 18–20.

Kully E. A. (1997). *Conducting Research via the Internet.* Chicago: Crestwood Associates.

McDaniel, Carl, and Roger Gates (2002). *Marketing Research: The Impact of the Internet.* Mason, Ohio: South-Western Educational Publishing, Chapter 6, pp. 182–93.

Media Marketing Consultants (1998) "MMC Online Survey Hosting" (http://www.mm consultants.com/surveyhost.htm/).

Mosley-Matchett, J. D. (1997). "Remember: It's the World Wide Web," *AMA Marketing News*, January 20, vol. 31, no. 2, p. 16 (http://www.jdmm.com/ama_1.html/).

Oppermann, M., (1995). "E-mail Surveys—Potentials and Pitfalls." *Marketing Research*, vol. 7, no. 3, pp. 28–33.

Parker, L., (1992). "Collecting Data the E-mail Way." *Training and Development*, vol. 46, no. 7, pp. 52–4.

Pope, N. K., Tam, T., Forrest, E. J., and Henderson K., (1997). "Survey Research on the Web." *The Fourteenth International Conference on Technology and Education.* Oslo, Norway, August 10–13, vol. 2, pp. 620–3.

Roller, M. R., (1996). "Virtual Research Exists, But How Real Is It?" *Marketing News*, vol. 30, no. 2, pp. 13, 15.

Romano, C. (1996). "Websites: If You Build It, Will They Come?" *Management Review*, vol. 85, no. 9, pp. 49–51.

SRI International, (1995). (http://www.sri.com/).

Solomon, M. B., (1996) "Targeting Trendsetters." *Marketing Research*, vol. 8, no. 2, pp. 9–11.

Sproull, L., and Kiesler, S., (1986). "Reducing Social Context Cues: Electronic Mail in Organizational Communication." *Management Science*, vol. 32, no. 1, pp. 1492–512.

SurveyOnline.com, (1997). (http://www.surveyonline.com/).

Unger, R., (1996). *Brand with the New Technology: Part I.* Paper presented at the Retail Advertising Conference. Chicago, Illinois.

Waller, Richard, (2001). "How Big Is the Internet" (http://www.waller.co.uk/web.htm/).

Watt, J., (1997). *Using the Internet for Quantitative Survey Research.* Quirks.com. (Watt provides an exceptionally good analysis of Internet survey methods. It is from his analyses that much of this section was drawn.)

Weissbach, S., (1997). *Internet Research: Still a Few Hurdles to Clear.* Quirks.com.

Woodall, G., (1996). *Market Research on the Internet.* Great Falls, Virginia: Rockbridge Associates, Inc.

8

An Introduction to Internet Newsgroups

Newsgroups and discussion lists are valuable to researchers because they are an excellent venue for monitoring consumer opinions as well as soliciting expert advice. Moreover, they are an incredibly valuable archive of information, containing the accumulation of years of participants' concerns and convictions. In addition to providing a fertile ground for collecting consumer and competitor intelligence, newsgroups and discussion lists provide the survey researcher with a pool of pre-screened special-interest subjects who otherwise could be hard to identify. This chapter focuses on the research applications that newsgroups and discussion lists offer the market researcher.

Chapter objectives

This chapter aims to:

- Explain what newsgroups are and how they are organized.

- Outline proper netiquette for interacting with and posting to newsgroups.

- Explain how to conduct surveys within newsgroups.

- Provide a directory of useful Internet resources on newsgroups and discussion groups.

Introduction

Newsgroups, also known as **Internet discussion groups** (IDGs), are one of the richest sources of online information.

> Whether you're a rank beginner or an old hand on the Net, newsgroups—chat forums that run over the open-ended "Usenet" discussion network—will give you the scoop on your concern, from computer conundrums to Beanie Baby hunts. (Keizer, 2000)

Today, Internet users have direct access to over 80,000 newsgroups, where people **post** hundreds of thousands of messages a day and over 650 million postings (dating back to 1995) are archived (Gunn, 2001). Through them researchers can communicate with a few dozen to a few million individual persons on almost any topic conceivable. **Usenet** organizes thousands of newsgroups into topic areas, with discussion of virtually anything, including food recipes, politics, sex, and computers. Newsgroups are like a global electronic community bulletin board system on the Internet. With so many newsgroups in existence, there should be at least one newsgroup out there that is relevant to any marketing research project.

It is interesting to note that newsgroups are easy to create, but nearly impossible to delete, and that hundreds of hierarchies each have a different procedure. When someone posts an article, or posting, to a newsgroup, that article is sent out via computers for other people to read. A newsgroup is a posted discussion group on Usenet, a worldwide network of newsgroups. Newsgroups are almost an entirely text-based network. Newsgroup postings are sent much like e-mail is sent between people, but the message is sent directly to a **server**, which delivers it globally to thousands of servers. This allows the posting to be viewed by millions of people worldwide.

Newsgroups are categorized into several large "trees," each of which is broken down into layers of specific topical subtrees. Within each newsgroup, messages are posted by its participants. These messages are the real content of newsgroups: they look like personal e-mails but are posted for the entire newsgroup audience to access.

Discussion group mailing lists are similar to newsgroups, except that the messages are delivered directly into the personal e-mail boxes of subscribers, instead of being posted to an electronic bulletin board. The other difference is that mailing lists can be kept private and restricted to only those people the researcher wants to participate, whereas newsgroups are accessed by anyone around the world who has an interest in the newsgroup.

There are two types of newsgroups: **unmoderated**, which are completely open, allowing anyone to participate in the discussion, posting anything they want (though keeping to the newsgroup's topic is usually appreciated); and **moderated**, meaning that there is a newsgroup **moderator** who reviews postings sent to their newsgroup before allowing them to appear. Moderated newsgroups almost always contain more focused discussions since the moderators want to keep the conversation on track. Moderated newsgroups also have fewer blatant advertisements, which can clog up newsgroup content.

Newsgroups are a great forum through which people interact, discussing various interests and passions with thousands of other people on the Internet. They are also undeniably a great resource (thousands of experts on various topics) for sharing ideas and for research purposes, which is precisely what this chapter will demonstrate.

Newsgroup Applications in Marketing Research

Performing like focus groups, but available only online, newsgroups are useful in marketing research. An enormous pool of knowledge and experience is available through newsgroup subscribers. Any problem or question can be posted to relevant newsgroups, with answers received from both dilettante and expert participants. The serendipitous nature of the exchanges often results in the generation of numerous related ideas and facts that could never have been compiled outside the newsgroup environment.

At the same time, newsgroups can assist researchers to screen samples for their surveys. Often individuals who participate in newsgroups have many similar psychographic and demographic features. Newsgroups assist researchers in finding appropriate samples, which are otherwise extremely difficult to find. **Lurking** (that is, reading messages without participating) in newsgroups is another means by which researchers can unobtrusively assess consumer attitudes and perceptions. Newsgroups can prove helpful in assisting researchers' environmental scanning and competitor tracking efforts, should discussion of their competitors and the industry environment be introduced as a discussion question or topic.

In addition, newsgroups can be used purely for marketing purposes, that is, where a researcher "uses" Usenet solely as a promotional channel. Their postings would be for purposes of sales solicitation as opposed to information gathering. This application is not the focus of this chapter, which is instead concerned with using the Internet for gathering market research, not garnering market share. For those interested in the former, the following are excellent resources:

- Online Success for Internet Business, "Power Marketing through Newsgroups" (http://www.webmastercourse.com/articles/newsgroups/).

- American Express Small Business Services—Small Business Exchange (http://home3.americanexpress.com/smallbusiness/resources/expanding/newsmail.shtml/).

Organization of the Hierarchy of Newsgroups

Newsgroups are divided into many hierarchies based on topical and regional categories. The names of newsgroups usually start with the topical or regional category they fall under, followed by one or two names that more specifically define the newsgroup. The first part is the most general (sci or comp), the following is more specific, with the last part completing the actual group name. Each part implies a further, more specific level. Understanding this hierarchy can help people find the intended newsgroup more swiftly. For example, the biz hierarchy is about newsgroups that focus on topics that are business related, such as biz.marketing.international, which is a newsgroup for people interested in conducting international trade and/or are looking for international business contacts online.

The Big Ten

Google Groups uses 10 major categories to reflect the interests of newsgroup subscribers at their website, (http://groups.google.com/).

FIGURE 8.1

Example of How Newsgroup Hierarchies Are Organized: The Biz Hierarchy

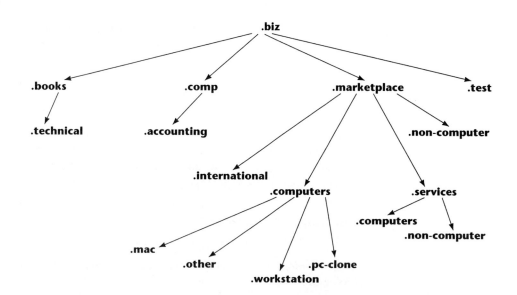

FIGURE 8.2
Organization of the
Biz Hierarchy as
Listed by Google

Source:
http://groups.google.com/
groups?group=biz/

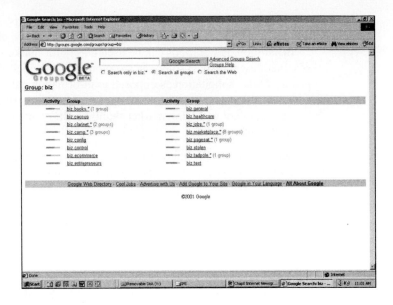

1. *Comp (computers):* Discussions about computers; topics of interest to both computer professionals and hobbyists; including topics in computer science, consumer information, software sources, and information on hardware and software systems.

2. *Rec (recreation):* Groups oriented toward the arts, hobbies, and recreational activities.

3. *Sci (science):* Discussions relating to research or application of the established sciences.

4. *Soc (society):* Groups primarily addressing social issues and socializing. There are many discussions related to many different world cultures.

5. *Talk*: For those people who love talking. Groups can discuss current issues or debate for weeks without any resolution.

6. *News*: Usenet describes itself—newsgroups discussing newsgroups. Groups concerned with the news network, group maintenance, and software.

7. *Misc (miscellaneous):* Groups on topics that are not classified into any of the other headings; or have themes from several categories, such as employment and health.

8. *Humanities*: Usenet discussions about humanities, fine arts, philosophy, literature, etc.

9. *Biz (business):* Business and commercial discussions including products, services, and reviews, as well as product development and integration.

10. *Alt*: Any conceivable topic. The alt hierarchy is a major hierarchy offered as an alternative to Usenet moderation and control. It contains groups regarding all sorts of topics created by people who wanted to bypass the "Usenet cabal" who control the previous groups. Many of these are highly unregulated groups, and can be very offensive.

Other Major Hierarchies

Newusers: If Usenet is a mystery to a new user, this would be the best place to start.

- *Bionet (biology net):* This is where biologists discuss their favorite body parts with other biologists.

- Info (information): This is the place to find the messages of mailing lists on Usenet.

Regional Categories

Newsgroups are also divided into regional categories, for example:

- *Ab*: Issues and topics of Alberta, Canada.

- *Ak*: Issues and topics related to Alaska.

- *Aus*: Topics on the Australasian region.

- Japan: Discussions on Japan and newsgroups in Japanese.

- Seattle: Affairs of Seattle, Washington.

- UK: Discussions on the United Kingdom.

A list of all newsgroups and a brief overview on them can be found at the Master List of Newsgroup Hierarchies v5.19 (http://www.faqs.org/faqs/top.html/).

Finding the Right Newsgroup/s

Finding the right newsgroup is the same as finding anything else on the Internet. Users can begin the search with their favorite search engine and search for *newsgroup* and/or *mailing lists*. After selecting their reference source, users can identify those specific newsgroups or mailing lists that include discussions on their particular topic of interest.

> For example, if your online company sells software, you may want to narrow your search to keywords such as software, computer software, computers, etc. This will allow you to find groups or lists of people who are already directly interested in your product or service—a targeted market. Also, don't neglect those groups who would use your software. For instance, if your software is used by fitness centers, you want to browse those newsgroups as well.
>
> When I want to find newsgroups related to my sites, I use Mailloop to search out the relevant groups. I just type in the keyword/s I'm looking for in the Newsgroup portion of Mailloop and the program does the rest. Mailloop will come up with a list of possible Newsgroups and will save the ones I want to keep in a list for future use. (Online Success for Internet Business, 2000)

Netiquette and Basic Guidelines for Using Newsgroups

Once the right newsgroup has been located, the benefits that newsgroups can offer can be maximized if, basic netiquette (proper behavior on the Internet) is followed. These are the general usage guidelines that must be heeded to avoid being flamed. Being flamed is to receive a rash of e-mail retorts of a most demeaning nature. The specific rules of conduct vary depending on the newsgroup. A visit to http://groups.google.com/googlegroups/basics.html/ will reveal instructions on:

- What Usenet is and where it came from.

- Navigating Usenet.

- How to avoid getting flamed.

Basic Netiquette

Newsgroups represent a significant information resource for marketing researchers. However, if a researcher behaves improperly when accessing and interacting with a newsgroup, they can expect swift and sure reprisals. Flames of hate mail may be directed to the offending researcher, their **Internet service provider** (ISP), the company, and the Internet community at large. Such an assault can ruin the reputation of the researcher, their company, and any prospects of continued future support from newsgroup members. Understanding some basic netiquette will help the researcher avoid these pitfalls and allow them to cultivate a long-term and mutually beneficial relationship with the newsgroup.

Find Out the Purpose of the Newsgroup

Some newsgroups are intended for discussions and some for announcements or queries. It is not a good idea to carry on discussions in newsgroups that are designated otherwise. Understand what the newsgroup is about before posting any announcements. Have a look at the Master List of newsgroup hierarchies at http://www.faqs.org/faqs/usenet/hierarchy-list/index.html/ and read a week's worth of messages, followed up by an examination of the Frequently Asked Questions (FAQ) list to see if the topic has already been dealt with.

Read the FAQs

Many newsgroups have a FAQ list that is posted periodically (usually every few weeks), and they are also usually cross-posted to news.answers. They usually have explicit expiration dates set, so they should not be considered expired until a new version has been posted. If a FAQ list cannot be found in either the newsgroup or news.answers, it probably does not exist. It is also possible to find FAQ archives on several websites that compile the FAQs of newsgroups. Note, however, that some of these archives are outdated and hence may not contain the FAQs for some newsgroups. The FAQs for certain newsgroups can be found by undertaking a search at Tile.net (http://tile.net/).

If a researcher's questions cannot be found in FAQs, it can be useful to find a knowledgeable user (or simply a more experienced user) in one of the groups and ask through private e-mail if the topic has already come up. Click on the "author profile" in Google Groups. It may not bear well for a researcher's reputation in the newsgroup if they bother thousands of people with the same question by posting before first checking the FAQs or the message archive.

FIGURE 8.3
Internet FAQ Archives

Source:
http://www.faqs.org/faqs/

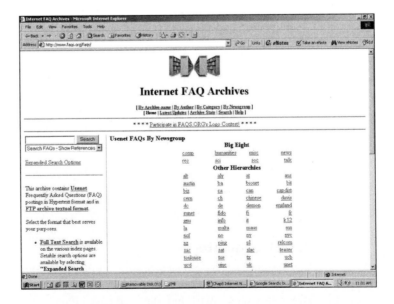

Maintain the Quality of Newsgroup Messages

It is important for the continual survival of newsgroups that quality messages, which relate to the newsgroup topic, are discussed. Improper postings result in a dilution of the quality of messages and a consequent decay of newsgroup participation and interest. This could eventually result in junk newsgroups, which are of little use. The following are several things that can be done to avoid the occurrence of such a scenario. These guidelines are drawn from Horton, Spafford, and Moraes (1999) and Templeton (1999).

- Do not post announcements regarding major news events. If you wish to discuss such an event on the Internet, use the misc.headlines newsgroup. If a posting is made that is totally irrelevant to the topic of the newsgroup, it will simply be deleted or, worse, seen as spam mail with the consequences that follow.

- Use e-mails for private messages. If someone makes an obvious mistake, do not make postings to the whole newsgroup telling them that the person has made a mistake. Use private e-mail to let the person know instead. If you are unhappy with what a user said, send a private e-mail rather than posting it. This applies as well to messages offering thanks, jibes, or congratulations that only need to be seen by the interested parties. The same goes for simple questions, and especially for any form of "me too" postings. As a general rule, use personal e-mail if the message does not contribute to the quality of the newsgroup.

- Do not include the entire text when replying. When replying or rebutting an article, do not include the entire text with your article. Cut out important bits to post along with your reply.

- Do not use newsgroups as a people directory. Do not look for particular persons in newsgroups by posting messages saying, "I'm looking for Mr. John Smith."

- Debates in newsgroups: If a debate occurs in a newsgroup, let other people join in to solicit their opinions on the issue. If you are involved, try to be the first one to stop debating if the debate is not getting anywhere and is just resulting in a deterioration of the quality of the newsgroup.

Commercial Postings and Announcements

The announcement of professional products or services on Usenet is allowed in certain newsgroups, provided suitable restraint is exercised. Researchers should check the FAQs and the moderator (if any) to ensure the product announcement is appropriate and permissible in the group. The subject should make it clear that the posting is a product announcement. Only one article should be included per product at the most, and preferably everything should be put into one article instead of into separate postings. The message should keep to technical facts, as advertising hype is especially frowned upon. Announcements or articles violating this policy may be rejected.

There exists an alternative hierarchy called biz specifically for commercial postings. This can be found in articles such as "Alternative Newsgroup Hierarchies, Part . . . .," posted periodically to several newsgroups, including news.lists. Users can also get these articles by an e-mail to mailserver@rtfm.mit.edu with only the following lines:

- Send usenet-by-group/news.answers/alt-hierarchies/part1.

- Send usenet-by-group/news.answers/alt-hierarchies/part2.

In most cases, newsgroups that end with *.marketplace are also suitable newsgroups to announce services or products, although it should be mentioned that several of the *.marketplace hierarchies are now moderated by some very competent people. These individuals scrutinize postings very closely, so users must be careful about their content or it will be rejected. Also, the *.marketplace should correspond to the product that a company intends to announce.

Copyright Issues

It is legal to reproduce short extracts of a copyrighted work for critical purposes in newsgroups, but reproduction of messages in whole is strictly and explicitly forbidden by international copyright law. Under copyright statutes, the author of an e-mail or any newsgroup posting possesses a copyright on e-mail that they write; posting it to the Internet or e-mailing it on to others without the permission of the author represents a violation of that copyright. More information on copyrights can be found at http://www.cs.ruu.nl/wais/html/na-dir/law/Copyright-FAQ/.html/ and is also discussed in Chapter 12 of this book.

Signatures

It is appropriate and often necessary that users include a signature file in all postings to newsgroups. A signature is a two- to five-line attachment that is included at the end of a message, providing the sender's contact details to readers. Signatures should be kept concise, as people do not appreciate seeing lengthy signatures or paying the Internet access bills to repeatedly transmit them. Two to four lines are usually plenty; any more and the sender is likely to offend others. It is all right to include an institution/business name, URL, the nature of the sender's business, and contact information. Drawings, pictures, maps, or other graphics should not be included in a signature as other readers may view it as rude.

FIGURE 8.4

Directory: law/Copyright-FAQ

Source:
http://www.cs.ruu.nl/wais/html/na-dir/law/Copyright-FAQ/.html/

FIGURE 8.5
Example of a
Signature File That Is
Attached to the End
of Postings

MH Peterson

E-mail: Agamemnon_mazerat@yahoo.com

Visit the Internet Marketing Research page:

http://groups.yahoo.com/group/Internet_Marketing_Research_Group

Spamming

Spamming is a term used to describe cross-postings of the same message to a large number of newsgroups or repeating the same message to the same newsgroup/s many times for the sole benefit of the poster. Such messages do not usually contribute content to newsgroups as they are either an advertisement that only benefits the individual posting the message or not pertinent to the group topic. Some messages are often just blatant commercials, and commercial announcements in noncommercial newsgroups are considered an act of spamming. If a user spams, their ISP will probably delete their account a few hours after they announce their product. Spamming usually results in getting flamed with abusive e-mails and, in some cases, the e-mail contains programs that block an ISP's server from functioning properly. Companies have been dropped by their ISPs, not only for spamming identical messages but also for mis-posting many slightly "customized" versions of the same message. Serious offenders find their entire companywide **domain name** blocked from newsgroups.

Researchers can avoid being spammers by choosing to post to groups that are relevant to their research project topic and whose audience would appreciate it. They should post only to those groups that appear to meet the needs of their research and try to limit those to less than four. Many servers allow only four, so users should research their posting and then post to those groups that will generate the highest quality responses. Since Usenet is regulated, a few hours after a spam posting is made, it will be erased by cancelbots that patrol newsgroups and keep Usenet free of spam.

Posting Messages

Be Polite and Nonintrusive

It is important that researchers do not try to be outrageous or say outlandish things in their article. Messages should be polite, reasoned, and to the point. Posting of information on Usenet is to be viewed as similar to publication. It will not take long to find that the sheer number of groups in some of the larger hierarchies can hide large volumes of information. The risk that an individual might attempt to become involved in an illegal activity is inevitable. However, users should try to avoid all such temptations. Even the act of attempting to solicit some types of information is illegal. Should the governing bodies that are responsible for maintaining the groups or the Internet policing groups catch a user, the consequences can be very painful. Even some types of marketing are illegal, and any schemes that are perpetrated on newsgroups can be prosecuted in a court of law.

Asking Questions in Newsgroups

All newsgroup messages asking questions should end the subject line with a question mark '?'.

Use Short Subject Topic Lines

When picking a subject for articles, researchers should keep it short yet make it as meaningful as possible.

Deleting Posted Messages

If a user posts an article and remembers something they've left out or realizes they've made a factual error, they can cancel the article and (if cancelled quickly enough) prevent its distribution. For example, if Netscape is being used as the newsgroup file manager, this is as simple as bringing up the post, highlighting it, and then clicking on file, followed by delete post.

Cross-Posting

If an article is really relevant to multiple newsgroups, then users can "cross-post" to the relevant newsgroups by posting the article only once with all newsgroups named on the Group header line in Google Groups. For example, posting to the groups news.newusers. questions, soc.men, and misc.biz would cause an article to be posted to these three groups simultaneously. Making separate postings of an article for each newsgroup a user wishes to reach tends to annoy readers. For an example of a cross-post, see page 159 in Chapter 9.

New Postings and Follow-Ups

All newsgroup users (also known as newsreaders) should have two ways to post a news article. First, there is an original posting; this is used whenever a member is starting a new topic. In Google Groups, users can click on Post New when they are reading a message. Second, there is a "follow-up" option; this is used when posting a response to another news article. This can be archived in Google Groups by clicking on Post Reply when reading a particular article. For those who do not want their postings to appear on the newsgroup, but want to send their message directly to the person, they can use the E-mail Reply option. It is important that these two posting methods not be confused. Researchers should not follow up articles without using the newsreader's follow-up mechanism. Conversely, the follow-up mechanism should not be used to post an article that is an unrelated thread.

If a posting does not appear immediately, this does not mean that it failed and that the user should try to repost it at once. Some websites have set up the local software to process news periodically. Thus, the article will not appear immediately. From experience, it usually takes several hours for postings to appear in Google Groups.

For help on posting in Google Groups, researchers should visit http://groups. google. com/googlegroups/help.html#posting/. It will provide users with all the information needed to make sure they post correctly.

The Twenty-Four Rules on Writing Proper Articles in Newsgroups

Again, this section is from Horton, Spafford, and Moraes (1999) and Templeton (1999).

1. Make your writing easy to read. Short and concise messages are the most effective. Remember the KISS principle (Keep It Simple Stupid)!

2. Leaving a blank line between paragraphs may help make your meaning clearer.

3. Choose your words carefully. Consider whether what you have written can be misinterpreted. Make sure you try your best not to use slang.

FIGURE 8.6

The Post New and Post Reply Functions in Google Groups for New and Follow-Up Messages, Respectively

Source:
http://groups.google.com/groups
?hl=en&safe=off&group=biz.
marketplace.discussion/ and/or
http://groups.google.com/groups
?hl=en&safe=off&th=7ed7e88
f3653ea26,4/

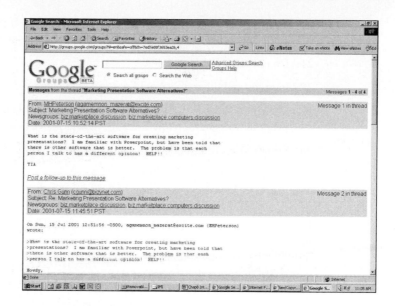

4. Do not input too many ideas and paragraphs all in one posting; people may get confused and your ideas may be diluted.

5. Avoid abbreviations and acronyms as people may not understand them.

6. Avoid passive, questioning, or negative sentences that take longer to read.

7. "Cute" misspellings are difficult to read, especially if the reader is not fluent in the language (for example, using *thankz* instead of *thanks*).

8. Be open and avoid subtlety in your writing style.

9. Use smiles :-), frowns :-(, winks ;-), and the like, to help avoid confusion.

10. Take a coffee break before posting something in anger or that might hurt or anger others.

11. Subject lines should be used very carefully and not be misleading.

12. Make references to the original article by using snippets of the original message in the body of your follow-up. Do not include the entire article that you are replying to.

13. It is much easier to read a mixture of uppercase and lowercase letters.

14. Leaving out articles such as *the*, *a*, *an*, for briefness could alter the meaning of your sentences and make it take longer to read. It saves you time at the expense of your reader.

15. Be careful of contextual meanings of words.

16. Make an effort to spell words correctly. Make it a habit to use the spell checker program.

17. If your article is longer than one screen, use subheadings to organize it.

18. Just before you post your article, reread it.

19. Remember, your current or future employers may be reading your articles. So might your spouse, neighbors, children, and other people close to you; post messages accordingly.

20. Keep your lines under 80 characters and under 72 if possible (so that the lines won't get longer than 80 when people include them to respond to your postings).

21. Do not justify your articles.

22. Pictures and diagrams should not use embedded tabs.

23. Refer to articles by Message-ID and never by article number. Article numbers vary on every news system, while Message-IDs are always preserved.

24. Submissions in a single case (all upper or all lower) are difficult to read.

Conducting Surveys in Newsgroups

For a simple answer to a question or two, a researcher should format the question to show that it is less formal and simply from a fellow newsgroup user. Posting a question from an individual (as opposed to some titled position in some department or company) is a good way to get unbiased reactions to marketing ideas. For example, "I want to know if anybody has had any experience with . . . ," "Does anybody have any strong feelings about . . . ," "What would you think of . . . ," are all good formats for leading into a few short, informal questions. However, researchers need to bear in mind the ethical implications of conducting research without letting the respondents know they are being researched.

In some cases a researcher may want to do more than ask questions and solicit opinions. Newsgroups can also be used as a tool by researchers to gather quantifiable statistical information. There are several things to keep in mind when doing so. Researchers will need to post an invitation to participate. There is a problem with posting lengthy multiple-question surveys on a newsgroup. If successful in generating a response, no matter how carefully a researcher instructs respondents to forward completed surveys to them instead of posting to the group, many will miss the instructions and repost to the group. The group will become clogged with copies of the survey and other users will be unhappy.

First and foremost, researchers must observe good netiquette in order to gain maximum response. Second, they should remember that newsgroups are a virtual community where many experts on the topic, and nonexperts who are interested in the topic, gather together. It is important then to be able to contribute something of value to the community while gaining something from the other members. In order to increase participation rates, researchers may want to use a give-and-take approach. For example, they could write a discussion of various approaches, pros and cons, and so forth, and then seek opinions or comments.

Third, and perhaps most importantly, incentives may need to be offered in order to gain participation from newsgroup members. A "pull" strategy needs to be employed in this case. With newsgroups, it might be beneficial to offer an incentive that is relevant and useful to newsgroup members; for example, access to a marketing journal for members of newsgroups who discuss topics on marketing can only be achieved after completing a survey. For more detailed information on proper netiquette when conducting surveys on the Internet, refer to Chapter 7.

Other Useful Websites and Links

Researchers can find out more about newsgroups by using the following websites:

The official home page of news.newusers.questions can be found at http://vancouver-webpages.com/nnq/ or http://www.aptalaska.net/~kmorgan/nnqlinks.html/. This is a Usenet

FIGURE 8.7
The Official Home
Page of News.
newusers.questions

Source:
http://www.aptalaska.net/~
kmorgan/nnqlinks.html/

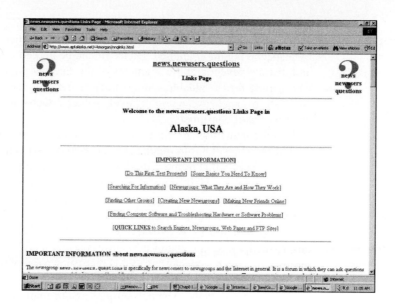

newsgroup whose purpose is the dissemination of questions and answers about Usenet and the Internet. Visitors should take note that some aspects of the FAQs may not have been updated and may no longer apply.

A newsgroup in which newcomers can ask questions about newsgroups and the Internet in general is news.newusers.questions newsgroup. Hopefully visitors will get useful answers, as it claims to be the "Q & A for users new to the Usenet." This newsgroup contains FAQs, links to many helpful websites and newsgroups, and news.newusers.questions policy and administrative documents.

The news.announce.newusers newsgroup contains explanatory postings for new users. Its purpose is to provide basic information with which all participants in Usenet should familiarize themselves in order to make Usenet a better place for all users.

An important tip is to read the introductory postings in news.announce.newusers before posting any messages to any newsgroup. In fact, the following postings in news. announce.newusers might be considered compulsory for new users:

• A Primer on How to Work with the Usenet Community

• Answers to Frequently Asked Questions about Usenet

• Emily Postnews Answers Your Questions on Netiquette

• Hints on Writing Style for Usenet

• Rules for Posting to Usenet

• What is Usenet?

Index of /public/usenet/news (http://sunsite.org.uk/public/usenet/news-faqs) is a website that stores a list of related FAQs that are posted at news.announce.newsgroup. Visitors may read those FAQs that are relevant to their area of interest. FAQs here include a list and brief description of all Usenet newsgroups. The news.answers newsgroup contains articles that will give users a better understanding of the breadth of information embodied in Usenet. The news newsgroup hierarchy is where information on newsgroups is obtained.

Summary

Newsgroups and discussion lists form virtual communities of people who are joined online by a special common interest. Hence, it can be argued that newsgroups represent unique and distinct psychographic segments of the Internet population. This makes newsgroups and mailing lists a valuable source of marketing data. By lurking in newsgroups or discussion lists, researchers can unobtrusively gather valuable information on the perceptions and experiences of consumers.

When conducting any form of research on newsgroups and mailing lists, researchers should keep two things in mind: (1) be courteous and (2) make sure that all interactions and postings are of value to the virtual community and not just pointless chatter. Researchers should also be especially careful to observe netiquette when they are posting a commercial message, announcement, or an invitation to participate in a survey. If a researcher plans to use newsgroups and mailing lists as a long-term resource for their market research purposes, good netiquette is essential for maintaining their long-term reputation. It also will ensure the long-term value of newsgroups as a research tool. Research efforts will be better rewarded if a researcher has a good reputation as an observer of good netiquette and you are a regular contributor to the newsgroup.

In most cases, there exist newsgroups and/or mailing lists that will be of assistance in finding the information desired, considering that there are around 80,000 newsgroups. Researchers may want to create newsgroups or discussion lists of their own, where no newsgroup or mailing list exists that suits their research purposes.

When conducting research in newsgroups, it is important to first gain an understanding of what the newsgroup is about by reading their FAQs and browsing approximately a week's worth of messages. Surveys posted in newsgroups should have some appropriate incentives; it helps if the researcher is a significant contributor to the newsgroup as well. Everyone plays a role in ensuring newsgroups and mailing lists continue to remain a viable part of the Internet for research, meaningful interaction, and entertainment.

Your online learning center has a case study on *Internet Newsgroups* available now at www.mhhe.com/forrest.

Discussion Questions

1. How do you think newsgroups and other segmented virtual communities can help researchers find the information they need?
2. What function do signature files perform? Why is it important to have a signature file attached to the end of your message?
3. Briefly explain what netiquette is. What would be the most important things to tell your boss about proper netiquette in newsgroups?
4. Why does netiquette exist?
5. As a market researcher, how would you invite people in newsgroups to participate in your surveys without being seen as a spammer?
6. Of the 24 rules of writing proper postings in newsgroups, choose three rules that you believe would be the most important to remember based on what you now know about netiquette. Why do you regard these as the most important?
7. Under what circumstances should researchers create their own newsgroups or mailing lists? How should a market researcher act in the virtual community once it is created to make it a useful market-scanning tool?
8. Briefly outline the steps market researchers should take when attempting to obtain information through newsgroups.
9. What is the difference between a newsgroup and a discussion list?

Internet Project

Find a newsgroup that relates to your main area of study. Go to http://groups.google.com/groups?group=biz/ and visit a few groups that catch your interest and follow some of the **threads** of postings within those groups.

- biz.books.* (1 group)
- biz.caucus
- biz.clarinet.* (2 groups)
- biz.comp.* (3 groups)
- biz.config
- biz.control
- biz.ecommerce
- biz.entrepreneurs

- biz.general
- biz.healthcare
- biz.jobs.* (1 group)
- biz.marketplace.* (8 groups)
- biz.pagesat.* (1 group)
- biz.stolen
- biz.tadpole.* (1 group)
- biz.test

Further Reading

Pfaffenberger, Bryan, (1995). *The USENET Book: Finding, Using, and Surviving Newsgroups on the Internet;* Massachusetts: Addison-Wesley.

References

Eisen, L. S., (2001). "The Master List of Newsgroup Hierarchies, v5.19" (http://www.faqs.org/faqs/usenet/hierarchy-list/index.html/).

Google, Inc., (2001). "Basics of Usenet" (http://groups.google.com/googlegroups/basics.html/).

Google, Inc., (2001). "Navigating Usenet" (http://groups.google.com/googlegroups/basics.html#navigating).

Google, Inc., (2001). "Avoid Getting Flamed" (http://groups.google.com/google groups/basics.html#flamed).

Google, Inc., (2001). "Usenet Glossary" (http://groups.google.com/googlegroups/glossary.html/).

Google, Inc., (2001). "Google Groups FAQ" (http://groups.google.com/googlegroups/help.html/).

Google, Inc., (2001). "Posting FAQ" (http://groups.google.com/googlegroups/posting_faq.html/).

Google, Inc., (2001). "Posting Style Guide" (http://groups.google.com/googlegroups/posting_style.html/).

Google, Inc., (2001). "Advanced Group Search" (http://groups.google.com/advanced_group_search/).

Gunn, Chris. (2001) Business newsgroup moderator.

Horton, M., Spafford, G., & Moraes, M., (posted December 28, 1999. "Rules for Posting to Usenet" (http://www.faqs.org/faqs/usenet/posting-rules/part1/).

Keizer, Gregg, (2000). "The Insiders Guide to Newgroups" (http://home.cnet.com/internet/0-3805-7-1564164.html/).

Offutt, A. J., Spafford, G., & Moraes, M. (2001). "Hints on Writing Style for Usenet" (http://www.faqs.org/faqs/usenet/writing-style/part1/).

Online Success for Internet Business (2000). "Power Marketing to Newsgroups" (http://www.webmastercourse.com/articles/newsgroups/).

Templeton, B. (Posted December 28, 1999). "Emily Postnews Answers Your Questions on Netiquette," (http://www.faqs.org/faqs/usenet/emily-postnews/part1/).Woods, G., Spafford, G., & Lawrence, D. (1997). "How to Create a New Usenet Newsgroup" (http://www.faqs.org/faqs/usenet/creating-newsgroups/part1/).

9

Applied Research Methods for Newsgroups and Discussion Groups

The goal of Internet marketing research is to extract the information necessary to effectively market to companies or individuals, either on the Internet or in person. This chapter is intended as an example of the methods that might be used, within the context of newsgroups, to achieve this goal. The following examples provide proven techniques that will yield results.

Chapter Objectives

This chapter aims to:

- Provide a practical, step-by-step guide for conducting research in newsgroups.

- Use a three-level plan for detailed methodology: newsgroup searches, posting to newsgroups, creating a new newsgroup or discussion group.

Introduction

When approaching newsgroups, it is important to keep a specific goal in mind. What is it that you, as a researcher, are trying to accomplish within the newsgroups? Newsgroups are so vast—and there are so many opportunities to click through areas, explore, and utilize the array of tools available to researchers—that it is very easy to simply lose track of time. Soon a researcher may well lose track of his or her research goals altogether. A systematic approach to newsgroup researching is very useful. The following is one approach to newsgroups and alternatives for meeting research goals.

Three Main Methods of Researching Newsgroups

Method A: Newsgroup Search

Each newsgroup has a search function, which is very useful for information gathering. In large newsgroups, such as Google Groups, there are so many people working within the newsgroups that the postings for common areas of research are plentiful. A search of the groups is an incredibly powerful tool.

Method B. Newsgroup Posting

When a search yields no information, or information that needs further clarification, and e-mailing the people who have posted on similar subjects is unproductive, posting in a newsgroup is the next option. Researchers should be certain to adhere to the following steps and be careful to use proper netiquette so as not to be flamed out before having the opportunity to learn how to navigate in newsgroups.

Method C: Create a New Newsgroup

Should the above options fail to provide the information a researcher is searching for, or they simply would like to establish a single location on the Internet to collect information related to their interests, a researcher will want to create their own newsgroup.

Step-by-Step Guide to Conducting Research in Newsgroups and Discussion Groups

The following steps are the starting point for a research project conducted using the Internet. These should be read and the sections worked through to establish a systematic approach. Without some direction, as mentioned above, it is simply too easy to become distracted by the sheer number and variety of postings in one of thousands of newsgroups.

Step One: Read Introductory Postings

A good suggestion for new users of newsgroups is to read the introductory postings in news.announce.newusers and browse through the postings at news.answers to get a better understanding of the nature and scope of newsgroups.

Step Two: Perform an Advanced Search for Relevant Newsgroups

Utilize Method A as described above. Do an advanced search following the guidelines provided in this chapter. Often the amount of information available is amazing. Use Google Groups (http://groups.google.com/), Tile.net (http://tile.net/news/), and other search tools to ascertain the newsgroup/s most relevant to a particular area of research. Try using several different relevant keywords to conduct the search. For example, if searching for marketing newsgroups, users may want to try *marketing, selling, advertising, consumer behavior*, and so on. Remember to take into consideration the different terms and/or spellings of keywords (as noted in Table 2.3, page 27). Researchers should take note of the various newsgroups that are relevant to the area of research.

Step Three: Read the FAQs

Before posting, users should make sure they read the FAQs of the newsgroup/s, either at the websites listed in the previous chapter or by reading the FAQs that are posted regularly at the website. Many times questions that are nonspecific will be found in the FAQs. If no

FAQs are found—either at the websites, or in the newsgroups—it could mean that there are no FAQs for that particular newsgroup.

Step Four: Read Postings in Relevant Newsgroups

Take some time to read the postings at the newsgroups the search in Step Two yielded. Try reading at least one to two weeks' worth of postings to get a feel for the newsgroup and the types of topics that are discussed there.

Step Five: E-Mail an Expert

If it appears that a question may be a common one in the newsgroup/s, but no answer could be found in the FAQs or in any of the postings in the newsgroup, it may be useful to e-mail the "local experts" (people who are active in the newsgroup and seem knowledgeable).

Step Six: Do a Posting

If an answer still cannot be found, it may be best to do a posting. Make sure the posting ends with a question mark in the subject heading if asking a question. Refer to the section on netiquette in Chapter 8 before proceeding to write a posting so as to avoid offending anyone and gaining a bad reputation.

Once again, do not expect the posting to appear immediately in the newsgroup. Just wait patiently and replies to the posting will be e-mailed within a day or two. It could also be useful to do some test postings for practice or for fun in some newsgroups that have names that end with test. Do not expect responses to test postings.

Step Seven: Conduct a Survey

Perhaps these steps may not have yet uncovered the information needed, or the research project needs more in-depth information. It may simply be a case of now needing to conduct surveys to gather primary data. Whatever the reason, users may want to start off by ensuring that the newsgroup permits surveys. Study the FAQs and then ask the moderator of the newsgroup (if any) whether surveys are permissible. Chapter 8, which talks about Internet surveys, will help researchers get the best possible return from their online survey efforts.

Step Eight: Create a New Newsgroup

There may be an occasion where better information can be revealed by monitoring the responses of a particular group of people with a specific interest over a long period of time. Newsgroup/s on that particular topic may not yet exist; for example, there may not be a newsgroup for the researcher's company or the sort of product the company is selling. Given such a scenario, researchers might want to go through the process of creating a newsgroup to serve that purpose. Remember that it is common practice to post to the closest related newsgroup if a newsgroup on an exact topic does not exist. Many times an existing newsgroup that is well established and has loyal visitors will generate more feedback than a new newsgroup, even if the topic is not an exact match. Once again, be careful not to get flamed before presenting the idea to the newsgroup (see the section on netiquette in Chapter 8).

Method A: Advanced Search Methods

One of the most powerful tools for research within the newsgroup format is the advanced search. This is particularly true with the larger newsgroups like Google Groups, whose advanced search page can be found at http://groups.yahoo.com/. Chris Gunn, moderator of several of the biz groups provided the following example of a brief method to put a Google search engine to work.

Let's use selling shoes as an example.

Run an advanced search using All Words for *Buy Shoes* and the other advanced search options empty. Write down the total messages found.

Hit the Back button and run another search for *Buy Cheap Shoes* with *inexpensive* in the Any Words field.

Whoops, some of the results include movies. Add it to the Without the Words field, and that will trim the count. Now we're down to 65,000 messages matching that search. That's a very nice sized number when building a trend analysis.

Add other words such as *FL* and *Florida* to sample a geographic area.

Write the totals down and repeat the search for *expensive*.

Now you have numbers for how many are posting messages about shoes, how many want cheap, and how many want expensive. Add more numbers for brand names and types of shoes. Use time spans to see changes from 1998, 1999, 2000, and 2001.

With a little patience you can get an idea which shoes you have in stock are most likely to do well in advertising or perhaps what you should plan on adding to the inventory.

Searches of this nature are worth mastering. The information to be gained can be geography-, product-, or even media-oriented. When the pool of information is very large, the opportunity to gain some very useful data arises. It is worth noting the conclusion to the message sent by Chris Gunn: "I do not recommend using searches like this to harvest e-mail lists. Many of the resulting addresses will be folks like myself who know how to file complaints in the right places to remove e-mail accounts, websites and entire domains." As the contributors to this book have pointed out at every opportunity, this type of technology can be abused. However, should a user choose to abuse it, they may well suffer some fairly costly consequences, so please use proper netiquette.

Method B: Posting to a Newsgroup

This section will provide an example of research techniques in the context of a question to a newsgroup. Purpose of research: To establish resources and tools for Internet marketing research on the Internet and within the newsgroups.

Step One: Check Out Newsgroups

New users of newsgroups should use Google Groups (http://groups.google.com/) to check out the following newsgroups and their FAQs in order to gain some general knowledge about newsgroups: news.newusers.questions, news.announce.newusers, and news.answers.
Tip: Use the Browse Groups function in Google Groups, the page for which can be found by clicking the link below the headings of the Big 8 on the Google groups home page. Type *news* in the prompt box (shown in Figure 9.1).

Step Two: Search for Information

Search for information in newsgroups on marketing and marketing research with exactly the same methodology as described in Method A. This search will determine the availability of this information within the newsgroups, if this information has been posted by other

FIGURE 9.1
The Browse Groups
Function in Google
Groups

Source:
http://groups.google.com/

newsgroup users. Utilizing the advanced search to begin, users will be able to click the Back button and modify the search without having to reenter all the information.

For example, an initial search is made in which the topic words submitted include *marketing* and *research*. This generates 906 responses, which include student projects, job postings, people seeking employment, and even radio advertisements. Much of this extra information is spam and is in unmoderated newsgroups. Obviously, further revision of the search is required.

An initial search can be revised by clicking the Back button; then using the Not Including the Words field to exclude *job*, *employment*, *position* and *consulting*, then clicking the Submit button again. The example search again returns enormous numbers of group postings.

When another search is submitted with the word *Internet* added to the topic line, the number of subjects returned drops to only 251, which is still too many subjects to bother reading. Further revision of the search is now possible by returning to the starting window and adding *Internet Marketing Research* to the Find Exact Wording line. This search returns exactly one subject. Unfortunately, unless a user is multilingual, this brings them no closer to resolution in the search for Internet marketing research tools and software, as the website is not in English. So, with no luck finding information on the topic, further efforts must be made to find the information. This involves posting to a newsgroup.

Step Three: Posting for Information

With the knowledge that the information required is not available in the newsgroups, a posting is the next option. The question is, Where should a question be posted to gather the information required? This information is obtained by looking at the location of the topics closest to the topic being researched. Many times there will be several locations. Remember, netiquette requires that postings be limited to avoid getting flamed. Find the location that is nearest to the search area and cross-post to no more than three other groups. This should provide sufficient exposure to determine if the information is available or, at the very least, if anyone cares. Unfortunately, one of the negative aspects of newsgroups is that individuals within the group may be focused on topics other than the topic a researcher posts. For this reason, finding the newsgroup that most closely follows the interests of the research project is very important.

As mentioned, a search will reveal areas on which it might be worth concentrating. Of those found when the results were more closely focused, the biz hierarchy, or the category for discussing business and business-related topics, was the most useful for researching this topic. Other areas to consider might be the comp, or computer-related section. Each section contains subheadings; for example, within the comp hierarchy is com.software and com.internet. Neither of these topics provided subheadings that appeared to be appropriate for this topic. Upon further review of the biz hierarchy, several groups looked much more promising. Several of the results pointed to a group called biz.marketplace.

Note that there are eight subgroups within the biz.marketplace shown in Figure 9.2. Of these, one in particular, biz.marketplace.discussion, has postings that are compatible with the topic. In addition, the spamming in this group is minimal due to the watchful eye of what is obviously a very involved moderator. So this is one of the groups to post to. Another group that looks promising is the biz.marketplace.comp.discussion group. It is best to look through the groups to see the content of the last few months to be certain that it is compatible with the question to be posed to the group's audience. At this point it is a good idea to check with a local group expert if uncertain.

Step Four: Ask the Experts

By this stage, you may still be uncertain whether some newsgroups are really accepting of the product/service announcements. This is the stage to now try e-mailing some of the experts. Asking some of the more experienced users can also help to discover if there are any other newsgroups that are relevant. It may also be worth finding and asking the moderator of the newsgroup to gain more information. The moderator will respond from a position of authority, while another user of the group might simply guess and intentionally or unintentionally lead you astray.

It would be appropriate to find some names that appear relatively often in the newsgroup and to find users who appear to be providing many answers to the queries of others (which would make them appear knowledgeable). In Google Groups, it is possible to find out more about a particular author by clicking on their posting and then clicking on Author Profile to get a list of where that person has been making their postings and how many postings have been made. This will give you a good idea as to whether that particular per-

FIGURE 9.2
Google Groups biz.marketplace

Source:
http://groups.google.com/group s?hl=en&safe=off&group=biz. marketplace/

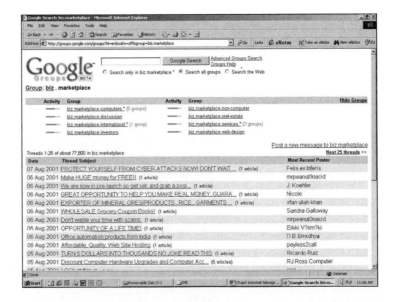

FIGURE 9.3

Example of an Author Profile in Google Groups

Source:
http://groups.google.com/groups
?hl=en&safe=off&q=author:
cgunn%40bizynet.com+/

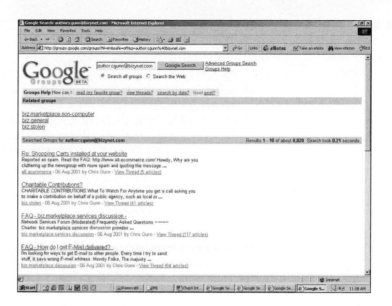

FIGURE 9.4

Copy of an E-Mail Sent to Chris Gunn, the Moderator of Several of the biz. Groups

> Dear Chris,
>
> I am interested in finding the most versatile and easy-to-use software for creating marketing presentations. In my search of the Google Groups, I have not seen any information on this topic. In an attempt to follow proper netiquette, I wanted to e-mail an expert first.
>
> I want to avoid posting to the wrong group, but I need help finding the best software for marketing presentations and could use your opinion as to which groups I should post to get the most help. I believe that you are savvy enough to point me in the right direction. Any help you are able to give would be greatly appreciated.
>
> Thank you in advance,
> Marc Peterson

son is an "expert" for the newsgroup (*Note*: make sure the person's posting is fairly recent, otherwise they may not be able to be reached due to possible changes in their e-mail address).

Now that the expertise of the person has been ascertained, they can be e-mailed by simply clicking on the e-mail address next to their name.

Remember that the person being e-mailed is being asked for a favor, so make sure the message is courteous. It would be wise to follow the procedures outlined here to ensure that newsgroups continue to be a useful information resource that is not cluttered up with useless messages.

A day or two later (depending on the frequency that the person responds to their e-mail), a reply should be received regarding the question. The reply received from Chris Gunn is shown in Figure 9.5.

FIGURE 9.5:
E-Mail Reply
Received from Chris
Gunn in Response to
Query

Re: Presentation Software?
Date: Sat, 14 Jul 2001 17:40:12 -0500
From: Chris Gunn <cgunn@bizynet.com>
Organization: BIZynet International Business Network
To: The Petersons <ursa@alaska.net>
References: 1
On Sat, 14 Jul 2001 13:57:17 -0700, you wrote:
>I want to avoid posting to the wrong group, but I need help
>finding the best software for marketing presentations and
>could use your opinion as to which groups I should post to
>get the most help. I believe that you are savvy enough to
>point me in the right direction. Any help you are able to give
>would be greatly appreciated.

Howdy Marc,
Your best presentations would probably be by using a website.
If you want to market an online site, the biz.ecommerce
newsgroup would work. Questions for any kind of business
marketing should work well on biz.marketplace.discussions.
The FAQs for all of the biz newsgroups are at
http://www.bizynet.com/FAQ-News.htm
Chris http://www.bizynet.com
BIZynet Coordinator cgunn@bizynet.com
Moderator of biz.general, biz.marketplace.discussion,
biz.healthcare, biz.marketplace.web-design,
biz.marketplace.international & others

Users should add the new information this has revealed to a checklist.

Step Five: Post an Article

With the information gathered from the "expert" in Step Four, it may now be possible to further revise the approach. Either way, it is now time to post to the newsgroups that will provide the feedback needed to conclude the search for information. It is important that a review of the goal be performed at this point as the search for prerequisite information may have derailed any efforts to focus on the goal.

With this information in mind, it is now necessary to register with the newsgroup service in question, in this case Google Groups. This can be done by simply clicking on the Post a New Message link, which presents the choice of entering log-in information or registering as a new user. If this is the first time a user has posted on the newsgroup, they will need to register with the service. New users will be walked through a series of screens, each requesting them to fill out required information. Upon conclusion, information will be e-mailed that will allow them access to the newsgroup. They can then click the link in their e-mail and proceed to the website to post their first message.

One response was received to the posting that was made in Figure 9.6, and it is shown in Figure 9.7 as an example of how people will respond to a posting.

As the response to the initial question left the door open for further clarification, the subsequent question in Figure 9.8 was an attempt at gathering further information. This method of finding information and developing a topic is extremely useful. It should be noted that this is one strength of newsgroups: they provide an effective method for acquiring feedback on a variety of issues in a reasonable amount of time, for little or no cost.

FIGURE 9.6:

A Cross-Posting to biz.marketplace.discussion, biz.marketplace.computers.discussion

Source:
http://groups.google.com/groups?hl=en&safe=off&th=7ed7e88f3653ea26,4/

> Messages from the thread "Marketing Presentation Software Alternatives?" Messages 1–4 of 4.
> From: MHPeterson (agamemnon_mazerat@excite.com)
> Subject: Marketing Presentation Software Alternatives?
> Newsgroups: biz.marketplace.discussion, biz.marketplace.computers.discussion
> Date: 2001-07-15 10:52:14 PST
> What is the state-of-the-art software for creating marketing presentations? I am familiar with PowerPoint, but have been told that there is other software that is better. The problem is that each person I talk to has a different opinion! HELP!!
> TIA

FIGURE 9.7:

Response to the Posting in Figure 9.6

Source:
http://groups.google.com/groups?hl=en&safe=off&th=7ed7e88f3653ea26,4/

> From: Chris Gunn (cgunn@bizynet.com)
> Subject: Re: Marketing Presentation Software Alternatives?
> Newsgroups: biz.marketplace.discussion, biz.marketplace.computers.discussion
> Date: 2001-07-15 11:45:51 PST
> On Sun, 15 Jul 2001 12:51:56 -0500, agamemnon_mazerat@excite.com (MHPeterson) wrote:
> >What is the state-of-the-art software for creating marketing
> >presentations? I am familiar with PowerPoint, but have been
> >told that there is other software that is better. The problem is
> >that each person I talk to has a different opinion! HELP!!
>
> Howdy,
> It makes a big difference as to whether you plan on making the presentation on a CD or online using a website. A website will give you the widest audience and flexibility.
> Better is a matter of skill level and experience. Everyone is going to tell you what they've learned to use is the easiest. None of the programs are easy or will they give you professional results unless you are a skilled marketing expert who has done dozens of effective presentations.
> If you have at least 500 hours of your time (one month) to devote to it, PowerPoint is a good program to get started with. You may find PowerPoint doesn't let you do everything you want. If you shift to another program, you've still gained an understanding of how presentation software works, what you want to accomplish, and the illustrations to use.
> You may find it more cost effective to hire someone who can create what you need in less than a week.
> Chris http://www.bizynet.com
> BIZynet Coordinator cgunn@bizynet.com
> Moderator of biz.general, biz.marketplace.discussion, biz.healthcare,
> biz.marketplace.web-design, biz.marketplace.international & others

FIGURE 9.8:
**Repost to
Newsgroups to
Further Clarify
Points**

Source:
http://groups.google.com/group
s?hl=en&safe=off&th=7ed7e88
f3653ea26,4/

> From: MHPeterson (agamemnon_mazerat@excite.com)
> Subject: Re: Marketing Presentation Software Alternatives?
> Newsgroups: biz.marketplace.discussion,
> biz.marketplace.computers.discussion
> Date: 2001-07-19 21:20:13 PST
> Hello,
> If PowerPoint is the starting point for presentations off-line,
> what is your recommendation for starting a website for a
> marketing presentation? Are there several possible options?
> Thanks in advance!

FIGURE 9.9:
**Response for Further
Clarification**

Source:
http://groups.google.com/group
s?hl=en&safe=off&th=7ed7e88
f3653ea26,4/

> From: Chris Gunn (cgunn@bizynet.com)
> Subject: Re: Marketing Presentation Software Alternatives?
> Newsgroups: biz.marketplace.discussion,
> biz.marketplace.computers.discussion
> Date: 2001-07-20 12:12:36 PST
> On Thu, 19 Jul 2001 23:19:39 -0500,
> agamemnon_mazerat@excite.com (MHPeterson)
> wrote:
> >Hello,
> >If PowerPoint is the starting point for presentations off-line,
> >what is your recommendation for starting a website for a
> >marketing presentation? Are there several possible options?
>
> Howdy,
> First off: Avoid FrontPage or anything from Netscape like the
> plague. For a graphical (WYSIWYG) interface and fairly decent
> HTML results, DreamWeaver seems to be the best option. If
> you want to get really serious about it and build fast and
> efficient Web pages, get a copy of Hippie. You'll find lots of
> good advice on the biz.marketplace.web-design newsgroup.
> Thanks, Chris http://www.bizynet.com
> BIZynet Coordinator cgunn@bizynet.com
> Moderator of biz.general, biz.marketplace.discussion,
> biz.healthcare,
> biz.marketplace.web-design, biz.marketplace.international &
> others

Figure 9.9 shows the response that was received.

Make sure all the rules of good netiquette are observed in all postings, as shown in the previous messages.

Canceling a Post   Since the message was posted to a Usenet newsgroup, the sender may wish to cancel this message in the future. Google Groups reported in 2001 at (http://groups.google.com/ googlegroups/posting_faq.html/) that they provide an option to enable the nuking (removal) of an author's own posts from message groups. If the author of a message in the Google Groups archive would like to remove it, they should send an e-mail to groups-support@google.com that contains the following items:

- Their full name and contact information, including an e-mail address that can be verified.

- The complete Google Groups URL (or message-ID) for each message to be suppressed.

- A statement that says, "I swear under penalty of civil or criminal laws that I am the person who posted each of the foregoing messages or am authorized to request removal by the person who posted those messages."

- Their signature (electronic).

Users can prevent their future posts from being added to the Google Groups archive by typing "X-No-archive: yes" in the header or the first line of the message.

For this exercise in researching on the Internet, posting to a newsgroup provided useful feedback. However, if a researcher required more information, or needed to provide a format for specific exchanges of information within a select group of people for an ongoing project, an excellent option may be to start an autonomous newsgroup, using Method C.

Method C: Create a New Newsgroup

When researching on the Internet, there are times when it may be better to let the information come to the researcher, rather than going to the information. We have discussed the two methods that a researcher might use to gather information actively. However, it is possible to establish a forum in which a researcher can gather information that is relevant to the topic being researched. One very good option is for a researcher to start their own discussion group. It is possible to start a newsgroup in the Usenet-based newsgroup, but the process is very involved and cumbersome unless the user does so in the alt hierarchy. Unfortunately, the sheer number of groups in the alt category makes it likely that a user will be lost unless they have a group of individuals who simply want a location to post to where information can be shared but does not have to be maintained in an Intranet.

When the determination has been made that a discussion group or newsgroup would be a useful tool as part of the research project, a researcher must then determine the best location for the group to achieve its goals. When considering an example, perhaps it would be useful to illustrate the establishment of a discussion group and monitor its evolution over the next several months, and perhaps until the next edition of this book. Not only will this provide an example of how researchers can do this on their own, but researchers can be active participants in the development, contributions, and discussions within the group. The decision must start with what the format should be.

While it is possible to start a newsgroup in the alt hierarchy, this is a cumbersome process, and as pointed out previously, once a newsgroup is established, it is nearly impossible to cancel. The group is active for a period and then continues to float in cyberspace without a purpose and serves only to clog up the hierarchy. Instead, for the purpose of this book, a much better choice would be a discussion group. Discussion groups have two advantages in this case. First, the discussion groups at Yahoo! Groups (http://groups.yahoo.com/) are very convenient to set up and use. Second, and even more useful, if an individual subscribes to a discussion group, it is Yahoo!'s option that enables any postings to the group to be e-mailed directly to a member's e-mail account. When pressed for time, e-mail is usually the most convenient method for maintaining contact with the rest of the world. A discussion group allows researchers to maintain their surveillance of information posted to the group without taking the time and effort to go to the website.

With the rationale established, the next step is to consider what the group will be named. As marketing researchers, the approach to this aspect of research should be very exciting. Remember that the goal is to be concise and yet descriptive. In this way, people will notice the newsgroup and perhaps even visit and contribute, but the name will not be so long as to be forgotten or considered unwieldy.

After some consideration, the title for our group will be Internet Marketing Research Group. This is the term researchers will look for, and yet it is concise. The purpose of the website will be to establish a forum for contribution and feedback for this text and related matters and findings on the Internet. The process is begun at Yahoo! Groups (http://groups.yahoo.com/).

The Yahoo! Groups home page allows visitors to proceed in a number of directions. Visitors can search for information as in the previous example with Google Groups, or it is possible to browse through categories of hierarchies to find other groups that might contain the information required, or a group that contains the information the researcher wishes to gather. In this way, they may be able to avoid having to start their own group. In the middle of the page, as seen in Figure 9.10, are the words "Start a New Group!" Clicking this link leads to the starting page. The starting page contains fields to fill out to describe the group. Following are the questions users will need to address to establish their group.

The first step is for the creator to determine where to place the page to most effectively generate interest from other readers. If an Internet Marketing Research group were established in a cross-stitch hierarchy, you can reasonably assume that the website will be very quiet. On the other hand, if the group is named *Marketing Aces!* and is located in the Free Advertising hierarchy, it will likely be inundated with spam until any useful information is lost in the flood of postings. The hierarchy needs to be representative of the research goals so that useful information is gathered from individuals interested in the topic. The section below is a step-by step process for selecting the location of the group within the group hierarchies.

Step 1 of 4: Classify the Group

This can be achieved by browsing or searching for the category that best describes the group. Creators should be as specific as possible when selecting the category. It is normally requested that groups containing sexual content be placed in the Romance and Relationships category. The Yahoo! group categories are:

- Business & Finance.

- Computers & Internet.

- Cultures & Community.

FIGURE 9.10:
Yahoo! Groups Home Page

Source:
http://groups.yahoo.com/

FIGURE 9.11
Yahoo! Groups Sign-
In Page

Source:
http://groups.yahoo.com/start/

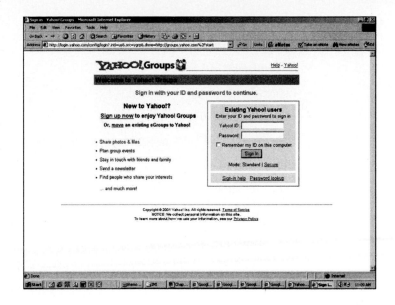

- Entertainment & Arts.

- Family & Home.

- Games.

- Government & Politics.

- Health & Wellness.

- Hobbies & Crafts.

- Music.

- Recreation & Sports.

- Regional.

- Religion & Beliefs.

- Romance & Relationships.

- Schools & Education.

- Science.

- World.

The relevant group in this instance would be *Business & Finance*. Having selected this category, the user would be asked to select from the following subcategories:

- Business Schools.

- Companies.

- Consumer.

- Employment and Work.

- Financial Professionals.

- Free Stuff.

- Home Business.

- Industry Associations.

- Investments.

- Labor.

- Marketing and Advertising.

- News and Media.

- Other.

- Public Relations.

- Real Estate.

- Small Business.

- Trade.

- Transportation.

- Stock Sectors.

At this point, the *Marketing and Advertising* hierarchy can be selected for the group, or it can be placed in a more specific category that is more appropriate. This would also provide the added benefit of allowing the group to be found when other researchers search under the section titles *Internet Marketing and Advertising* below.

- Direct Marketing.

- Internet Marketing and Advertising.

- Public Relations.

- Television Advertising.

The final page presents the creator with the choice of placing the group in the *Internet Marketing and Advertising* hierarchy. The Internet Marketing Research Group (http://groups.yahoo.com/group/Internet_Marketing_Research_Group) will then be located in the *Internet Marketing and Advertising* hierarchy within the *Business & Finance* hierarchy.

Step 2 of 4: Describe the Group
The following fields need to be filled out to create a new group in Yahoo!

- Name your group, which establishes the name that will appear on the group page and in search results.

- Enter your group e-mail address, which confirms the e-mail address to be used for the group's e-mail.

- Describe your group, which allows the creator to write a description that will appear at the top of the group page. This may be edited later in the group's settings.

- Select primary language, which designates the main language to be used by members of the group. This is a decriptor that will not affect message formatting or content.

- Select directory listing type, to allocate the way it will be listed in Yahoo!'s directory, making it accessible to other Yahoo! Groups members. For a group to be private, the creator must select Unlisted. Listed means it will be displayed in the directory.

- Select membership type, as a creator can allow anyone to join the group (open), or they can approve all members (restricted). These options may be edited later in the settings. If a closed membership is selected, only invited members can join. If this option is selected, it cannot be changed later.

- Select moderation type, the options for which are that members can post freely (unmoderated), the moderator approves all messages (moderated), or the creator can be the only one who can post messages (newsletters). These options may be edited later in the settings. Yahoo! also has a mailing list tool to send messages to members.

Step 3 of 4: Select the Yahoo! Profile and E-Mail Address

This step is used to assign the creator as the group's moderator. It also requires the provision of an e-mail address to which all postings will be sent for approval by the moderator, should they be an active moderator, or simply for information, should they choose to leave it open for submissions in Step 1. Either way, the creator has to tell the system who they are and where it can find them now that they are the boss.

Step 4 of 4: Invite People to the Group

Should a group be created with the intention of establishing a location for submissions to be shared with the viewing community, this step will be very useful. Users are able to provide information on the people to be included in the group so that they will be alerted to the new group and its location. This saves time and hassles for the creator and those intended to be assimilated into the group. If the creator is simply fishing for people in the group community, this step can be skipped by clicking the Skip This Step button at the bottom of the screen.

Completing the Group

The group has, by this point, been created at http://groups.yahoo.com/group/Internet_Marketing_Research_Group. Please feel free to subscribe! All postings to the group will be e-mailed to the subscribers, and feedback can be posted to provide a forum for discussion on marketing research on the Internet. Again, in the next edition of this book, the development of this discussion group will be reviewed.

FIGURE 9.12
Internet_Marketing_
Research_Group
Home Page

Source:
http://groups.yahoo.com/group/
Internet_Marketing_Research_
Group/

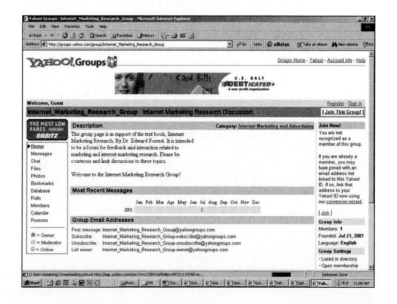

Summary

Newsgroups provide a very useful resource for gathering information. Many of the groups are full of very knowledgeable people who are able and willing to contribute to the group. If postings to the newsgroups are well placed, properly constructed, and follow proper netiquette, a person's research experience in newsgroups will be both productive and enjoyable. Further exploration of the websites will also provide a better foundation for research elsewhere.

The examples in this chapter provide a structure for research within the newsgroup, and discussion group format. The three methods discussed—searches, posting to newsgroups and creating a new newsgroup—provide tools that will contribute to a user's research efforts.

Your online learning center has a case study on *Applied Research Methods for Newsgroups and Discussion Groups* available now at www.mhhe.com/forrest.

Internet Project

Select one of the three main methods of researching newsgroups outlined in this chapter.

1. Newsgroup search.
2. Newsgroup posting.
3. Create a new newsgroup.

Conduct a brief Internet intelligence gathering exercise on a topic of personal interest to you.

References

Eisen, L. S. (2001). "The Master List of Newsgroup Hierarchies, v5.19" (http://www.faqs.org/faqs/usenet/hierarchy-list/index.html/).
Google, Inc. (2001). "Basics of Usenet" (http://groups.google.com/googlegroups/basics.html/).
Google, Inc. (2001). "Navigating Usenet" (http://groups.google.com/googlegroups/basics.html#navigating).
Google, Inc. (2001). "Avoid Getting Flamed" (http://groups.google.com/googlegroups/basics.html#flamed).
Google, Inc. (2001). "Usenet Glossary" (http://groups.google.com/googlegroups/glossary.html/).
Google, Inc. (2001). "Google Groups FAQ" (http://groups.google.com/googlegroups/help.html/).
Google, Inc. (2001). "Posting FAQ" (http://groups.google.com/googlegroups/posting_faq.html/).
Google, Inc. (2001). "Posting Style Guide" (http://groups.google.com/googlegroups/posting_style.html/).
Google, Inc. (2001). "Advanced Group Search" (http://groups.google.com/advanced_group_search/).
Gunn, Chris. (2001). Business newsgroup moderator.
Horton, M., Spafford, G., & Moraes, M. (Posted December 28 , 1999). "Rules for Posting to Usenet" (http://www.faqs.org/faqs/usenet/posting-rules/part1/).
Offutt, A. J., Spafford, G., & Moraes, M. (2001). "Hints on Writing Style for Usenet" (http://www.faqs.org/faqs/usenet/writing-style/part1/).
Templeton, B. (Posted December 28, 1999). "Emily Postnews Answers Your Questions on Netiquette" (http://www.faqs.org/faqs/usenet/emily-postnews/part1/).
Woods, G., Spafford, G., & Lawrence, D. (1997). "How to Create a New Usenet Newsgroup" (http://www.faqs.org/faqs/usenet/creating-newsgroups/part1/).

Chapter 10

Online Focus Groups

In the past five years, advances in bandwidth and video-streaming have made one of marketing's most reliable and heavily used research tools, the focus group, even more attractive and user-friendly for conducting research on and through the Internet (Nucifora, 2000). Numerous organizations that specialize in qualitative assessment of consumers' attitudes and perceptions now offer their services exclusively on the Internet. Skeptics remain unconvinced that virtual focus groups can ever fully replace real-world face-to-face research sessions; however, getting caught up in such arguments misses the point. Online focus groups simply offer researchers another viable and valuable means to conduct research. It can readily supplement (as opposed to supplant) traditional methods of qualitative consumer studies.

Chapter objectives

This chapter aims to:

- Provide an understanding of the general nature of focus group research and how to conduct focus groups on and through the Internet.

- Delineate the advantages and disadvantages of Internet-based focus groups.

- List Internet-based organizations that allow you to participate in online focus groups.

- List Internet-based organizations that can be employed to conduct online focus groups.

- Discuss a range of resources that may be used to learn more about online focus groups.

Focus Groups

There are two main data-collection methods used in market research: quantitative and qualitative. Quantitative research is employed when researchers use identical questions and structured response alternatives, usually collected in numerical form from larger, more representative samples and subjected to empirical analysis. Qualitative research, on the other hand, involves gathering data from free-format responses elicited by open-ended questions, in-depth probing, and subjective observation. Qualitative research is often used to measure such things as experiences, emotions, opinions, and other nonquantifiable data. The most popular form of qualitative research is the **focus group** (Perreault & McCarthy, 2000). Focus groups are controlled by a moderator, who leads 8 to 12 participants in a probing discussion of a product, concept, problem, or item of concern.

> The goal of focus group research is to learn and understand what people have to say and why. The emphasis is on getting people to talk at length and in detail about the subject at hand. The intent is to find out how they feel about a product, concept, idea or organization; how it fits in their lives; and their emotional involvement with it. (McDaniel & Gates, 2002)

The focus group process had its beginnings in the group therapy method utilized by psychiatrists. It was based on the premise that individuals would be more willing to discuss a problem that was shared by other members of a group. As a market research tool, focus groups are used to elicit information that cannot be gained using traditional question/answer surveys because they are too complex, ambiguous, or require further explanation. Focus groups are used for a variety of reasons but are especially popular for gaining consumer reaction to new products or ideas.

Most market researchers agree that there are three essential elements involved in conducting effective focus group sessions:

- A skilled moderator.

- Screened respondents.

- A suitable interviewing facility.

The moderator is the person who will be facilitating the group interaction. Normally he or she needs to prepare or be provided with a discussion/interview guide that outlines the key issues to be addressed. The interview guide lists major areas of inquiry that enable the group to remain focused on the topic being explored.

It is important to select the most appropriate sample possible, and a screening method is usually implemented for selecting participants. Some researchers claim that it is best if the participants are not previously acquainted, although others argue that this does not affect the quality of information gathered. Focus group interviews are generally agreed to be most effective when the number of group participants ranges from 8 to 12.

Deciding on the appropriate number of focus groups to run is also an important consideration and depends largely on the scope of the project. However, the objective is to have as few groups as possible while attempting to maximize the amount of information elicited and to maintain the focus of discussion for each group. Most focus group interviews last for one to two hours. Two hours is generally accepted as the outside limit as the quality of information elicited tends to deteriorate after this amount of time.

The focus group session is usually audiotaped or videotaped to assist the assessment of the results. The taping of focus group interviews provides an extremely useful means of collecting and analyzing data. Transcripts can be made of the tapes, and the responses of participants can be interpreted and categorized in a manner useful to the researcher.

Online Focus Groups

As was the case with survey research, many market researchers engaged in focus group studies readily saw the inherent benefits of the Internet: "lack of geographic barriers, lower costs (about half as much), faster turnaround time and intangibles such as increased openness on the part of respondents when they do not have an interviewer staring them in the face" (McDaniel & Gates, 2002). Yet, despite such demonstrable benefits, there are other researchers who maintain that without direct, person-to-person interaction, focus group research will always come up short. After an exhaustive review of the pluses and minuses of online focus groups, Silverman concludes:

I think that the inevitable conclusion is that online groups, particularly asynchronous bulletin board and list serve groups, have a definite place, but that place is extremely limited and limiting. The usual justifications for online groups, namely, their ability to include difficult-to-recruit, geographically dispersed participants is spurious at best, and dishonest at worst, when compared to telephone groups. That's why, with the exception of a series of list serve type groups conducted worldwide almost twenty years ago, I have not been able to recommend them in good conscience to clients. (Silverman, 2000)

Indeed, critics of online focus groups go so far as to suggest that the research community does itself an injustice by calling qualitative sessions conducted over the Internet "focus groups." McDaniel and Gates (2002) list seven points of contention regarding this issue.

- *Group dynamics.* In cyberspace, it is difficult, if not impossible, to create any real group dynamics, particularly when the participants are reading from computer screens rather than interacting verbally.

- *Nonverbal inputs.* Experienced moderators use nonverbal inputs from participants while moderating and analyzing sessions. It is not possible to duplicate the nonverbal input in an online environment.

- *Client involvement.* Many organizations use the focus group methodology because it gives clients an opportunity to experience some direct interface with consumers in an objective environment. With online focus groups, clients can only monitor written responses on a computer screen.

- *Security.* With a traditional focus group, the moderator and client know who is in the room, assuming that appropriate screening has been done. With online focus groups, there is no way to be sure who is sitting at the computer.

- *Attention to the topic.* Another important benefit of the traditional focus group process is that the participants in the group understand that they are expected to stay in the room for the full two hours of the session and contribute to the discussion. However, in an online environment, the moderator can never be sure that the participants are not watching TV, reading a book, or eating dinner while the session is proceeding.

- *Exposure to external stimuli.* A key use of focus groups is to present participants with advertising copy, new product concepts, prototypes, or other stimuli in order to get their reactions. In an online chat situation, it is almost impossible to duplicate the kind of exposure to external stimuli that occurs in the live focus group environment.

- *Role and skill of the moderator.* Most marketing professionals agree that the most important factor in the quality of traditional focus group research is the skill of the moderator. The techniques available to a moderator sitting alone at a computer terminal are much more limited because of the lack of face-to-face involvement with participants.

So far, such criticisms have remained valid. However, with the advent of broadband Internet connections, proliferations of Web-cam technology, and real-time video-streaming, these limitations have begun to fall by the wayside. As Nucifora reports:

The advent of video-streaming technology now means that focus groups can be observed "live" from the comfort of one's desk. The focus group technique itself remains unchanged. Participants gather at a location to discuss and talk under the guidance of a facilitator. However, observers no longer need to be on site, behind the mirror to view the proceedings. A camera captures all the action close-up, including facial expressions, and broadcasts the action via video streaming to an unlimited number of viewers who can watch real-time from the comfort of their desktop computers at any time, any place. Observers normally require a password to gain access to the proceedings and have the option of commenting on the discussion via text with other observers. Once the focus group session is completed, the data are saved to a server where the client on an on-demand basis can view it. Material can also be indexed for easy retrieval by subject matter and stored on CD-ROM. (Nucifora, 2000)

Accordingly, many organizations and market researchers find online focus group sessions a useful technique for the reasons listed in the next section.

Advantages of Online Focus Groups

Financial Advantages

A simple cost–benefit analysis reveals that online focus groups possess several economic advantages over their real-world counterparts. Focus groups are often a very costly exercise, with the client company having to pay for such expenses as rental of a suitable facility, catering, incentive payments, transcripts, and videotaping or audiotaping. Sometimes, selecting the most appropriate group members from a large geographic area means that air travel, car rental, and hotel accommodation costs are also incurred. Online focus groups alleviate these expenses to a great extent. Facility costs are virtually nonexistent, no catering is required, and transcripts of discussions are available within minutes of completing the session. Incentive payments may also be reduced, as there is less inconvenience to the participant. In addition, people can join the group from any location; hence, there are no travel costs involved.

Efficiency Advantages

The entire online focus group process—from recruitment to data output—can be conducted in a very short period of time. Screening and scheduling via e-mail substantially reduces field time, and transcripts and data analysis can be made available much sooner. One online researcher reported that she "received 2,700 responses within one day of sending out a so-called screener e-mail to approximately 6,000 users in the company's database of 500,000 Internet homes." (McDaniel & Gates, 2002). In addition, online focus group participants can communicate in a place and time that is most convenient for them.

Diversity of Group Participants

Another advantage of online focus groups is that participants can be recruited from diverse geographical locations as well as from different social and demographic groups. For example, some real-world focus groups suffer negative effects when participants of considerably different ages are forced to interact. Similar difficulties may arise when participants of different gender, race, religion, and/or color are brought together. The electronic medium can substantially reduce such problems, as the anonymity of group members is preserved to a large degree. It is also likely that consumers who are usually averse to participating in focus groups, such as those who are too busy or dislike group interaction, may be persuaded to join in an online discussion. Such difficult-to-reach consumers might include executives and professionals whose opinions are sometimes the most valuable. Taking part in an online focus group may be more convenient as they can remain in their office or at home. Other arguments for the practicality and payoffs of using online focus groups include those listed in Table 10.1.

Disadvantages of Online Focus Groups

Screening Problems

One of the shortcomings of conducting market research over the Internet is that researchers can never really be sure that respondents are who they say they are.

TABLE 10.1
Advantages of Online Focus Groups

Participants	Anyone in the world with a computer and modem can participate.
Time commitment	No traveling to a facility, so busy respondents are more likely to be available.
Openness of respondents	Lack of face-to-face contact may lead respondents to express true feelings in writing. Traditional focus groups always include "natural talkers," who dominate the discussion, despite a good moderator's attempt to equalize participant contributions. Other participants will be less comfortable voicing opinions in a group; they may express themselves more freely when not face to face with their peers. The online focus group has a built-in leveling effect, in the sense that shy participants can express themselves as freely as more outgoing participants.
Transcripts	Word-for-word transcripts are available almost immediately, allowing capture of complete sentences/thoughts.
Respondent recruiting	It is easier to obtain all types of respondents. It is possible online to reach populations that are traditionally inaccessible because of time or professional constraints, for example, groups such as doctors, lawyers, and senior business executives. They do not need to take time from their busy schedules to visit a focus group facility but, rather, can participate from the privacy of their own home.
Client travel costs	Expenditures for return airline tickets to distant cities, meals, hotels, and taxis are avoided. Clients merely log on in their own office, or even at home, to observe the research in progress.
Communication with moderator	Observers can communicate privately with the moderator on a split screen. During the traditional focus group, the client observes the discussion from behind a one-way glass; communication with the moderator is impossible without interfering with the discussion. An online focus group, however, offers a remarkable opportunity for two-way interaction between the moderator and the client. Rather than speaking into the room with a note scribbled on a piece of paper, the client can address the moderator directly, clearly, and efficiently, without interrupting the group dynamic.
Client involvement	Clients can read live dialogue and transcripts.
Online groups easier to moderate	Telephone groups are probably the hardest to moderate, followed closely by face-to-face groups. Online groups are the easiest by far because they do not require the moderator to think on his or her feet as quickly.
Bulletin board style allows for participation on respondents' schedule	The bulletin board style, as distinct from the chat room style, is where the participants return to the session periodically, often once or twice a day, and participate in an ongoing group anywhere from several days to several weeks or even months in duration. In this way, participation comes to the participants, rather than having the participant remember to visit a particular website periodically. The basic difference here is that the group is taking place asynchronously, that is, without everyone being online at the same time.
More available in certain places than telephone conferencing facilities	In the few cases where the computer is available but telephone conference calls are not, obviously online groups are the way to go. With respect to participants in telephone groups from many so-called Third World countries, as long as they can get to a phone that can reach the United States, they can participate in a conference. However, this would be much more expensive than online groups.
Can be used to corroborate findings from in-person groups—done in only one or two markets	Both telephone and online groups can be conducted in as many locations as there are participants. So a group of nine participants can be from nine different towns or even countries. Or they can be as narrow as from one office building in Los Angeles.

Source: Compiled from Silverman (2000) and McDaniel & Gates (2002)

Technical Limitations

There are a number of unique features of focus group discussions that cannot be replicated in an electronic environment. For example, eye contact is not possible; hence, it may be difficult for the moderator to gauge the feelings of the group and to decide if the discussion should deviate from the discussion guide. Retaining the full attention of participants is also a potential problem as other things may distract them when sitting in front of a computer at home or work. In a real-world focus group, the moderator usually has the undivided attention of participants. Interpreting qualitative data is a complex process and involves analyzing not only verbal communications but also nonverbal information such as silences, tone of voice, contradictions, and level of energy. Transcripts of online discussions are usually entirely text-based, and the extra information that can be gained from audiotaping or videotaping is not available. If the subject matter is highly emotional, it may be difficult to obtain appropriate feedback.

When Are Online Groups Appropriate?

It is really up to the researcher to determine when an online focus group should be used. This will, of course, depend on the research objectives and the type of product or idea being discussed. However, online focus groups appear to be most effective when qualitative feedback is needed quickly, participants are from widely dispersed locations, and/or ideas for questions to be included in a quantitative survey are needed. They may be particularly conducive to concept testing, especially of text or images, as this information can be sent to the participants either prior to commencement or during the course of the discussion using **pop-up** style browser windows.

A typical online focus group scenario may run something like this:

- Respondents are identified by e-mail or via the Web.

- They are screened and, if deemed suitable for a particular focus group, are contacted via e-mail and directed to a specific Internet address.

- Participants are greeted electronically and instructed as to how they may proceed.

- A **chat room** window is used in which participants can type their messages in response to other comments or questions from the moderator.

- A picture of an advertisement (for example) may be shown to participants by using a pop-up window, and group members are asked to comment on it.

- The client company can watch the discussion as it unfolds on their screens (the electronic equivalent of a one-way mirror).

- Finally, a transcript of the discussion can be supplied within minutes, although analysis of results may take longer.

Conducting focus groups is not as simple as it sounds. Of course, any company can set up a page on its website where visitors can interact with one another and discuss topics relevant to the firm's products or services. In fact, this is a very useful tool to gauge market reaction and get new ideas. However, if a researcher is interested in generating more rigorous qualitative data and analysis, it is strongly recommended that they employ the services of a company that has a demonstrated ability to conduct this type of research. Considerable organization is required to set up a focus group, and a skilled moderator is usually an important component of any worthwhile discussion.

Online focus groups are not appropriate for satisfying all qualitative research objectives. However, the potential savings in cost and time make this methodology very appealing to companies with limited research budgets and/or companies that need to get qualitative information quickly. It is ideal for situations where there is little need for face-to-face interaction between participants and the method will satisfy research objectives. Nevertheless, any use of online focus groups should still be preceded by a thorough description of the intended objectives of the research in conjunction with budget and time considerations. In the same way that focus groups are just a tool in the market researcher's toolbox, so too online focus groups should be considered yet another tool. They should only be used when appropriate and not as a complete substitute for other methods.

Conducting an Online Focus Group

If a company feels the need to set up and run their own online focus group, they will require the use of a chat room facility at the very least. If thinking about downloading a chat software program to use for a focus group, think twice. If the software must be downloaded and run as a separate application, then all of the group participants must also download the software onto their computers—which is something they may not be very comfortable doing! The following websites are suggested, as they provide chat room facilities on their server or enable others to host chats on their own website without the use of stand-alone software.

CustomForum (http://www.delphiforums.com/) is a service provided by Delphi Forums, Inc. It offers packages to users that include limited space on the Delphi server that can be used to conduct online discussions. They can be in either a message board format or real-time chat format. Access to the chat room can be password-protected, which is essential if wanting to run a private focus group.

ParaChat (http://parachat.com/parachat.htm/) provides free chat rooms and is a service offered by M Square, Inc. According to their website, Free ParaChat rooms are:

FIGURE 10.1
Delphi Forums, Inc.

Source:
http://www.delphiforums.com/

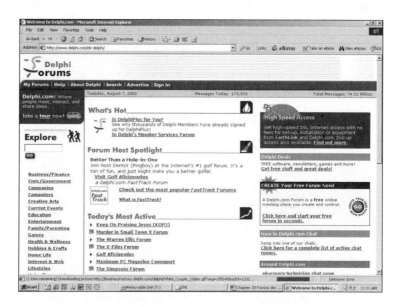

FIGURE 10.2

**Example of a
ParaChat Chat Room**

Source:
http://parachat.com/pchat1.htm/

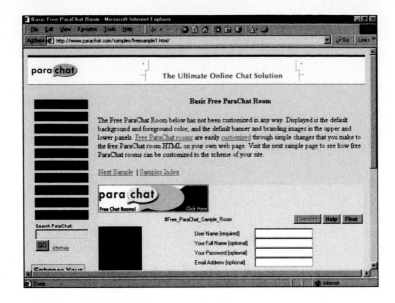

- Easy to set up: Copy and paste a few lines of HTML to your Web page.

- Easy to use: no software downloads—works with your browser.

- Seamlessly integrated with your website, as the chat room is embedded within your Web page and is fully customizable.

  Beseen.com (http://www.beseen.com/chat/index.html/) lets visitors create a chat room for free that can be linked into a company's own website. The company simply creates a hyperlink on one of their own Web pages, and when a user clicks on it, they are presented with a chat room page. According to Beseen.com, their features are:

- Your very own customizable Internet messaging system.

- A chat room where you can talk to your customers, meet friends, or simply visit relatives.

- The ability to add chat to your website or just get a room to use as a freestanding Web destination.

- No programming required, easy setup, and simple maintenance.

- A totally free chat room, customized to your look and feel.

Participating in Online Focus Groups

There are many companies that allow people to actually participate in an online focus group discussion, and some will even pay participants. All that is needed is to register with them; and then a group facilitator will lead new participants through the process—online, of course. It may be worthwhile to participate in an online focus group before committing an organization's resources to such a research project.

TABLE 10.2
Google Listing of Volunteer Focus Groups

Web Pages	Description
Consumer product ratings network (http://www.ratings.net/)	Consumers can earn points toward contest prizes by providing online ratings, reviews, and reports on products and services.
Harris Poll Online (http://vr.harrispollonline.com/register/register.asp/)	The Internet-based extension to the prestigious Harris Poll offers an opportunity to express your views, hopes, and opinions. Influential decision makers in government and business will hear what you think.
Cyber Dialogue (http://members.cyberdialogue.com/index.html/)	Turn your opinions into cash. Earn money for taking surveys and participating in online focus groups.
SurveySite (http://www.surveysite.com/)	Specializes in online market research including e-mail and online surveys, website evaluation, online focus groups, and conjoint analysis.
Greenfield Online (http://signup.greenfieldonline.com/)	Speak out and express yourself. Your participation directly influences the way companies develop products, policies, and services.
NFO Interactive (http://www.mysurvey.com/)	Market research gathered by online surveys.
GlobalTestMarket (http://www.globaltestmarket.com/)	An online marketplace where consumers from around the world participate in the development of new-to-the-world products and services.
American Consumer Opinion (http://www.acop.com/)	As a member, you will help evaluate new products, test new advertising, and tell companies what you like, don't like, and want in the future.
SurveySavvy (http://www.surveysavvy.com/)	Surveys members for their opinions on the products and services they use. Payment for member participation and for the participation of those whom members refer.
iCameo (http://www.icameo.com/)	iCameo provides Internet market research for firms, and pays survey participants generously.
Forum Modalis (http://www.forummodalis.com/)	Business and IT professionals sharing their opinions on products, services, and concepts. Participants are rewarded with cash and prizes. All opinions and information offered are strictly confidential.
MBS Internet Research Center (http://www.mbsinternet.net/)	Earn cash for filling out online surveys! Give your opinion and make money at the same time. Your identity is protected; company claims it never gives out contact information.
iOpinion (http://www.iopinion.com/)	Participate in online focus group discussion forums and online surveys.
SurveyGuy.Com (http://www.surveyguy.com/)	Provides online surveys and polls for businesses, organizations, and market research professionals.
Onesight (http://www.onesight.com/)	Onesight conducts market research surveys on behalf of leading companies. Consumers who are interested in shaping the products and services offered by these companies have joined their market research panel to take these surveys.

Web Pages	Description
Trendsetters (http://trendcreators.com/)	Trendsetters specialize in helping clients adapt to rapidly changing markets through carefully targeted customer-centric research.
Interactive Rewards (http://www.interactiverewards.com/)	Get paid for taking online surveys. They pay a minimum of $40 if you participate in an online chat discussion and pay cash or hold contests if you answer an online survey.
Paid2Survey.Com (http://www.paid2survey.com/)	Get paid for filling out surveys online.
IonsInfotech Services (http://www.ionsinfotech.com/)	The pioneer of Internet-based market research in India. It leverages the people on the Web as well as off-line panelists who make for diverse content in marketing and management decision making. Residents of India only.
Survey Payday (http://www.surveypayday.com/)	Online surveys for market research, website reviews, and public opinion polls. Perfect for small businesses or new sites that need affordable and reliable market research or site reviews.
Opinion Surveys UK (http://www.opinionsurveys.co.uk/)	Provides tools for creating opinion surveys, customer surveys online.
Cash4Answers (http://www.cash4answers.com/)	Cash4Answers.com is an online market research panel. Members are asked to fill out online questionnaires on a host of subjects. In return participants can earn cash and/or enter drawings for prizes.
KNOTs (http://www.knots-eu.com/)	The quality consumer panel for online research where members can earn rewards by sharing opinions in online research studies.
Brand Institute Inc. (https://www.brandinst.com/secure/memberservices.htm/)	Brand Institute is always looking for new participants in its online market research groups. Participants are asked to fill out online surveys from time to time and are reimbursed for their time and efforts.

Source: http://directory.google.com/Top/Business/Marketing/Market_Research_Suppliers/Online_Surveys/Volunteer_Focus_Groups/

Some Organizations That Conduct Focus Groups

Greenfield Online (http://www.greenfield.com/) not only conducts online focus groups but also actively recruits participants. People can register with them by simply filling out an online application, meaning they will then be added to Greenfield Online's database. If they invite the person to participate, the individual will be required to fill out an online survey as part of the screening process. FocusChat™ is Greenfield Online's proprietary qualitative research tool that provides the ability to conduct focus groups online and learn what consumers think of products or services, explore consumer attitudes, test new concepts or products, and hear what consumers think about one company versus their competitors. Greenfield Online also has three-dimensional imaging technology "which allows panelists to get up close and personal with your products."

CustomerSat, Inc. (http://www.customersat.com/index.html) is a market research firm that takes a unique approach to the focus group paradigm. They believe that conventional

FIGURE 10.3
Example of a
Greenfield Online
Focus Chat

Source:
http://www.greenfield.com/dem
os/FocusChat.html/

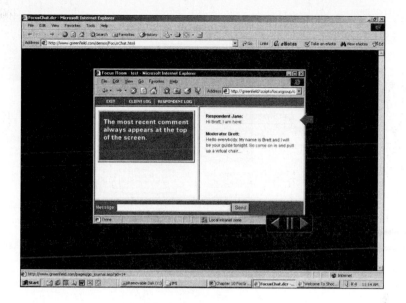

focus groups, of one to two hours in duration and with 8 to 12 participants from the same geographical area, are somewhat limited. CustomerSat, Inc.'s online focus groups (branded WebFocus™) offer an alternative. WebFocus™ Groups include up to 30 participants spanning the globe, eliminating geographical biases. Participants can volunteer their thoughts from the comfort and convenience of their home, office, or anywhere else they choose to use the Internet, rather than having to find an unfamiliar place in rush-hour traffic. In addition, instead of having to start at a fixed time, they can participate whenever they wish—before work, during the day, over lunch, or in the evening—usually for 10 to 20 minutes per day. WebFocus™ groups last from four days to a week, so participants can reflect on ideas overnight and provide richer, deeper, and more thoughtful insight.

CustomerSat, Inc. sees the potential for audience diversity as one of the strengths of Internet-based research. The website also provides a range of free market research resources such as tutorials, articles, sample surveys, links, and workshops, with an emphasis on Internet survey techniques and developments.

SurveySite, Inc. (http://www.surveysite.com/) is an Internet-based market research organization that offers online focus groups as part of its overall research approach. They use experienced moderators and are able to introduce text, graphics, sounds/jingles, video, or multimedia during a focus group discussion. The company also uses **pop-up survey** software to collect data on the World Wide Web. This technique randomly selects website visitors and pops up a small window asking them if they want to take part in a brief online survey. SurveySite, Inc. claims that this gives a true random sample of website visitors. Their services include customer relationship management research, website evaluation, e-commerce/shopping cart analysis, and customer/employee surveys. SurveySite, Inc. offers a variety of research methods such as Web-based surveys (in multiple languages), e-mail surveys, Internet panel research, online focus groups, and their unique product FocusSite: The Two Day Focus Group™.

Online focus groups are a cost-effective alternative to conventional face-to-face focus groups. Generally 8 to 10 people are invited to join for a specified period of time (90 minutes to two hours). The controlled environment of the chat rooms allows participants to view text, graphics, sounds/jingles, video, or multimedia for evaluation and testing. On the

FIGURE 10.4
CustomerSat, Inc.'s
WebFocus™ Groups

Source:
http://www.customersat.com/
000svc.html

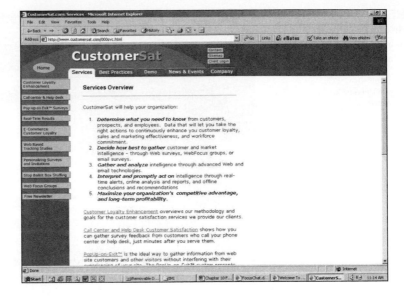

FIGURE 10.5
SurveySite, Inc.'s
Online Focus Groups

Source:
http://www.surveysite.com/new
site/docs/onlinefocus.htm/

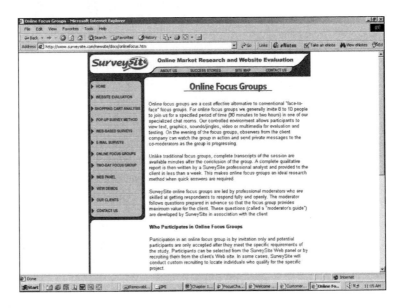

evening of the focus groups, observers from the client company can watch the group in action and send private messages to the co-moderators as the group is progressing.

Harrisinteractive (http://www.harrisinteractive.com/) has an online panel of more than 7 million people with diverse backgrounds, behaviors, and attitudes. Its panel members originate from more than 200 countries.

Metadexes of Market Research Firms

The *GreenBook* (http://www.greenbook.org/) is an established print-based directory of market research firms produced by the American Marketing Association. It is also a website that lists thousands of market research firms throughout the world that are indexed and cross-indexed. The website enables the user to search for companies that conduct specific types of research using such parameters as company name, research services offered, market specialties, industry specialties, computer programs, trademarked products and services, geographic location, and key personnel listings.

The *GreenBook® Volume I, Worldwide Directory of Marketing Research Companies and Services* (http://www.greenbook.org/index.cfm/) includes the full range of marketing research companies and services worldwide. It can help researchers select the best services for their needs. The *GreenBook® Volume II, Worldwide Directory of Focus Group Companies and Services*, now in its tenth year, offers comprehensive listings of facilities, moderating, and more.

@ResearchInfo.com (http://www.researchinfo.com/) is a directory of market research firms and resources that can assist researchers in finding the "right" company. Visitors can search by type of research conducted, geographical area (mainly U.S.), and/or type of industry.

Quirk's Marketing Research Review (http://www.quirks.com/) contains the Researcher SourceBook™, which has listings of more than 6,500 firms providing marketing research products and services. It has a directory that is searchable by company/contact name and geography/specialty.

Zarden Market Research Direct-A-Net (http://www.zarden.com) provides a very robust directory for finding market research companies. It allows searching through its directory by type of service provided, alphabetical order, and state/country.

Volition (http://www.volition.com/opinions.html/) lists over 30 online market research firms that will pay for people's opinions, with cash, prizes, and/or points given for participating in their surveys and related research activities.

Other Online Focus Group Resources

Roger J. Rezabek's "Online Focus Groups: Electronic Discussions for Research" (http://qualitative-research.net/fqs-texte/1-00/1-00rezabek-e.htm) states the following in its abstract:

FIGURE 10.6
GreenBook

Source:
http://www.greenbook.org/

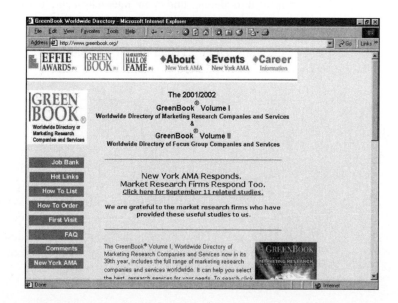

As part of a dissertation research project, an online focus group was created in order to help determine questions and issues to be asked [in] in-depth interviews of distance learning students about their motives, barriers and enablers in their decision to enroll in adult distance learning courses. The focus group used asynchronous discussion through a listserve for approximately two and a half months, and identified several key issues that were explored in the [in-] depth interviews. An FAQ for Online Focus Groups is included. (Rezabek, 2000)

Tech Ed also presents information about online focus groups in the paper "What's Different about Useability Focus Groups: When and Why Should We Use Them?" (http://www.teced.com/upa_2001_sig.html/), which was written by a Special Interest Group (SIG) at the Useability Professionals Association 2001 Conference. According to the website, this SIG:

Provides for useability professionals to discuss when to use this methodology—and when not to use it, how to design useability focus groups, how to facilitate useability focus groups, and how to analyze the resulting data. The facilitators believe that useability focus groups actually have much in common with other ethnographic methods (we challenge the assumption that focus groups are only good for marketing research).

orcFOCUS (http://www.orcfocus.com/html/about_1.htm/) provides an example of what users would see in an online focus group and lets them observe how they work.

Summary

Many research firms are now conducting qualitative research on and through the Internet. Online focus groups often provide a faster and cheaper means of collecting qualitative data than using the real-world equivalent. However, there are also screening and technical limitations. Fortunately, the benefits to most organizations far outweigh the costs, certainly in terms of:

- The lack of geographic barriers.

- Lower costs (up to half as much).

- Faster turnaround time.

- Worldwide and versatile recruitment.

- Improved moderator and client interaction and involvement.

- Increased openness on the part of participants.

Your online learning center has a case study on *Online Focus Groups* available now at www.mhhe.com/forrest.

Discussion Questions

1. Why are focus groups such a popular method among market researchers for collecting qualitative data?

2. Do you think that the integrity of qualitative research is threatened or enhanced as a result of the growing popularity of online focus groups? Explain your argument.

3. The emergence of online focus groups means that conventional focus groups can now be avoided entirely. Discuss your view of this statement with the class.

4. Describe some of the problems that may be encountered when conducting do-it-yourself online focus group discussions. What steps could be taken to alleviate these problems?

5. What are some of the advantages and disadvantages of conducting product or copy testing via the Internet?

6. What has been the effect of increases in Internet bandwidth, (enabling real-time audio and video capability), on the use of online focus groups as a qualitative research technique?

Internet Project

Select one of the following Web services and conduct your own online focus group. CustomForum (http://www.delphi.com/dir-delphi/).

- ParaChat (http://parachat.com/parachat.htm)..

Further Reading

Greenbaum, Thomas L. (1998). *The Handbook for Focus Group Research*, 2nd ed. Thousand Oaks: Sage Publications, Inc.

Krueger, A., and Casey, Mary Anne (2000). *Focus Groups: A Practical Guide for Applied Research*, 3rd ed. Thousand Oaks, California: Sage Publications, Inc.

Morgan, David L., (1997). *Focus Groups as Qualitative Research*, 2nd ed. Thousand Oaks, California: Sage Publications, Inc.

References

Dutka, A., (1994). *AMA Handbook for Customer Satisfaction.* Lincolnwood, Illinois: NTC Business Books.

HyperNews HTTPD Log Analysers, (1998). *HTTPd Log Analysers* (http://www.hypernews.org/HyperNews/get/www/log-analysers.html/).

Malhotra, N. K., Hall, J., Shaw, M., and Crisp, M. (1996). *Marketing Research: An Applied Approach.* Sydney: Prentice-Hall.

McDaniel, Carl, and Gates., Roger (2002). *Marketing Research: The Impact of the Internet.* Mason, Ohio: South-Western Educational Publishing, Chapter 5, pp. 125, 140–7.

Neuman, W. L., (1994). *Social Research Methods*, 2nd ed. Sydney: Allyn and Bacon.

Nucifora, Alf (2000). "Marketing on a Shoestring: Online Focus Groups Bring the Action to Your Desktop." *The Business Journal*, September 18, Charlotte, North Carolina (http://charlotte.bcentral.com/charlotte/stories/2000/09/18/smallb3.htm/).

Perreault William D., and McCarthy, Jerome (2000). *Essentials of Marketing.* New York: McGraw-Hill, p. 165.

Rezabek, Roger J. (2000). *Online Focus Groups: Electronic Discussions for Research*, January vol. 1, no. 1 (http://qualitative-research.net/fqs-texte/1-00/1-00rezabek-e.htm/).

Silverman, George (2000). "Online vs. Face to Face vs. Telephone Groups" (http://www.mnav.com/online.htm/).

Van Nuys, David (1999). "Online Focus Groups Save Time, Money" (http://sanjose.bcentral.com/sanjose/stories/1999/11/29/smallb4.html/).

Chapter 11

Websites, Sources, and Data—Reliability and Validity

Question: Why are Web/home pages like belly buttons?

Answer: Because everyone has one.

One of the many jokes regarding the Internet highlights the problem of searching for and evaluating information using this tool. Simply put, anybody and everybody can post anything, under a real or pseudo-identity, at any time and on any subject. Ensuring the reliability and validity of data is a necessary undertaking in every research endeavor, and in this regard the Internet poses distinct problems for any researcher. Due to its open and freewheeling nature there are no enforced review procedures or information-filtering mechanisms. The Internet does provide instant access to an ever expanding global repository of information. However, this instant and direct access, coupled with the ease of publication, necessitates that Internet information be thoroughly screened and scrutinized by the researcher.

Chapter objectives

This chapter aims to:

- Compare information found online and off-line, and discuss the disadvantages and advantages of accessing information on the Internet.

- Review the ways used to cope with information overload such as meta-information.

- Provide an understanding of the need to evaluate information on the Internet, and insight into the varying quality of information available and the lack of filtered information.

Information on the Internet

The obvious advantages of obtaining research information from the Internet include the wide variety of information that is available, the speed of access, and the fact that it can be accessed cheaply. Another major advantage is that Internet information is often more timely than printed material due to ease of publication, and it can be updated on a regular basis. The Internet provides the means for researchers to access considerably more information than is feasible with print-based resources.

The ease of access to information through the Internet can also prove to be a disadvantage if researchers do not have the skills and knowledge needed to evaluate and filter the information. Information overload will prove to be troublesome for those without the skills. There are also problems of reliability of Internet information, as it generally bypasses the traditional review process that printed material in the traditional domain has to endure. Due to the ease of publication, questions about quality and stability are raised. Anyone can publish on the Internet, making it imperative that information be evaluated for reliability and validity.

Unlike traditional libraries, information on the Internet is not formally cataloged and there is no central control over what the online library stocks. Moreover, information on the Internet is constantly changing and can easily be deleted. Thus arise the problems of reliability and validity. Internet researchers are going to need to develop information skills to be able to determine the credentials of the source, reliability of the website, and, thus, the accuracy of the data obtained at the website and supplied by the source.

Three paradigms have emerged that researchers can employ to guide their evaluative efforts: the five Ws, the ten Cs, and AOC criteria (see Table 11.1).

Who (Credibility/Authority)?

First off, can the author of the information on a website be identified? It is necessary to know the author if the user is going to assess the website's "authority." Is there a name on

TABLE 11.1
Website, Source, and Data Evaluation Paradigms

The Five Ws (Lauer, 1999)	The Ten Cs (University of Wisconsin–Eau Claire, 2001)	AOC Criteria (Alexander & Tate, 1996)
Who	Content	Authority
Where	Credibility	Accuracy
What	Critical thinking	Objectivity
When	Copyright	Currency
Why	Citation	Coverage
	Continuity	
	Censorship	
	Connectivity	
	Comparability	
	Context	

the document to indicate who the author is and any biographical detail? If not, there may be a link to another Web page where the author's biographical details can be found.

A number of questions need to be asked to establish author credibility. What is their level of education or training? Do they have a title or position of employment? Do they have a ranking or position among their peers? These points need to be established so that the level of authority and expertise with which the author speaks can be determined and taken into account.

The level of responsibility the author takes for the information must also be established. If the author takes little responsibility, then it is easier for them to make unproven claims. By searching for and reviewing their other works, the user can develop a further understanding of the author and their publications. This will help researchers to obtain some insight into the areas in which the author concentrates. Although the author may not always be identifiable, in this case the Web-master can be contacted and asked who the author of the page is and whether any biographical details can be obtained.

Internet information does not necessarily have to be authored by a person or persons; it may be authored by an organization. If this is the case, it will be necessary to identify the function the organization performs—corporate, governmental, nonprofit, or educational. A clue as to what type of organization has published the information can be found in the URL extension **.com, .org, .gov,** or **.edu.** With organizational information, the level of authority, expertise, and responsibility also needs to be established.

- Is this organization in a position to comment on the topic?

- Is the organization recognized and respected?

The organization can usually be identified by the name on the header or footer of the Web page. An unidentifiable author does not necessarily mean that the information is unreliable, but care must be taken in using the information. In this situation, it is advisable to find other reliable documents to support the information.

Where (Comparability/Connectivity/Copyright/Citation/Accuracy)?

"The 'where' question is linked to noting the accuracy of the information" (Lauer, 1999). The task of determining how accurate the information is falls to the researcher because no information standards currently exist on the Internet. If the information is accurate, that means it is correct, comprehensive, timely, consistent, and comparable with other reliable work in the area.

Comprehensive

The researcher must make a concerted effort to ensure that the information is complete and comprehensive. How in-depth is the coverage?

Consistent and Comparable

Are the figures and information presented consistent? Inconsistencies may imply poor information quality. The information should be comparable with other reliable sources (Lauer, 1999). A number of questions need to be answered here:

- Does the author let the reader know where the information came from?

- Did the author provide citations?

- Do the citations appear to be accurate and valid?

- Is it possible to double-check the citations because the author linked to them?

- Does the author provide links to related websites that can be used to continue research?

- If information is obtained from an electronic journal, is that journal peer-reviewed?

- What sort of reputation does the journal maintain?

- If an organization sponsors the website, how reputable is that organization?

- If the publisher is difficult to identify, then is the website linked to other reputable sources?

- Does the information receive expert evaluation?

Evidence

Is there any evidence to support the claims made or statistics and information presented? Are the appropriate points referenced and documented? Is there evidence of a wide variety of sources used to support any arguments that are made?

Supporting Information

It is important to establish what supporting information has been used. If statistics are given or claims are made, are the original documents cited? Is there a bibliography to show what sources were used? How reliable are they? It is especially important when using statistics that they are obtained from a reliable source.

The aim of identifying the source is to determine the extent of quality control that the information has undertaken. As information on the Internet continues to grow at a rapid pace, it is increasingly important to know the quality of information accessed. The demand for peer-reviewed information will be evident and so will the rating of websites based on recognized criteria.

Researchers should be wary of websites that do not cite where they got their information or provide links to other websites that corroborate or add to what they are saying (Lauer, 1999). In addition, the lack of identified sources, as well as poor spelling and grammar, can all be used to assess the quality of any information obtained.

What (Content/Objectivity)?

A critical task is to assess the objectivity of the information presented on a given website. Does it show imbalance and/or any conflict of interest? Information must always be evaluated for bias. For example, if a company is writing something about itself, it is probably less reliable than an independent source writing about that organization. The information is, no doubt, presented from a certain perspective and with its own agenda. Other considerations include:

Tone

Does the information use emotional language? What is the tone of the writing? If the writer is using emotional language, this could suggest that the information presented may not be objective.

Purpose

What is the purpose of the information? Is it designed to educate, inform, or persuade? Is the information for entertainment, commercial, or informational purposes? If the purpose and goals of the website are not clear, further clarification may be required.

Plausibility

Biased and emotional language can be indicators of lack of objectivity and therefore plausibility. The purpose and reason for the information need to be taken into account when considering how useful the information is. A reader might also ask, Is this page mostly fact or mostly opinion? Does the author attempt to overgeneralize or simplify information to detract from fact? Do any of the facts appear out of context? Are they applied in a way to persuade the reader? Are there links to the organization sponsoring the page? Or does this seem like a lone person trying to voice their opinion? Is the page actually an advertisement disguised as information?

When (Continuity/Currency)?

Timeliness is extremely important when determining the currency and relevancy of information on the Internet. The changing nature of information on the Internet requires constant monitoring. It is important to determine when the information was written, published, and when it was last updated. Information based on highly changeable areas like technology, the sciences, and the economy needs constant updating. When a document was first published and last updated should be indicated on the website. A credible website should include the date that it was created and the date it was last updated. If the dates are not given on the page, then it is sometimes possible to view them in the directory in which the document is placed. If all else fails, it may be necessary to contact the Web-master to get these details. When using databases to access information, the researcher must also be aware of the timeliness of the database because there are lag times between publications. Reliable sources are usually ones that give the last date that the website was revised (Edwards, 1998).

Why (Context/Critical Thinking/Coverage)?

Certainly, important questions to consider are, Why is the information posted on the Internet? What purpose is it serving? Can it be corroborated by other sites or sources on the Internet? According to Lauer, "The 'why' question is answered by evaluating what coverage this information has across the wide spectrum of the Internet" (1999).

- Does this website provide valuable information?

- Or should I keep researching?

- Is this new information to me?

- Is it something I haven't yet discovered?

- Can I corroborate this information, meaning, can I confirm its reliability by finding similar information elsewhere, from places I trust?

Websites about Websites

In addition to numerous articles, books, manuscripts, lectures, and tutorials, there are a multitude of websites that will guide you in the fine art of website evaluation.

- Virginia Tech University Libraries—Bibliography on Evaluating Internet Resources (http://www.lib.vt.edu/research/libinst/evalbiblio.html/).

- Information Quality WWW Virtual Library (http://www.ciolek.com/WWWVLInfo Quality.html/).

- UCLA College Library—Thinking Critically about World Wide Web Resources (http://www.library.ucla.edu/libraries/college/help/critical/index.htm/).

- Cornell University Library—Critically analyzing Information Sources (http://www.library.cornell.edu/okuref/research/skill26.htm/).

- Kathy Schrock's Guide for Educators: Critical Evaluation Information (http://discoveryschool.com/schrockguide/eval.html/).

Meta-Information

There is a general lack of review and information-filtering services on the Internet. To date, the researcher is required, for the most part, to do much of the screening; albeit, there are a few websites that evaluate, rate, and review other websites. Evaluation tools are available, but careful consideration should be given as to what criteria are being used to rate and review the websites.

In order to cope with the information explosion, the researcher must acquire the means to summarize and index information. **Meta-information** is a way of achieving this and can be described as information about information. High-quality meta-information is important in that search and evaluation time can be reduced. Currently meta-information takes two forms: evaluative and summary.

Evaluative Meta-Information

Evaluative meta-information evaluates and judges the information based on a set of criteria. Figure 11.1 shows how Internet marketing websites have been evaluated through the Argus Clearinghouse, which is (in March 2002) transferring its listings into the main Internet Public Library (IPL) (http://www.ipl.com/). Argus Clearinghouse websites are rated for resource description, resource evaluation, guide design, organization schemes, and meta-information.

FIGURE 11.1
The Argus Clearinghouse

Source:
http://www.clearinghouse.net/

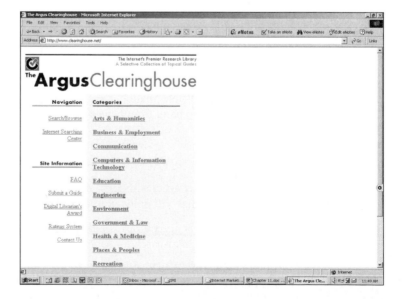

Figure 11.2 shows how the Marketing Virtual Library is rated on the Argus Clearing-house. It also shows who reviewed the site, where they are from, when it was reviewed, and also when it was last updated.

If a researcher wants to depend on others' evaluation of websites, there are a number of search engines that list and rank sites based on their "popularity" with Internet users. If researchers equate popularity with utility, Direct Hit is a search engine they can employ. As described at its website, Direct Hit's technology:

> works by anonymously monitoring which websites Internet searchers select from the search results list, how much time the searchers spend at these sites and a number of other metrics, such as the position of a site relative to other sites. The sites that are selected by searchers are boosted in their ranking, while the sites that are consistently ignored by searchers are penalized in their rankings. In this manner, the Direct Hit effectively harnesses millions of

FIGURE 11.2

The Marketing Virtual Library

Source:
http://www.clearinghouse.net/
cgibin/chadmin/viewitem/Busin
ess___Employment/marketing/
marketing__general_?1070+/

FIGURE 11.3

Direct Hit

Source:
http://www.directhit.com/about/
products/index.html/

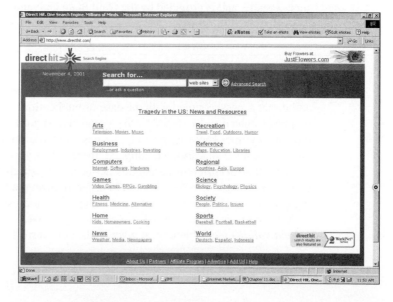

FIGURE 11.4
Top99sites.com

Source:
http://www.top99sites.com/

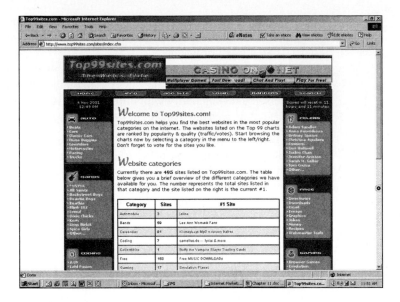

human decisions being made each day by the millions of daily Internet searchers to provide more relevant and better-organized search results.

Another search engine is Top99sites.com, which assists users in finding the "best websites in the most popular categories on the Internet. The websites listed on the Top 99 charts are ranked by popularity and quality (traffic/votes)."

Summary Meta-Information

Summary meta-information provides content summaries or abstracts which allow researchers to get an idea of what the source contains without having to go through all the information. Financial Data Finder (http://www.cob.ohio-stae.edu/fin/osudata.htm) is one such website, and is provided by the Ohio State University. It provides an alphabetical listing of financial information websites and gives a summary of each.

Summary

The Internet brings the advantage of instant global access to information that is incomparable to that of traditional print or broadcast, which is preedited and evaluated. This instant and direct access, coupled with the ease of publication, necessitates that Internet information be evaluated and assessed by the researcher. Anyone can create a website and post anything at anytime. There are no editors, rules, or restrictions. As a consequence, information on the Internet is of varying quality and therefore of varying reliability and validity.

A number of different paradigms delineate criteria that researchers can use when accessing information on the Internet. In order to glean the best and most applicable marketing data, researchers must adopt information evaluation skills.

Your online learning center has a case study on *Websites, Sources, and Data—Reliability and Validity* available now at www.mhhe.com/forrest.

Discussion Questions

1. What are the differences between information found online and off-line?

2. What are some of the major advantages and disadvantages of obtaining research information from the Internet?

3. Why is meta-information so useful when researching on the Internet? What are the two main types of meta-information? Find some websites that provide meta-information. How useful is the website? What type of meta-information does the website use?

4. What are some of the major considerations when searching for information on the Internet?

5. Why is it important to evaluate information, especially on the Internet?

6. How can the five Ws evaluation criteria help with information evaluation? Summarize the criteria in your own words.

7. Search the Internet for two market research websites and evaluate them. If the information does not comply with the five Ws criteria, comment on how this may affect decisions based on this research.

Internet Project

Select one of the three paradigms presented in this chapter:

- The five Ws.

- The ten Cs.

- AOC criteria.

Select any website and evaluate it accordingly. In addition, note if and how that website was evaluated by:

- Direct Hit (http://www.directhit.com/).

- Top99sites (http://www.top99sites.com/).

Further Reading

Alexander, Janet E., and Tate, Marsha A. (1999). *Web Wisdom: How to Evaluate and Create Information Quality on the Web.* Mahwah, New Jersey: Lawrence Erlbaum Associates, Inc.
Jones, Steve (ed), (1998). *Doing Internet Research: Critical Issues and Methods for Examining the Net.* Thousand Oaks, California: Sage Publications, Inc.

References

Alexander, Janet E., and Tate, Marsha A. (1996). "Evaluating Web Resources" (http://www2.widener.edu/Wolfgram-Memorial-Library/webevaluation/webeval.htm/).
Anagnostelis, B., and Cox, J. (1996). "Data on the Internet: Evaluating the Quality or 'Less Is More," July, University of Nottingham (http://omni.ac.uk/agec/ukolug.html/).
Aranzen, M. A. (1996). "Cyber Citations: Documenting Internet Sources Some Thorny Problems." *Internet World,* September (http://www.internetworld.com/print/monthly/1996/09/cybercitations.htm/).
Auer, N. (1998). "Bibliography on Evaluating Internet Resources," March, Virginia Polytechnic and State University (http://refserver.lib.vt.edu/libinst/critTHINK.HTM/).
Brandt, D. S. (1996). "Evaluating Information on the Internet," Purdue University Libraries (http://thorplus.lib.purdue.edu/~techman/evaluate.htm).
Calishain, T., and Nystrom, J. (1998). "Official Netscape Guide to Internet Research," Florence, Kentucky: International Thompson Learning.

Descy, D. E. (1996). "Evaluating Internet Based Information," Widener University (http://lme.mankato.msus.edu/class/629/wid.html/).

Edwards, J. (1998). "Tips for Evaluating a World Wide Web Search," February, University of Florida Libraries (http://www.uflib.ufl.edu/hss/ref/tips.html/).

Fuld, L. (1996) *The New Competitor Intelligence.* Cambridge, Massachusetts: Fuld & Co. (http://www.fuld.com/chapt1.html/).

Grassian, E. (1998). "Thinking Critically about World Wide Web Resources," May, UCLA (http://www.library.ucla.edu/libraries/college/instruct/critical.htn/).

Harris, R. (1997). "Evaluating Internet Research Sources," November, Southern California College (http://www.sccu.edu/faculty/R_Harris/evalu8it.htm/).

Kirk, E. (1996). "Evaluating Information Found on the Internet," John Hopkins University (http://milton.mse.jhu.edu:8001/research/education/net.html/).

Lauer, Diane (1999). "The Five W's of Web Site Evaluation" (http://www.geocities.com/mrslauer/fivewww/webeval.html/).

Lescher, J. F. (1995). *Online Market Research.* U.S.: Addison-Wesley Publishing Company.

Lewis, S. (1997). "The Complete Internet Researcher," May, American Association of Law Libraries (http://www.aallnet.org/products/crab/biblio.htm/).

Rettig, J. (1995). "Putting the Squeeze on the Information Firehose: The Need for Neteditors and Netreviewers," November, College of William and Mary (http://www.swem.wm.edu/firehose.html/).

Rettig, J. (1996). "Beyond 'Cool': Analog Models for Reviewing Digital Resources." *ONLINE,* September.

Scholz-Crane, A. (1997). "Evaluating World Wide Web Information," March, State University of New Jersey (http://crab.rutgers.edu/~scholzcr/eval.html/).

Smith, A. (1998). "Evaluation of Information Sources," June, The World Wide Web Virtual Library (http://www.vuw.ac.nz/~agsmith/evaln/evaln.htm/).

Tillman, H. (1997). "Evaluating Quality on the Net," November, Babson College (http://www.tiac.net/users/hope/findqual.html/).

Tyburski, G. (1997). "Publishers Wanted, No Experience Necessary: Information Quality on the Web," June, Law Library Resource Exchange (http://www.llrx.com/columns/quality.htm/).

University of Wisconsin—Eau Claire (2001). (http://www.uwec.edu/library/Guides/tencs.html/).

Chapter 12

Ethical Concerns and Legalities

Anyone and everyone who uses the Internet should have some awareness and understanding of the myriad of ethical, legal, and moral concerns that the Internet has raised. Market researchers in particular have an obligation to be sensitive to and cognizant of such issues as data security, user privacy, consumer protection, intellectual property, fair use, trademarking, and copyright laws. Attention to and appreciation for these concepts and practices not only is proper netiquette but can be a legal obligation.

Chapter objectives

This chapter aims to:

- Provide understanding of the current debate as to whether information transmitted through the Internet should be controlled.

- Examine the significance of providing security and protection for data transmitted through the Internet and the strengths and weaknesses of various measures proposed for this purpose.

- Give an understanding of the magnitude of fraud on the Internet and action proposed to provide protection to consumers and minimize losses to industry.

- Outline the unique characteristics of digital technology that have caused difficulties in the enforcement of existing copyright laws.

- Discuss the proposed action to curtail copyright infringements on the Internet.

- Provide an understanding of defamation on the Internet and legal issues in the enforcement of existing laws.

- Develop an understanding of the debate over transmission of pornographic and offensive material on the Internet and action proposed to keep children away from such material.

Introduction

Over the last decade, the Internet has evolved into a broad-based personal and enterprise-wide communication resource. Its usage is relevant to virtually every domain and topic of potential interest. Compared with previous technological changes, the Internet has the following unique features:

- Its rapid proliferation.

- The multiplicity of communication channels.

- The enormous volume of information and range of services available.

- The ease with which trans-border transactions can be conducted.

The phenomenal growth of the Internet has alarmed many observers. As it is, many people believe that the exchange of vast quantities of information between tens of millions of users worldwide poses a dramatic threat to confidentiality, privacy, and civil liberties. Moreover, it has been argued that the underlying technology used in the Internet—with an emphasis on flexibility and durability—is inherently insecure (Fletcher, 1995). The proponents of this school of thought have emphasized a need for bringing the same kind of control to the Internet that monitors society as a whole—namely, moral tenets and legal repercussions (Christy, 1996), just as church and jail provide the means for controlling the behavior of different elements of society to improve the overall quality of life.

However, it has long been felt that excessive controls would hinder the development of the global marketplace of ideas, which the Internet naturally embodies. If the Internet is going to serve as a free and open information exchange for the emerging global village, it should be immune to excessive restrictive measures. Yet, there is growing consensus that increased national legislation must be applied to Internet commerce. However, there remains disagreement as to the extent to which such national laws can be stretched to cope with the more novel problems created by the developing technology.

A major concern of the key stakeholders of Internet commerce is how the security of commercial transactions over the Internet can be maintained and how the consumer's interests can be protected. Key issues that have legal implications are security, consumer protection, intellectual property and copyright laws, trademarks, defamation, obscenity, and privacy. These issues are discussed in this chapter. They are interrelated and therefore some overlap will be necessary.

Security

The most commonly raised legal issue is the security and protection from alteration of data transmitted through the Internet. While copyright law certainly applies to products and content that are available online, it has not been interpreted in terms of online content distribution. It is feared that sophisticated hackers or criminals can intercept and alter information being transmitted, as the Internet was not devised with data security in mind. This possibility, in the context of commercial communication, has resulted in fears that commercial information such as contract papers, regulatory filings, or credit card numbers can be altered, forged, or stolen, wrecking havoc on the parties whose data have been intercepted. It is argued that unless the framework for legitimate commerce is preserved and adequate protection for copyrighted works ensured, the Internet will not reach its potential as a global marketplace. It is estimated that the annual loss of online data, due to the work of hackers, is over $10 billion worldwide. A number of technological solutions are suggested to ensure data security on the Internet. One of the solutions involves **encryption schemes**, defined by CNet as follows:

> Encryption is the process of changing data into a form that can be read only by the intended receiver. To decipher the message, the receiver of the encrypted data must have the proper decryption key. In traditional encryption schemes, the sender and the receiver use the same key to encrypt and decrypt data. Public-key encryption schemes use two keys: a public key, which anyone may use, and a corresponding private key, which is possessed only by the person who created it. With this method, anyone may send a message encrypted with the owner's public key, but only the owner has the private key necessary to decrypt it. PGP (Pretty Good Privacy) and DES (data encryption standard) are two of the most popular public-key encryption schemes. (CNet, 2001)

In such schemes, the information to be transmitted is run through a sophisticated mathematical algorithm that encodes the data; in order to decipher the data, a recipient must have the key to the algorithm through which the data must run. The data intercepted by parties without keys to encryption schemes are useless to them. However, the use of encryption schemes has a number of limitations. The first problem is that it is necessary for both parties in a transaction to have access to the keys. Therefore, for many customer transactions, such as ordering a product and giving a credit card number, encryption schemes are impractical because the customers are unfamiliar with the scheme and do not have the encryption key available. Most customers do not have the necessary encryption software on their computers. A second problem is that many of the encryption schemes are easier to decode than was previously thought. This can be overcome by use of additional hardware or software, which, in turn, adds a number of complications including increased costs.

The development of *secured communication services provided by third parties* is an alternative to encryption schemes. In this case, the third party provides either dedicated lines or their own encryption or other security routines. One party, such as an organization offering goods or services for sale, subscribes to the scheme and makes it available to all other parties who wish to enter into a transaction. Although such schemes offer a high degree of security, they impose additional costs on the transaction, which results in increased prices.

Similarly, third parties can guarantee the authenticity and accuracy of transmissions. In such a scheme, a transmission is sent to the third party guarantor, who then authenticates it and transmits it to the ultimate recipient, along with a certification that the transmission is genuine and accurate. The justification for such a scheme is that the third party guarantor, being highly specialized, is capable of developing and offering encryption and authentication techniques sufficiently sophisticated to deter any attempts at fraud. However, similar to the previous approaches, such a scheme may result in additional costs.

The insurance industry provides a classic example of the difficulties involved with ensuring security for data transmitted through the Internet. Although the industry is gaining confidence about doing business in cyberspace, at the outset of Internet commerce many companies remained concerned about using the Internet to accept applications for insurance policies, particularly obtaining a legally acceptable signature from customers (Christy, 1996). In the United States recent legislation eliminated this impediment to electronic commerce. On March 30, 2000, President Bill Clinton signed the Electronic Signatures Act (U.S.). The act accorded online "electronic" signatures the same legal status as a formal signature on a paper document.

Symbolically, Clinton used new digital signature technology developed by SG-Tech PenOp (http://www.sg-tech.net/penop.htm) to sign the legislation. The system software "links people to documents by capturing all the details of a signing event and binding it to the electronic document"; the "handwritten digital signatures . . . serve as legal and irrefutable audit trails of who signed what, when, where and why."

Consumer Protection

The growing evidence of fraud on the Internet has caused much concern among key stakeholders of Internet commerce. According to Internet Fraud Watch (http://www.fraud.org/internet/2001stats10mnt.htm), the amount of money consumers are losing to Internet fraud, like telemarketing fraud, is increasing. For the first 10 months of 2001, losses overall were US$4,371,724, an increase from the US$3,387,530 lost in 2000. Online auctions are, far and away, the most prevalent form of fraud committed on the Internet.

While significantly less numerous in actual occurrences (at 0.05 percent), credit card fraud continues to be a major concern among Internet consumers. Despite the convenience of being able to peruse a wide variety of merchandise from the comfort of their homes, select an item, and pay for it in a matter of minutes, many credit card holders are uncertain about whether to buy or not to buy on the Internet. And even consumers who do shop online continue to wonder, Just how great is the risk of being intercepted by hackers or of dealing with an unscrupulous merchant? The credit card industry's reaction to such concerns has been to develop schemes designed to utilize technology for authenticating the parties involved in payment card purchases on any type of online network, including the Internet.

Observers believe that 100 percent security can never be guaranteed, even with the new encryption standard in place. According to a report by Forrester Research Inc., most companies should expect to lose US$1 per US$1,000 of transactions to Internet-based fraud (Martin, 1996).

Similar to credit card transactions, the phenomenon of **cyberbanking** presents many new legal and regulatory issues. Today, millions of people around the world have access to financial services via the Internet. Legal and regulatory issues arise from the ability of banks and nonbank entities to gather, transfer, and store money through mechanisms outside of the banks' regulatory framework that traditionally has governed banking relationships.

TABLE 12.1
Internet Fraud Watch's Top 10 Frauds, 1999–2000

Top 10 Frauds, 1999	Percent	Top 10 Frauds, 2000	Percent
Online auctions	87.0	Online auctions	78.0
General merchandise sales	7.0	General merchandise sales	10.0
Internet access services	2.0	Internet access services	3.0
Computer equipment/software	1.0	Work at home	3.0
Work at home	1.0	Advance fee loans	2.0
Advance fee loans	0.2	Computer equipment/software	1.0
Magazine sales	0.2	Nigerian money offers	1.0
Information adult services	0.2	Information adult services	1.0
Travel/vacations	0.1	Credit card offers	0.5
Multilevel market/pyramids	0.1	Travel/vacations	0.5

Source: http://www.fraud.org/internet/intstat.htm/

Cyberbanking raises issues of the safety of customers' money, privacy of customers' financial records, verification of the customers' financial transactions and information, and customers' rights and remedies in the event of errors or fraud. For money resting in cyberspace overnight or longer before arriving at its destination, and for money stored or invested for safekeeping, the issues are exceedingly complex.

For those interested in the ongoing issue and evolving phenomenon of cyberbanking, visit the Cyber Banking website (http://www.globalchange.com/cyberb_index.htm/).

Other Websites Relevant to Consumer Fraud and Protection

Consumer.gov (http://www.consumer.gov/) contains consumer information and publications. The publications available online at this website are maintained by the U.S. Federal Trade Commission, a federal watchdog agency.

The Internet Fraud Complaint Center (IFCC) website at (http://www.ifccfbi.gov/) provides a convenient and easy-to-use mechanism to report suspected Internet fraud to law enforcement authorities.

The National Consumers League (http://www.natlconsumersleague.org/) provides useful information and advice about shopping online and how to avoid Internet fraud. Visitors can also report suspected fraudulent websites and scams with an online form.

Econsumer.gov (http://www.econsumer.gov/) is administered by the U.S. Federal Trade Commission. Specifically designed to address cross-border, international e-commerce disputes, Econsumer.gov will record the complaints and pass them along to civil and criminal fraud fighters around the world.

Scambusters.com (http://www.scambusters.com/) is an action alert network that digs up dirt on Internet and telecommunications fraud, ranging from "services" that charge astronomical prices for domain name registration to con artists who partner with Caribbean-based companies to rake in the proceeds of crooked pay-per-call charges.

Intellectual Property and Copyright Law

Intellectual property is a key element in the success of modern businesses. Copyright law protects intellectual property and includes a wide array of material (such as writings,

FIGURE 12.1
Cyber Banking

Source:
http://www.globalchange.com/
cyberb_index.htm/

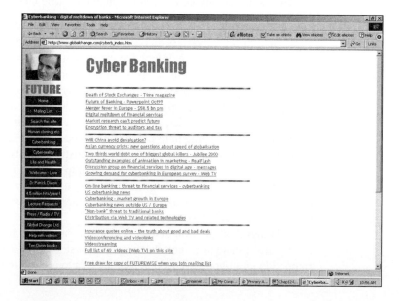

artwork, music, films, and computer programs) that extends to broadcast material, which is quite separate from the copyright of the material that is transmitted. The copyright automatically belongs to the creator or the owner from the time of its creation; and international treaties, such as the Berne Convention for the Protection of Artistic and Literary Works, provide protection for copyright owners (Lawrence et al., 1998). Copyright law in general rewards copyright owners with an economic return, so as to encourage the individual effort devoted to creative activities that will advance public welfare. In order to achieve this goal, the copyright laws grant copyright owners the exclusive rights to reproduce, distribute, perform, and display their works. Copyright laws protect the copyrighted works by stipulating that any violation of the copyright law constitutes infringement and by prescribing an array of remedies to compensate owners for statutory or actual damages (Ching, 1998).

In the past, copying intellectual products was relatively time-consuming. However, with the advances in digital technology and the development of the Internet, it is increasingly easy to copy or alter all sorts of information and art, from music to data to computer software. Some observers regard the Internet to be just one gigantic copying machine. Any individual can, in theory, copy or alter any digitized work and distribute it in a few keystrokes to hundreds of friends. In this situation, the pirate and the potential customer may often be the same person. Particular characteristics of the Internet are unique in comparison with the traditional media and, thus, make copyright law difficult to implement. These characteristics are as follows:

- Barriers to entry are low: anyone with a computer and the necessary accessories can get onto the Internet.

- Communication on the Internet was designed to be free of direct human control, and the Internet facilitates transmitting messages without any constraint.

- Information on the Internet is delivered quickly and economically anywhere there is a link.

- The Internet interconnects innumerable groups of linked computer networks, so that the connection is not only national but also international.

- The Internet accommodates **pseudo-anonymity** and anonymity. Pseudo-anonymity occurs when a user communicates on the Internet with a pseudonym or nickname. Users can also use anonymous e-mail to hide their true identities.

These characteristics, particularly the very nature of electronic communication, make it impossible to set up barriers among connected computers and make it harder to decide who is liable. On such an open, interactive system, it is difficult to determine whether the materials have copyright clearance. While the information transmitted in real time makes scanning ineffective, pseudo-anonymity and anonymity make tracing the true identity of the infringer difficult. The only way the user's identity can be discovered is by checking through the access provider, or if the user reveals it themselves. Therefore, violating copyright laws without being held liable is much easier for the Internet user (Ching, 1998).

Some attempts have been made to estimate the loss of sales due to pirated copies. Every year Business Software Alliance (BSA) compares sales of computers with sales of software. Working on a rule of thumb that a PC uses an average of three packages—a word processor, a spreadsheet, and perhaps one other—it is estimated that pirated products supply *half* of the global market.

Although this situation demands urgent measures to protect intellectual property, there are several practical issues that require consideration. Copyright law confers two main rights: (1) to authorize reproduction; and (2) to authorize the distribution of those copies.

Therefore, an important issue is the nature of electronic transmission: is it reproduction, distribution, or both? Copyright law makes a distinction between reproduction for public use (with the rightholder's permission) and reproduction for private use (within certain limits). Currently it is possible to download a perfect copy of a whole database or a video clip, and therefore, an important issue is whether that distinction is allowed. In regard to distribution, the current copyright law protects the right to control the first sale of the copy, but not subsequent sales. Yet, with the current possibility of perfectly copying the initial copy again and again, the question is, What copying is allowed?

In regard to the enforcement of law, there are further difficulties. First, it may be hard to track down the source of illicit material. Second, once tracked, it may be hard to decide who is liable. A major issue relating to these two considerations is determining jurisdiction in relation to where the infringement actually took place (Fletcher, 1995). If the parties communicate through a third party, such as an online service provider, does the infringement take place on the third party system, or on one of the parties' systems? Likewise, if the parties communicate directly across the Internet, then the question arises as to where exactly the infringement occurs. Such questions are difficult to answer, and the questions become much more complex when the parties sit in different jurisdictions. The answers to these questions then depend on both the national laws and their rules on the conflict of laws.

A number of steps are suggested to help copyright owners protect their property on the Internet and to mitigate potential liabilities (Jeremy, 1996).

1. Companies with Internet access need to implement new policies governing their employees' use of their systems. Because of the risk of copyright liability, they should impose formal restrictions on the downloading of software and other copyrighted material.

2. With regard to the uploading of defamatory material by employees, the very severe civil and criminal sanctions to which this exposes the employer mean that businesses should consider making it a dismissal offense. Guidelines should also be laid down about the risks of publishing confidential or copyrighted material (particularly in relation to technical and sensitive commercial matters). Staff must be instructed not to use e-mail and other facilities frivolously or maliciously.

3. Companies using the Internet for promotional or distribution purposes should consider including formal copyright notices identifying the copyright owner and specifying the uses that may be made of the material.

4. Companies should take steps to register their corporate name and principal trademarks as Internet addresses. They should also undertake regular searches of the register of domain names to ensure that no third party is trading on their goodwill.

5. Local networks should be systematically monitored on a continuing basis to ensure that any offending material is removed at the earliest opportunity.

In the recent past, copyright owners increasingly have been filing suits targeting service providers, and in a number of cases the court decided that online service providers were liable for infringements. However, it is operationally impossible for ISPs to review such volumes of data representing millions of messages; and even if they were able to do so, the content review would impair the immediacy of the transmission. The cost of content supervision would have to be shared by all subscribers, which may lead to increased costs and threaten the affordability and ubiquity of access to the information superhighway. Additionally, providers and operators do not know whether these materials are copyrighted and whether the uploader had the rights to such works. The ISPs do not originate, manage, or review the content of the information; they do not know what information or messages they are transmitting or distributing on a real-time basis. Therefore, it is difficult for service providers to discover an infringement of a copyrighted work (Ching, 1998).

The Copyright Society of the USA (http://www.law.duke.edu/copyright/index.htm/) has as its main function the "gathering, dissemination and interchange of information concerning protection and use of rights in intellectual property." The website provides hundreds of links to copyright-related websites including general copyright and licensing information, international agreements and treaties, statutory and legislative materials, case law and courts, licensing organizations, events, and publications.

In the foregoing context, the conclusions of some of the recent U.S. court cases will have an adverse effect on the speed and cost of infrastructure development. It is observed that courts have had no standards with regard to the issue of copyright, and it appears that they set new standards on a case-by-case basis. It is also believed that current copyright law hardly keeps pace with technology. While current copyright law does not adequately protect copyright owners from the potential economic loss, it also fails to create a balance between the interests of the copyright owners and interests of manufacturers of new technology. In the global arena—although there are several treaties such as the Berne Convention, the Rome Convention, and the Geneva Phonogram Convention—copyright infringements still take place on the Internet (Ching, 1998).

Ching (1998) suggests that the following be incorporated into copyright law, so as to balance the interests of copyright owners and online service providers.

- It is the subscribers' or the information providers' direct responsibility to abide by copyright law. In other words, content providers and subscribers who upload or download materials would have full responsibility for compliance with intellectual property laws, for producing information, and for making it available on the system.

- Online service providers and operators should be held to a standard of liability based on contributory infringement, but not based on the strict standard of liability for direct infringement. Because service providers simply act as facilitators for user-originated communications, technically and practically they are not capable of controlling their subscribers' uploading and downloading of copyrighted works or any infringing behavior.

FIGURE 12.2
The Copyright Society of the USA

Source:
http://www.law.duke.edu/
copyright/index.htm/

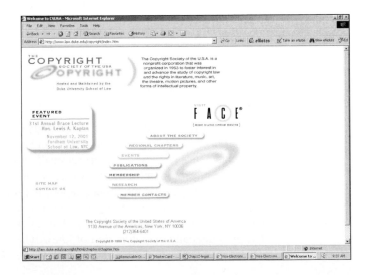

- An Internet service provider should be held liable for infringement of copyright if (a) the provider has actual knowledge that a work that is being transmitted, or has been transmitted, on its system is an unauthorized work, and (b) the provider has the ability to stop the transmission or remove the unauthorized work from its system after a reasonable time, but fails to do so.

- If protection of copyright works is undertaken with assistance of technological devices, such as header-based systems, the uploaders should be fully liable for the infringement, but they should be allowed "fair use" of the copyright work. In other words, if the work is used for criticism, comment, news reporting, teaching, scholarship, or research, then the uploaders do not need the permission of the copyright owners.

A number of technological solutions have been suggested to protect copyrighted works against infringements such as reproduction, display, manipulation, performance, and distribution. Technological protection for copyrighted works can be implemented through hardware, software, or a combination of the two; by controlling access; by using digital signatures; and through online copyright contracts. Widely recommended technological measures are the use of encryption technology, **digital object identifier** (DOI), and **header-based systems** (Ching, 1998). The use of encryption technology was discussed in the previous section of this chapter.

A DOI system prevents users from uploading unauthorized works and is used to provide identification for digital content. It was developed by the Corporation for National Research Initiatives. Copyright owners and their product lines can be identified with a combination of a designated prefix and suffix (Ching, 1998).

A header-based system is a program developed to check if uploaded information is authorized and if an individual download is permitted. A header is an electronic tagging of a digitized work. Headers can be used to control access and use of copyrighted works at the users' workstation. Headers provide information about copyright such as the permitted use, the permission information, authentication of website address, the price for each type of use, and the copyright owner's electronic address to identify and provide protection for copyrighted works. If this technology is used, then every file or document uploaded should contain a header. The software for headers also should be designed to block the intended actions of users if they do not provide correct permission information. Copyright owners will retain control of the work (options include allowing the work to be viewed at no cost but requiring users to pay a fee to copy or print the work; different rates may be set for viewing, copying, or printing) and will not have to fear piracy. This method would not intrude upon the fair use rights and the first sale rights of the public. Similarly, ISPs do not have to monitor each transmitted file and wonder if uploaded data are authorized or not. The program can deal with it automatically (Ching, 1998).

Observers believe that the primary means for limiting infringement and for protecting copyrighted works may be education and wide dissemination of information about copyright. The educational process should cover all Internet users and will include those attached to educational institutions, public organizations, and private firms.

The foregoing headaches will not drive content companies out of business but may destroy some of their profits. Observers believe that there is no real solution for pirating intellectual property in the foreseeable future.

For further information on these and other related copyright matters, the Australian Copyright Council (ACC) maintains a website at http://www.copyright.org.au/). As delineated in the *Australian Copyright Council 1999 Annual Report*, their objectives are to:

- Assist creators and other copyright owners to exercise their rights effectively.

FIGURE 12.3
Australian Copyright
Council

Source:
http://www.copyright.org.au/

- Raise awareness in the community generally about the importance of copyright.

- Research and identify areas of copyright law that are inadequate or unfair.

- Seek changes to law and practice to enhance the effectiveness and fairness of copyright.

- Foster cooperation among bodies representing creators and owners of copyright.

Trademarks

Over the last few years trademark disputes, particularly those relating to the registration of domain names on the Internet, have gained prominence in Internet-related legal issues. Any institution that intends to operate a website must register a domain name with either its national domain name register or an ISP. A domain name is a unique address that enables other Internet users to locate a computer or network on the Internet. For example, if Global, Inc. maintains a website in the United Kingdom, its domain name may be Global.com.uk.

The primary legal issue arising from the registration of domain names is who has the right to use what name under what circumstances. Certain countries are designated to maintain their own registry; domain names registered in those countries include an identifier—such as .uk for the United Kingdom, .au for Australia, and .nz for New Zealand—whereas domain names registered with Verisign do not (Maddox, 1996).

Initially, registration was handled on a first-come, first-served basis, with no questions asked as to whether third party rights were being appropriated or infringed. Thus, the first entity to request the Global.com domain name generally has the right to use it. While this system benefited from administrative ease, it raised serious concerns for companies whose trademarks or service marks could be appropriated for another's domain name. At one stage organizations like McDonalds and MTV were surprised to find their names had been claimed as Internet domain names by someone else before these entities realized they needed to preserve their names on the Internet.

However, under the registration rules adopted worldwide in July 1995 and administered by the United States, an applicant must agree to be subject to the terms of the governing policy statement then in force, and as amended from time to time. The applicant also must certify that (Mantle & Radin, 1996):

- Use or registration of the domain name does not interfere with or infringe the right of any third party in any jurisdiction with respect to trademark, trade name, company name, or any other intellectual property right.

- Applicant is not seeking to use the domain name for any unlawful purpose, including tortious interference with contract or prospective business advantage, unfair competition, injuring the reputation of another, or confusing or misleading a person.

For a complete and full explanation of the legalities, processes, and procedures of trademark registration of Internet domain names, see the *Trademark Registration of Internet Domain Names—Examination Guide No. 2–99* (http://www.uspto.gov/web/offices/tac/domain/).

Why is it important for businesses to have their trademark as the domain name? Because trademarks denote the source of particular goods and services. Trademarks simplify the process through which consumers acquire product information and therefore lower the search costs involved in distinguishing among different sellers and differentiating among goods the consumers may never have seen before. By relying on trademarks to identify various product characteristics, the consumer need not scrutinize each individual good every time they make a purchase. Moreover, since consumers benefit from lower search costs, sellers can capture some of this surplus by charging higher prices. However, confusion in the marketplace eliminates these economic gains. When trademarks convey misinformation, consumers' search costs rise substantially (Oram, 1997). Domain names were initially intended to offer a user-friendly means by which to identify and locate particular Internet sites. However, with the expansion of Internet commerce many observers believe that they serve the trademark function of identifying the source of particular products or services.

Under the Trade Marks Act 1994 (U.K.), it is an infringement of a registered mark to do any of the following acts in the course of trade:

- Using a sign that is identical with the trademark in relation to goods and services identical with those for which the mark is registered.

- Using an identical sign in relation to similar goods and services, if there is a likelihood of confusion on the part of the public.

- Using a similar sign in relation to identical goods or services, again if there is a likelihood of confusion.

- Using an identical or similar sign, in relation to dissimilar goods or services, where the mark has "a reputation in the United Kingdom" and the use of the sign without due cause takes unfair advantage of the distinctive character of the mark.

Therefore, the misuse of trademarks gives rise to liability for trademark infringement. Similar to other legal issues, the application of trademark law to the use of business names on the Internet is subject to jurisdictional and practical difficulties. Again, a number of jurisdictional problems arise. Is the offending action committed where the message is first posted (in which event the copyright owner may not have a registration in the relevant territory) or where it is received? It is arguable that under U.K. law any infringing material accessible from the U.K. could give rise to liability. Whether the prospective defendant has assets in the U.K. capable of satisfying judgment and indeed whether the defendant's home jurisdiction would impose liability at all are entirely different matters (Jeremy, 1996).

Internet stakeholders are relieved to note that some degree of international consensus is emerging toward the development of international principles to ensure more effective trademark protection. The International Ad Hoc Committee (IAHC) and the World Intellectual Property Organization (WIPO) are continuing discussion on the harmonization of national laws concerning trademarks and Internet domain names and on the establishment of an arbitration and mediation panel to adjudicate domain name disputes.

Observers of Internet commerce are of the view that until national and international laws are well settled, businesses should register their chosen domain names early and vigorously protect against unauthorized use of their trademarks and service marks by others.

Cornell Law School's Legal Information Institute (http://www.law.cornell.edu/topics/trademark.html/) provides an overview of trademark law and a menu of links to other resources.

Defamation

A wide array of defamation issues now confronts online service users and the ISPs themselves. Defamation is the publication of a false and derogatory statement about another person without lawful justification (Lawrence et al., 1998). The print and broadcasting media are obliged to carefully monitor their output to avoid litigation by individuals or companies protecting their interests. It is also necessary for website owners and bulletin board participants to be careful in the transmission of information. Again, the question remains, In which jurisdictions were the postings made and received? Which person is responsible under the laws of that jurisdiction or jurisdictions for the defamation? The situation becomes more complicated if the offender lived in one country, posted the information on a website located in another country, used an ISP in yet another country, or chose to remain anonymous or used a fictitious name. All these could be quite feasible on the Internet and would make it exceedingly difficult, if not impossible, for the offended party to obtain legal remedy.

Two defamation issues are of particular interest. The first is whether the dissemination of defamatory material in this manner constitutes **libel** or **slander**. The second is the scope

FIGURE 12.4
Cornell Law School's Legal Information Institute—Trademark Law Material

Source:
http://www.law.cornell.edu/topics/trademark.html/

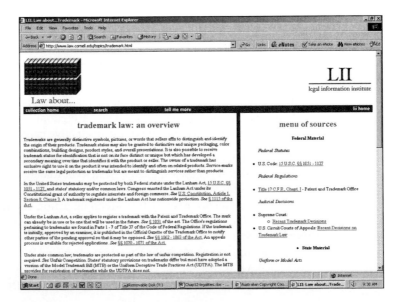

of a computer owner's liability for defamatory statements published on his or her server. Most European jurisdictions distinguish libel and slander as two separate classes of wrongful acts, and some (the Netherlands, for example) provide criminal as well as civil sanctions. Libel involves defamation in print or some other permanent form, whereas slander concerns transitory (principally oral) statements and requires proof of special damages before a plaintiff can seek relief. It is arguable that placing defamatory material on, say, a bulletin board is capable of amounting to libel since this form of defamatory statement is permanent: it remains on the bulletin board and is accessible to the public unless and until steps are taken to remove it. As to whether a computer owner should be held liable for the defamatory messages loaded onto the server, there have been conflicting decisions in two recent court cases. Observers are of the view that until proper legislation comes into force, only one solution is likely to be commercially palatable to network operators. It is for network operators to reserve for themselves the right to delete defamatory material, while making it clear that the ultimate responsibility for such statements rests with subscribers (Jeremy, 1996).

The Australasian Legal Information Institute offers its own search facility (see Figure 12.5), which can be used to search for any laws pertaining to defamation, libel, obscenity—or any law on anything, anywhere in the world.

Obscenity

Obscenity, particularly pornography on the Internet, has become an explosive issue over the last few years. It has sparked debates about free speech versus child protection, free enterprise versus social good, and free market versus fair business practices. A major issue is how to best protect children while allowing adults to set their own standards of behavior and taste. The magnitude of the problem is highlighted by the fact that any child can easily access sites giving suicide methods, instructions for making bombs, or hard core pornography. It is also believed that any user of the Internet, regardless of their age, can post pornography or sexual invitations to any unmoderated Usenet groups.

FIGURE 12.5
AustLII's World
Law Index/Search

Source:
http://www.austlii.edu.au/links/
World/

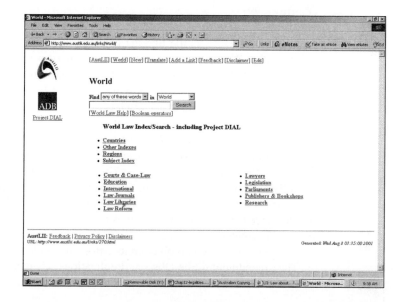

Erotic commerce has grown continuously since the Internet's commercial inception in the early 1990s. By the mid-1990s there were an estimated 28,000 websites offering adult entertainment to a wide range of customers. As of 2000, a Nua Internet Survey reported that:

> Despite perceived social taboos, online pornography is alive and kicking and there's still money to be made in it. . . . It's difficult to tell exactly how much money can be made, however. What were the total revenues from Internet pornography in 1999? Pluck a figure from thin air and you're as likely to be right as the analysts, whose estimates on this topic vary wildly. Jupiter says the online porn peddlers earned US$176 million last year, while Forrester says US$900 million, and Datamonitor offers US$1.39 billion as a likely figure. Recently released figures from Nielsen NetRatings indicate that 18 million U.S. Internet users visited porn sites in April. That's over three times as many than in April 1999.

There are two legal issues relating to obscenity on the Internet. First is establishing criminal liability of the publishers of pornographic material. Second is the jurisdictional difficulty in the enforcement of law.

In regard to criminal liability it is often argued that the distribution of pornography on the Internet is beyond control and that regulation and other methods of supervising ISPs are required (Palfrey, 1997). Observers argue that even if regulation is introduced, it will not necessarily solve the problem of their criminal liability. For example, the introduction of regulatory controls in Singapore still resulted in a prosecution of an end user under preexisting criminal laws, and the commercial intermediary was not charged with an offense (*The Times,* 1996). A major issue in establishing criminal liability on ISPs is whether they are "publishers" or "carriers" of pornographic material. Those supporting the view that ISPs are carriers argue that their role is much more like telephone companies that provide a connection between two terminals. It is not their responsibility to police what goes down the telephone line. The debate has become polarized between the terms *publisher* and *carrier,* and this perspective has influenced arguments concerning the potential criminal liability of ISPs. The traditional argument against using the existing criminal law and prosecuting ISPs is that they are mere carriers, implying that this status absolves them from criminal liability. Seeking to distance ISPs from any suggestion that they are publishing is the usual counterargument against a criminal prosecution of any commercial intermediary (Palfrey, 1997).

As is the case with other legal issues related to the Internet, the principal legal difficulty relating to obscenity on the Internet is that in any given case one of a number of jurisdictions applies. The transmission of pornography over the Internet is subject to broadly the same kinds of regulation as other methods of distribution. For example, if an individual in Denmark uploads certain explicit material onto a bulletin board, the material might well comply with more liberal obscenity legislation of their jurisdiction. However, it could still be illegal to transmit it via a U.K. network. Some important questions that may immediately arise are, Where does the publication take place? Which law applies? and How can the U.K. courts restrain the lawful activities of a citizen of another member of the European Union? In the United Kingdom, the Criminal Justice and Public Order Act 1994 (U.K.) has recently extended the scope of the Obscene Publications Act 1959 (U.K.) to cover the electronic transmission of data that on resolution into viewable form is obscene. Most people would agree that this therefore applies to material distributed over the Internet, so the fundamental problem is not with the substance of the law but rather with the practical and jurisdictional difficulties involved in its enforcement (Jeremy, 1996).

The amendment to the Obscene Publications Act means that liability for the transmission of obscene material extends to the organization whose facilities are used to access the

Internet. This requires business organizations to exercise due care in permitting their employees to use the Internet. It is suggested that the uploading of obscene material by employees be made a dismissable offense. Indeed, some firms have already gone so far as to impose an absolute ban on employees accessing the Internet from their premises other than in the strict course of their duties (Jeremy, 1996).

Recently, the U.S. government's Communications Decency Act 1996 (U.S.), which was aimed at regulating the Internet, has sparked a debate. The act was intended to stop pornography and other objectionable material from being transmitted via the Internet. The proposed legislation imposes penalties on people who transmit pornographic material via computer networks that are accessible to children. The maximum penalty for such an offense would be up to two years in jail and a fine of up to US$250,000.

Parties opposing this legislation cited it as a threat to freedom of speech, which is guaranteed by the U.S. Constitution. Thousands of Internet users protested by turning Web pages black when President Bill Clinton signed the bill into law in February 1996. The American Civil Liberties Union, the Citizens Internet Empowerment Coalition, and several online services and free speech groups challenged the law. The act was cited as the most sweeping censorship of any medium in U.S. history. A key argument was that federal officials are unfit stewards of young people, and with rare exceptions they have not exhibited any genuine interest in moral values. Subsequently, three federal judges ruled against major parts of the Communications Decency Act, imposing a temporary restraining order banning the Justice Department from enforcing the provisions of the act. This is cited by groups opposing the act as a victory for the freedom of speech.

These lobbying groups suggest that parental control is the most appropriate approach to keep adult material away from children. Parents can do a number of things to keep pornography out of their homes. Internet users can subscribe to growing numbers of parental control programs. These filter out offensive materials by screening keywords or simply limiting kids to a "white list" of approved websites (Sirico, 1996). Software such as Net Nanny and Cyber Patrol promise to block access to inappropriate websites, Usenet bulletin boards, chat rooms, and e-mail. Online services such as America Online and CompuServe offer similar features as part of their standard service. A system that rates websites, called Platform Internet Content Selection (PICs) has also been developed and is being used by Web browsers such as Microsoft's Internet Explorer (Oppenheim, 1997).

Australia has proposed controversial changes to their censorship laws with the Broadcasting Services Amendment (Online Services) Bill of 1999. This would see the Australian Broadcasting Authority (ABA) manage the search for and prosecution of those Australians responsible for illegal and offensive material on the Internet.

Privacy

Privacy is a complex concept and has been defined by S. Adler in *Privacy Issues in Telecommunications* as "the right not to be disturbed, the right to be anonymous, the right not to be monitored and the right not to have one's identifying information exploited" (Gattiker et al., 1996). Over the last few years, with the phenomenal growth of the Internet, the privacy of individuals using the Internet has received much attention. Of greatest concern is the fact that the use of electronic networks for commerce creates information trails that allow customers' transaction information to be easily tracked. This in turn diminishes information privacy, that is, an individual's control over the manner in which personal information is obtained, disclosed, and used. In a recent policy statement, the U.S. government urged organizations that do business electronically to establish voluntary Internet privacy protection to prevent excessive government regulations. The industry should develop codes of conduct to assure the public that Internet transactions are secure and that information submitted over the Internet would not be misused. In the recent past, a number of organizations have adopted this path, and the following are the privacy regulations announced by the U.S. Direct Marketing Association (DMA) (http://www.the-dma.org/consumers/):

- All marketers should post an easy-to-read, easy-to-find privacy policy online describing how they use information collected online.

- The notice should provide consumers with the means to limit disclosure of individual information that is collected online.

- Unsolicited marketing e-mail needs to be permitted as long as marketers exercise responsibility and responsiveness to consumers, that is, by sending e-mail to those consumers who appreciate the process and, at the same time, assuring consumers on an individual basis the capability to control and limit unsolicited e-mail.

- Online e-mail advertisements need to be clearly identified and must conform to the policies of forums that sponsor newsgroups, chat rooms, and bulletin boards.

- Marketers and data compilers that "harvest" consumer information need to disclose this practice and provide consumers with the opportunity to opt out.

However, this approach to self-regulation of Internet privacy has come under attack and some observers suggest that voluntary self-regulation of privacy on the Internet is like a fox guarding the henhouse. They stress the need for government presence in governance of the Internet. On this point, perhaps the most sweeping legislation and government attention to the issue of privacy has been offered by the Australian government with its passage of the Privacy (Private Sector) Regulations 2001.

Another source of information and discussion on the issue of privacy is the Electronic Privacy Information Center website (http://www.epic.org/), which provides extensive privacy news, resources, and links to online privacy resources.

FIGURE 12.6
U.S. Direct Marketing Association (DMA)

Source:
http://www.the-dma.org/consumers/

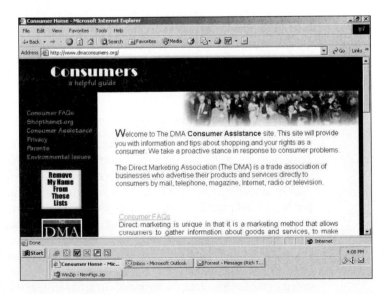

FIGURE 12.7
Electronic Privacy
Information Center

Source: http://www.epic.org/

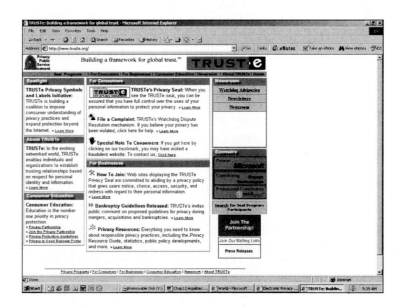

FIGURE 12.8
TRUSTe

Source: http://www.truste.org/

Other websites providing information and services include TRUSTe (http://www.truste.org/), which defines itself as "an independent, nonprofit privacy initiative dedicated to building users' trust and confidence on the Internet and accelerating growth of the Internet industry." They have developed a "seal" program to address users' concerns about on-line privacy.

Summary   The Internet has raised a myriad of ethical, legal, and moral concerns. At the forefront of the debate are such issues as:

• How to protect freedom of expression while keeping users safe.

- Defining the responsible party or parties when a law is broken.

- How to enforce legislation in a medium without boundaries.

Market researchers in particular have an obligation to be sensitive to and cognizant of such issues as data security, user privacy, consumer protection, intellectual property, fair use, trademarking, and copyright law.

Your online learning center has a case study on *Ethical Concerns and Legalities* available now at www.mhhe.com/forrest.

Discussion Questions

1. What is the most commonly raised legal issue relating to the Internet?
2. What are two technological solutions that have been developed to ensure data security on the Internet?
3. What is cyberbanking? Find and evaluate an example of this service on the Internet.
4. What characteristics of the Internet make copyright law difficult to implement?
5. What steps can be taken to help an individual to protect their property on the Internet?
6. What is the primary legal issue arising from the registration of domain names?
7. Define defamation, slander, and libel; discuss how the Internet impacts these legal concepts.
8. To what degree, and in what ways, are you concerned about your privacy on the Internet?

Internet Project

Go to the Internet Fraud Watch website (http://www.fraud.org/internet/intstat.htm/) and prepare a summary report entitled "The Current State of Internet Fraud."

Further Reading

Heels, Erik J., and Klau, Richard P. (1998). *Law, Law, Law on the Internet: The Best Legal Web Sites and More.* Chicago: Illinois, American Bar Association.

References

Australian Copyright Council (1999). *Annual Report.* (http:// www.copyright.org.au/ PDF/AnnualReports/AR1999.pdf).

Ching, L. (1998). "Toward a More Balanced Online Copyright Policy." *Communication and the Law*, March, vol. 20, no.1.

Christy, T. (1996). "Signatures in Cyberspace: Closer to Reality." *Insurance and Technology*, July, vol. 21, no. 7, pp. 26–8.

CNet (2001). (http://www.cnet.com/Resources/Info/Glossary/Terms/encryption.html/).

The Economist (1996). "The Property in Mind," vol. 340, no. 7976, pp. 57–9.

Fletcher, I. F. (1995). "The Trouble with Bits—First Steps in the Internet." *The University of Chicago Law Review,* vol. 63, no. 5.

Foley, Kathy (2000). "Porn: Not What It Used to Be," August 21, Dublin, Ireland: NUA (http://www.nua.ie/surveys/analysis/weekly_editorial/archives/2000/issue1no140.html/).

Gattiker, U. E., Janz, L., Kelly, H., and Schollmeyer, M. (1996). "The Internet and Privacy: Do You Know Who's Watching." *Business Quarterly*, Summer, vol. 60, no. 4, pp. 79–84.

Jeremy, N. (1996). "The Law and the Internet in Europe." *Managing Intellectual Property*, May, no. 59, pp. 34-8.

Lawrence, E., Corbitt, B., Tidwell, A., Fisher, J., and Lawrance, J. (1998). *Internet Commerce: Digital Models for Business*. New York: John Wiley & Sons.

Mantle, R. A., and Radin, M. E. (1996). "Domain Name and Trade Mark Law." *Managing Intellectual Property, TradeMark YearBook*, pp. 19–20.

Martin, F. (1996). "Are Internet Fraud Fears Overblown?" *Credit Card Management*, May, vol. 9, no. 2, pp. 46–52.

Montana, J. (1996). "Legal Issues in EDI." *Records Management Quarterly*, vol. 30, no. 3, pp. 39–45.

Myers, M. (1996). "How Free Should the Internet Be?" *Network World*, August 12, vol. 13, no. 33, p. 28.

Nua (2000). (http://www.nua.ie/surveys/analysis/weekly_editorial/archives/2000/issue 1no140.html).

Oppenheim, C. (1997). "LISLEX: Legal Issues of Concern to the Library and Information Sector." *Journal of Information Science*, vol. 23, no. 1, pp. 73–80.

Oram, J. H. (1997). "The Costs of Confusion in Cyberspace." *Yale Law Journal*, December, vol. 107, no. 3, pp. 869–74.

Palfrey, T. (1997). "Pornography and the Possible Criminal Liability of Internet Service Providers under the Obscene Publications and Protection of Children Act." *Information and Communications Technology Law*, October, vol. 6, no. 3, pp. 187–99.

Sirico, R. A. (1996). "Don't Censor the Internet." *Forbes*, July 29, vol. 158, no. 3, p. 48.

The Times (1996). September 26, p. 13.

Glossary

agent A program that gathers information or performs some other service without the user's immediate presence and on some regular schedule. Typically, an agent program, using parameters the user has provided, searches all or some part of the Internet, gathers information the user is interested in, and presents it to them on a daily or other periodic basis.

Archie A program that allows users to search the files of all the Internet FTP servers that offer anonymous FTP access for a particular search string. Archie is actually an indexing spider that visits the anonymous FTP sites, reads all the directory and file names, and then indexes them in one large index. A user can then query Archie, which checks the query against its index.

ASCII (American Standard Code for Information Interchange) The most common format for text files in computers and on the Internet. In an ASCII file, each alphabetic, numeric, or special character is represented by a seven-bit binary number (a string of seven 0s or 1s). 128 possible characters are defined. It is the basis for coding simple text files.

attachment A file that is included with an e-mail message. Can be data, sound, and/or graphic files.

bandwidth Used in reference to the frequency-response characteristics of a communications-receiving system. All transmitted signals, whether analog or digital, have a certain finite, nonzero bandwidth. The same is true of receiving systems. Generally speaking, bandwidth is directly proportional to the amount of data transmitted or received per unit of time. The greater the bandwidth, the greater the amount of data that can travel in a given time period.

bookmarks Within a World Wide Web browser, a bookmark is a saved link to a website that has been added to a list of saved links. When users are looking at a particular website and want to be able to quickly get back to it later, they can create a bookmark for it. A browser can be thought of as a book with millions of Web pages and a few well-placed bookmarks that an individual has chosen. Microsoft Internet Explorer refers to bookmarks as "favorites."

Boolean operators When doing a search in a library or on the Internet, this term refers to a system of logical thought developed by the English mathematician George Boole (1815–1864). In Boolean searching, an AND operator between two words or other values (for example, *pear* AND *apple*) means the user is searching for documents containing both of the words or values, not just one of them. An OR operator between two words or other values (for example,

pear OR *apple*) means the user is searching for documents containing either of the words.

Boolean search A method of searching for information by using search terms with the operators AND, OR, NOT, and parentheses.

browser plug-ins Software that can be added to a browser program to increase its capabilities, such as a multimedia viewer. An extension of this is a helper application, which can serve the same purpose; however, it launches into another window and is run as a separate, external program.

buying power index (BPI) A weighted index consisting of population, EBI, and retail sales data.

chat Talking on the Internet in real time. Usually, this "talking" is the exchange of typed-in messages requiring one website as the repository for the messages (or "chat site") and a group of users who take part from anywhere on the Internet.

chat rooms Virtual spaces where chat is carried out.

.com Commercial.

Common Gateway Interface (CGI) A standard way for an Internet server to pass control to an application program and receive data back when it is done. It allows application programs to run on the user's behalf as part of his/her Internet connection, on any kind of operating system.

competitive intelligence The collection of information on a competitor in order to make more informed marketing and strategic decisions.

conditioned viewing A situation where the researcher is sensitive only to particular areas of interest while browsing through information.

consumer intelligence Any information that a researcher can obtain in order to understand and relate to consumers better.

cookies Information that the server application puts in the http header that accompanies its response to a browser request. The browser then stores this information and sends it back in any additional requests related to the whole transaction or series of requests and responses. It is a way for a website to remember that a user has visited the website and to retain some information about them.

copyright The legal protection against copying given to original works, which may be in printed or photographically or electronically stored words, music, visual arts, and performing arts.

customer retention   Retaining customers; when customers who transacted with the company return to make repeat transactions as opposed to going to competing firms to carry out transactions.

cyberbanking   Banking activities that are carried out on the Internet by bank customers. Includes all regular banking activities such as checking account balances, applying for loans, and other financial services.

cyberspace   The total interconnectedness of human beings through computers and telecommunication without regard to physical geography. The term sometimes just means "everyone and everything on the Internet."

database   Collection of data organized so that its contents can easily be accessed, managed, and updated.

defamation   See *libel.*

Delphi   In this context, forecasting future developments and trends by a qualitative method of repeat surveys on a select panel of experts whereby a consensus is reached.

digital dawn   The beginning of the information age.

digital object identifier (DOI)   A permanent identifier given to a Web file or other Internet document so that if its Internet address changes, users will be redirected to its new address.

digital signatures   Digital signatures are attached to any electronic message and are a means of identifying the sender. They can also verify that the message is authentic and has not been tampered with.

directories   See *subject catalog.*

discussion list   A mailing list where people can leave messages and expect to see responses to messages sent out simultaneously to a group of people through e-mail. Usually based on a specific topic, demographic, or geographic location.

domain name   A domain name locates an organization or other entity on the Internet. For example, www.totalbaseball.com locates an Internet address for totalbaseball.com at Internet point 199.0.0.2 and a particular host server named www. The *com* part of the domain name reflects the purpose of the organization or entity (in this example, commercial) and is called the top-level domain name. The *totalbaseball* part of the domain name defines the organization or entity and, together with the top level, is called the second-level domain name. The second-level domain name maps to and can be thought of as the readable version of the Internet address. A third level can be defined to identify a particular host server at the Internet address. In our example, "www" is the name of the server that handles Internet requests. (A second server might be called "www2.") A third level of domain name is not required. For example, the fully qualified domain name could have been "totalbaseball.com" and the server assumed.

downloading   The transmission of a file from one computer system to another, usually smaller, computer system. From the Internet user's point of view, to download a file is to request it from another computer (or from a website on another computer) and to receive it.

e-commerce (electronic commerce or EC)   The buying and selling of goods and services on the Internet, especially the World Wide Web. In practice, this term and a new term, e-business, are often used interchangeably.

early adopters   The second group of people to embrace new products and services according to the diffusion of innovation theory.

economic environment   The economic and/or business-related variables in the environment—such as business cycles, inflation, unemployment, interest rates, and savings—that affect the general economic conditions.

.edu   Education.

effective buying income (EBI)   Income left after paying taxes.

electronic agents   See *agent.*

e-mail (electronic mail)   The exchange of computer-stored messages by telecommunication. E-mail messages are usually encoded in ASCII text. However, nontext files, such as graphic images and sound files, can also be sent as attachments in binary streams.

encryption   The conversion of data into a form, called a cipher, that cannot be easily intercepted by unauthorized people.

encryption schemes   A system whereby information is encrypted and sent to the recipient, who possesses a unique key to decipher the encrypted information. Without the key, the information cannot, under normal circumstances, be decoded.

environmental intelligence   Information about a firm's external environment that may be used to help marketing decision making.

environmental scanning   The process of systematically collecting information about changing macro-environmental variables that are incorporated into an organization's marketing strategy, through the observation and monitoring of the firm's external environment.

experimental research   Obtaining primary data by altering certain variables in a matched group of respondents in order to find out cause and effect relationships.

e-zine   Short for electronic magazine but also used to describe e-mail newsletters and Web-based news sites. The term is similar to *zine,* an earlier usage in print media that derived from magazine and described "small press" or personally distributed magazines or newsletters.

FAQs (frequently asked questions) Collections of common questions and answers for a particular subject area. FAQs may have originated in many of the Usenet groups as a way to acquaint new users with the rules.

favorites See *bookmarks.*

file transfer protocol (FTP) The usual method of sending files to a server (or receiving files). FTP can also be used to update (delete, rename, move, and copy) files at a server. People who create Web home pages use FTP to get their files to the server where they will be accessed.

flaming On the Internet, flaming is giving someone a verbal lashing in public. Often this is on a Usenet newsgroup, but it can also be on a Web-based forum or perhaps even as e-mail with copies to a distribution list. Also refers to abusive, angry, and/or insulting messages.

focus groups Group discussions of usually 8 to 12 people, where a specified topic is discussed in order to gather qualitative data.

formal search A well-established, functional method to obtain specific information.

.gov Government.

hacking Often refers to attempts to crack someone else's system or otherwise use programming or expert knowledge to act maliciously. The original word, *hacker,* was intended as a term for capable programmers.

header-based system A program that checks for authorization of uploaded information and permission for individual downloads.

host See *server.*

html (hypertext markup language) The coding system used to create pages on the World Wide Web using a set of markup symbols or codes inserted in a file intended for display on a browser. The markup tells the browser how to display a Web page's words and images for the user.

http (hypertext transfer protocol) Set of rules for exchanging files (text, graphic images, sound, video, and other multimedia files) on the World Wide Web. Relative to the TCP/IP suite of protocols (which are the basis for information exchange on the Internet), http is an application protocol.

hyperlink On the Web or other hypertext systems, hyperlink is a synonym for both link and hypertext link. Possibly, the term originated because *link* was not considered specific enough, and it is shorter than *hypertext link.*

informal search Limited and unstructured effort to obtain specific information or information for a specific purpose.

information age According to Alvin Toffler, author of *The Third Wave,* because of advancements in information technology, humankind is moving into a new era, the information age, where information will be the primary wealth-generating asset.

information overload A situation whereby too much information is received, to a point where the information renders the organization/person ineffective due to a feeling of being overwhelmed by the amount of information received, leading to a further sense of helplessness.

information superhighway A proposal in the United States by the Clinton/Gore administration to deregulate communication services. The aim of this was to widen the scope of the Internet by opening carriers, such as television cable, to data communication. The term is widely used to mean the Internet, often being shortened to terms like *I-way* or the *infobahn.*

intelligent agents An agent that has the ability to learn a user's tastes and preferences over time, and present relevant data to them accordingly.

Internet A vast network that connects many independent networks of computers around the world using a set of protocols called TCP/IP (transmission control protocol/ Internet protocol).

Internet discussion groups (IDGs) Newsgroups and discussion lists.

Internet protocol (IP) The method or protocol by which data are sent from one computer to another on the Internet. Each computer (known as a host) on the Internet has at least one address that uniquely identifies it from all other computers on the Internet.

Internet service provider (ISP) A company that provides access to the Internet for individuals and other companies. ISPs normally have their own permanent high-speed Internet connection and a network of servers (mail, news, Web, etc.), routers, and modems. Subscribers can then dial into the ISP's network to gain Internet access, without having to maintain servers, file for domain names, or learn Unix.

Intranet A network that is contained within an enterprise. It may consist of many interlinked local area networks and also use leased lines in the wide-area network. It may or may not include connections through one or more gateways to the outside Internet. The main purpose of an Intranet is usually to share company information and computing resources among employees.

IP See *TCP/IP.*

knowbots See *agent.*

libel The vilification or defamation of another person in print or some other permanent form. Libel can occur on the Internet in newsgroups and mailing lists, or even websites, with messages intent on hurting the reputation of a target person or group.

log analyzer   Software program that analyzes server log data files.

lurking   Listening in to a mailing list, message base, chat room, or newsgroup without participating. Newcomers are encouraged to lurk for a while as they get the feel of things.

macro-environment   The environment that is said to be outside the firm's locus of control; this includes the social, technological, economic, and political variables in the environment.

mailing list   A list of people who subscribe to a periodic mailing distribution on a particular topic. On the Internet, mailing lists include each person's e-mail address rather than a postal address. Mailing lists have become a popular way for Internet users to keep up with topics in which they are interested. Many software producers and other vendors are now using them as a way of keeping in touch with customers. Mailing lists are sometimes also referred to as *discussion lists.*

market trends   General trends and patterns in the marketplace.

metadexes   Also sometimes called multiple indexes or meta-indexes. *Meta* is a prefix that in most information technology usages means an underlying definition or description. A metadex is hence a "description of an index" or, more accurately, an index (usually on a specific topic area) with categorized websites that are individually described.

meta-index   See *metadexes.*

meta-information   Information about information.

meta-search engines   See *searchbot.*

moderated   An IDG that has a moderator.

moderator   The person who facilitates group interaction. In the case of newsgroups and discussion lists, the moderator may also act as a filtering agent who allows only appropriate messages to be posted within the group.

monitoring   An appraisal of the effectiveness of a firm's current action/s.

multiple indexes   See *metadexes.*

multivariate analysis   The analysis of more than two variables at a time. (Survey Sampling, Inc.)

netiquette   Etiquette on the Internet. Since the Internet changes rapidly, its netiquette does too, but it is still usually based on the Golden Rule of treating others the way you wish yourself to be treated. The need for a sense of netiquette arises mostly when sending or distributing e-mail, posting on Usenet groups, or chatting. To some extent, the practice of netiquette depends on understanding how e-mail, Usenet, chatting, or other aspects of the Internet actually work or are practiced. This can be helped by a little preliminary observation.

newsgroups   Posted discussion groups on Usenet, a worldwide network of newsgroups. Newsgroups are organized into subject hierarchies, with the first few letters of the newsgroup name indicating the major subject category, and subcategories represented by a subtopic name.

nonparametric statistics   Statistics that do not incorporate estimates pertaining to population characteristics.

nonprobability sample   Samples where the selection of population elements is based on arbitrary quotas, volunteers, the judgment of the researcher, or any other technique in which sample elements do not have a known probability of being selected. (Survey Sampling, Inc.)

objectivity   For given information, the objectivity refers to the level of nonbias and balance of the information.

observational research   The systematic gathering of primary data through recording the patterns of behavior and actions in a given situation.

one-to-one marketing   The concept of segmenting markets down to a single person and carrying out appropriate marketing strategies to cater to the needs of each single customer. Made possible through databases and computerized interactions.

online focus groups   Focus groups that are conducted within a computer-mediated environment.

.org   Organization.

personal intelligence   Information that is most relevant to an individual's personal and/or professional needs.

physical environment   Our natural surroundings—earth, air, water, atmosphere, etc.

politico-legal environment   Legislation and other political influences that can affect marketing decision making.

pop-up   A graphical user interface (GUI) display area, usually a small window, that suddenly appears ("pops up") in the foreground of the visual interface. Pop-ups can be initiated by a single or double mouse click or rollover (sometimes called a *mouseover*) and also possibly by voice command, or they can simply be timed to occur. A pop-up window must be smaller than the background window or interface; otherwise, it would be a replacement interface.

pop-up surveys   Surveys on the Internet using pop-up technology.

post   Sending a message to newsgroup/s or online community board/s for other participants to read.

primary data   Firsthand data that are obtained by a researcher through his/her efforts. It is usually purpose-specific.

probability sample   Samples in which members of the population have a known chance (probability) of being selected into the sample.

protocol   The special set of rules for communicating that the end points in a telecommunication connection use when they send signals back and forth. Protocols exist at several levels in a telecommunication connection. There are hardware telephone protocols. There are protocols between the end points in communicating programs within the same computer or at different locations. Both end points must recognize and observe the protocol.

pseudo-anonymity   The anonymity that arises as a result of Internet users communicating on the Internet using a pseudonym or nickname.

recruited samples   Survey samples of which the makeup of respondents is already known and can thus be further screened and handpicked for participating in surveys.

risk assessment   The evaluation of the risks involved in a strategic marketing option, which can give the marketer a better assessment of the likelihood of success in the strategic option.

robots   In this context, refers to programs that search the Internet for specific information. Web robots, also known as spiders, can be used to compile a large, searchable database through repetitive searches for Web pages.

sample   A subset of a population from which data are collected and then used to estimate parameters of the total population. (Survey Sampling, Inc.)

scanning   The observation and monitoring of a firm's external environment to detect any change in trends and patterns that could represent an opportunity or threat to the firm.

screened samples   A survey sample that has been selected based on some predetermined criteria.

searchable index   See *search engine*.

search engine   In its general context, a search engine has two parts: (1) a "robot" or "crawler" that goes to every page or representative pages on the Web and creates a huge index; (2) a program that receives a user's search request, compares it to the entries in the index, and returns results to them.

searchbot   software that performs multiple searches on various search engines from a single query, instead of you having to search the various search engines one by one.

secondary data   Data that already exist as a result of previous research from sources other than the researcher him/herself. Secondary data do not usually provide the researcher with all the information needed to solve the problem at hand but often give the researcher a good background understanding and better insight into the problem.

Secure Electronic Transactions (SET)   MasterCard and Visa have agreed on a common security standard, SET, using technology from Netscape (SSL, or Secure Sockets Layer), Microsoft (STT, or Secure Transaction Technology), and Terisa System (S-HTTP, or Secure Hypertext Transfer Protocol) to allow safe credit transactions to be conducted over the Internet.

secured communication services   Where a third party provides dedicated lines, its own encryption system, or other security measures to ensure the secure transmission of data online.

self-selection   Bias that occurs in a sample due to the sample being formed by people who volunteer (hence who have strong opinions on the topic) to participate in the survey.

server   In general, a computer program that provides services to other computer programs in the same or other computers. In the server/client programming model, a server is a program that awaits and fulfills requests from client programs in the same or other computers. A given application in a computer may function as a client with requests for services from other programs and a server of requests from other programs.

signature file   A signature file is a short text file created for use as a standard appendage at the end of e-mail or Usenet messages. For example, it might include the sender's full name, occupation or position, phone number, fax number, e-mail address, and the address of their website, if they have one. Many people also include a favorite quote, company motto, or short personal statement.

skewed deviations   When the deviation from the mean is greater in one direction than the other.

skip pattern   Where there are questions that are not required to be answered if a particular response is given for a preceding question, a skip pattern will result in the questions that are not required to be answered not being displayed; hence, a "skip" occurs.

slander   Libel in a transitory form (a nonpermanent form).

Society of Competitive Intelligence Professionals (SCIP)   A worldwide organization aimed at people who create and manage business information.

sociocultural environment   Cultural and social factors that are influenced and formed by a combination of people's attitudes, interests, values, norms, customs, beliefs, aesthetics, and lifestyles.

spam   Unsolicited e-mail. From the sender's perspective, it is a form of bulk mail, often to a list culled from subscribers to a Usenet discussion group or obtained by companies that specialize in creating e-mail distribution lists. To the receiver, it usually seems like junk e-mail. In general, it's not considered good netiquette to send spam.

stop words   See *stoplist.*

stoplist   Search engines do not catalog certain words, these being termed stoplist words or stop words.

subject catalog   Directories (such as Yahoo) wherein links are arranged in subject hierarchies.

survey research   Obtaining primary data by asking people for the information that the researcher wants.

TCP (transmission control protocol)   When an html file is sent to you from a Web server, the TCP program layer in that server divides the file into one or more packets, numbers the packets, and then forwards them individually to the IP program layer.

TCP/IP (transmission control protocol/Internet protocol)   The basic communication language or protocol of the Internet. The higher layer, TCP, manages the assembling of a message or file into smaller packets that are transmitted over the Internet and received by a TCP layer that reassembles the packets into the original message. The lower layer handles the address part of each packet so that it gets to the right destination.

technographics   A new type of segmentation first conceived by E. J. Forrest in 1985. Derived from knowing the purchase behavior of consumers based on their use of technology.

technological environment   Technological advances and changes that can significantly impact a particular industry or a whole economy. Marketers need to accommodate for these advances and make changes in their marketing strategies.

thread   In this context, a sequence of responses to an initial message posting. This enables users to follow or join an individual discussion in a newsgroup from among the many that may be there. A thread is usually shown graphically as an initial message and successive messages "hung off" the original message.

trademark   Any symbol, name, figure word, mark, and the like, used by a company to distinguish their products from those products manufactured or sold by others.

transmission control protocol/ Internet protocol   See *TCP/IP.*

trend leaders   People who start new trends or fads; opinion leaders.

undirected viewing   Looking through information without a specific purpose. "Surfing" the Internet is an example of undirected viewing as it is exploratory and not goal-directed.

unmoderated   An IDG or an online focus group that has no moderator.

unrestricted samples   A sample where there are no controls or restrictions on who can participate in the survey.

URL (uniform resource locator)   The address of a file (resource) accessible on the Internet. Sometimes also called website address.

Usenet   A worldwide network of posted discussion groups known as newsgroups, and a set of rules for accessing and posting to them. Usenet's original protocol was UNIX-to-UNIX Copy (UUCP), but other protocols are more prevalent today. Most browsers, such as Netscape and Microsoft's Internet Explorer, provide Usenet support and access to any newsgroups that a user selects.

Values and Lifestyles (VALS™) psychographic segmentation   A system developed to profile people according to their lifestyles and, hence, needs. This sort of segmentation, called psychographic segmentation, is based on measuring the activities, interest, and opinions of people.

Veronica   A program that allows users to search the files of the Internet's Gopher servers for a particular search string. Like Archie, which is Veronica's equivalent program for FTP servers, Veronica is an indexing spider that visits the Gopher websites, reads all the directory and file names, and then indexes them in one large index. A user can then query Veronica, which checks the query against its index.

virtual communities   Groups of people who are joined together through communication over the Internet. These communities of people may be joined together through common demographics, geographics, or even a particular interest or cause.

Web   See *World Wide Web.*

Web browser   Software that will load and display a Web page. The principal browsers are Netscape, Microsoft Internet Explorer, Opera, Mosaic, and the text-only Lynx.

website   A related collection of Web files that includes a beginning file called a home page. A company or an individual indicates how to get to their website by making available the address of their home page.

wildcards   Often used by computers as placeholders for missing characters in file names. Microsoft Windows, DOS, and Unix use the asterisk (*) wildcard to represent any number of characters, while a question mark (?) represents a single character. For example, a search for *r*te* will cause the words *rite, rate,* and *rotate* matches to be taken into consideration while *r?te* would only bring up *rite* and *rate.*

World Wide Web   All the resources and users on the Internet that are using the http.

Sources: Technical terms are from http://whatis.com/, © TechTarget, Inc. Where specified, market research terms are from © Survey Sampling, Inc.

Index

* (wildcard), 26

A

AANA. *See* Australian Association of
    National Advertisers
ABA. *See* Australian Broadcasting Authority
Abbott Wool Market Segment Resource
    Locator, 75
ABI. *See* American Business Information
ABI/INFORM GLOBAL, 85
About.com, 26
ABS. *See* Australian Bureau of Statistics
ACC. *See* Australian Copyright Council
ACLU. *See* American Civil Liberties Union
ACNielsen, 82, 87
ACORN, 76
ACSI. *See* American Customer Satisfaction
    Index
Ad-Aware, 36
Adler, S., 207
ADMA. *See* Australian Direct Marketing
    Association
Adobe Acrobat Reader, 64, 75
Ads
    banner ads, 35
    pop-up ads, 35
AdShield, 36
Advertising World, 46
Advice, soliciting, 8, 153, 156–158
Agents, 11
Alexa, 34
ALIWEB, 18
"All the secrets," 45
AltaVista, 26
AMA. *See* American Marketing Association
American Business Information (ABI), 98
American Civil Liberties Union (ACLU),
    207
American Customer Satisfaction Index
    (ACSI), 81
American Demographics, 64
American Express Small Business Services,
    137
American Law Sources On-line, 58
American Market Research Council, 6
American Marketing Association (AMA), 6,
    178
AND (Boolean operator), 24
    example, 25
Anger, 145
Anonymity, 114, 116
    pseudo-anonymity and, 198
Arbitron, 86

Archie, 18, 24
Argus Clearinghouse, 20, 188, 189
Art of War, The, 93
ASCII text, 123
Asian Demographics, 64, 75
Asian Internet Marketing, 45
Atomica, 32
@ResearchInfo.com, 125, 128, 179
Aurora, 107
Australasian Legal Information Institute,
    205
Australia
    Privacy Amendment, 119
    Privacy Regulations 2001, 208
Australia Legal Information Centre, 58
Australian Association of National
    Advertisers (AANA), 57
Australian Broadcasting Authority (ABA),
    207
Australian Bureau of Statistics (ABS), 60,
    65, 75
Australian Copyright Council (ACC), 201
Australian Direct Marketing Association
    (ADMA), 57
Aware, 105

B

Bacon, Francis, 1
Bandwidth, 131
Berne Convention, 198, 200
Berners-Lee, Tim, 57
Better Business Bureau, 57, 58
Bidigital, 95
Bigfoot, 24
Bigpond, 42
Bionet, 138
B.I.P. *See* Business Intelligence Program
Blink, 38
Bookmark, 36
Bookmark management, discussed, 36–37
Boole, George, 24
Boolean operators, searching with, 24–26
BrainReserve, 80
Brand Institute, 176
Broadcasting Services Amendment
    Bill 1999, 207
BroadPage, 36
Browser
    personalizing and customizing, 37–38,
        39tb
    plug-ins, 33

BSA. *See* Business Software Alliance
Bureau of Business Research, 6
Bureau of Labor Statistics, 59, 84
Burke Incorporated, 85
Business Intelligence Program (B.I.P.), 78
Business Software Alliance (BSA), 198
Buying power, indicators, 58–59

C

Career sites, 99–100
CareerPath.com, 100
Central Intelligence Agency (CIA), 55
C.F.D. *See* Consumer Financial Decisions
CGI. *See* Common Gateway Interface
Chat room, 172, 177. *See also* Focus groups
CIA. *See* Central Intelligence Agency
Citizens Internet Empowerment Coalition,
    207
Claritas, 76
Clicking, 80
Clinton, Bill, 195, 207
CNET Digital Dispatch, 44
CNN, 43
CNNFN, 43
.com extension, 185
Common Gateway Interface (CGI), 117
Communications Decency Act 1996, 207
Comparative–shopping services, 100
Competia, 106
Competition. *See also* Competitive
    intelligence
    investigating, 98–99
Competitive intelligence
    defining, 93tb
    discussed, 12
    discussion groups and, 107–108
    in general, 8, 91–92
    Internet and, 94
        conducting on Internet, 94–106
    outsourcing, 102–105
    professional and educational sources,
        106–107
    system benefits, 92–94
Conferences, 99
Confidentiality, 118
Connect 4, 98
Consumer Financial Decisions (C.F.D.), 78
Consumer intelligence. *See also* Consumer
    research
    consumer media attitudes and use
        patterns, 85–86

Consumer intelligence—*Cont.*,
   consumer media attitudes—*Cont.*
      online media attitudes and use
         patterns, 86–88
      discussed, 12, 71–72
      Internet and, 72
Consumer product ratings network, 175
Consumer protection. *See also* Legal issues
   in general, 196–197
      Top 10 Frauds, 196tb
   relevant websites, 197
Consumer research
   in general, 72–73
   objectives, in general, 79–80
   objects, occasions, outlets
      in general, 81–84
      organizations and operations, 84–85
   occupations and markets
      electronic consumer evaluations,
         80–81
      in general, 73–75
      geo-demographic segmentation
         tools, 76–78
      psychographic segmentation, 78
      technographic segmentation, 79
Consumer Trends Institute, 79
Consumer.gov, 197
Cookies, 35, 130. *See also* Privacy concerns
   activating, 117
Copyright issues. *See also* Legal issues
   intellectual property and, 197–202
   newsgroups, 142
Copyright Society of the USA, 200
Cornell University Library, 188
Corporation for National Research
      Initiatives, 201
CRAYON, 43
Criminal Justice and Public Order Act 1994
   (UK), 206
Curtis Publishing Co., 6
Customers
   relation to vendors, 8, 72
   researching, 100
CustomerSat, 127, 128, 176–177
CustomForum, 173
Cyber Dialogue, 175
Cyber Patrol, 207
Cyberbanking, 196–197
Cyberspace, 12
CyberTrends, 66–67

D

Data
   primary data, 10
   secondary data, 10
Data encryption standard (DES), 195. *See*
    also Encryption
DataTimes, 101

DealTime, 100
Defamation. *See also* Legal issues
   discussed, 204–205
Deja news, 100
DES. *See* Data encryption standard
Descriptive research, 3. *See also* Marketing
    research
Diagnostic research, 3. *See also* Marketing
    research
Dictionary.com, 39
Digital object identifier (DOI), 201
Digital Women, 45
Direct Hit, 189
Direct Marketing Association (DMA), 208
Directory of International Statistics, 73
Discussion groups. *See also* Focus groups;
    Mailing lists; Newsgroups
   for competitive intelligence, 107–108
Dismal Scientist, 55
DMA. *See* Direct Marketing Association
DOI. *See* Digital object identifier
Domain name, 143
Download Accelerator, 34
Downloading
   file, 18
      browser plug-ins, 33, 34tb
Dun & Bradstreet, 104
Duncan, D. S., 6

E

e-business. *See also* e-marketing
   information about, 43–44
e-mail. *See also* e-mail survey
   flaming, 123, 139
   newsgroups and, 13, 141
E-mail List Publisher Resource Network, 124
e-mail survey. *See also* Survey
   discussed, 122–123
   in general, 114–115
e-marketing, discussed, 44–45
e-zines, discussed, 43
Eastman, R. O., 6
Economic environment. *See also*
    Environmental intelligence
   in general, 58–59
   Web sites, 59–60
Economics Network, 60
Econsumer.gov, 197
EDGAR, 96
.edu extension, 185
Electronic Privacy Information Center, 208
Electronic Signatures Act, 195
eLibrary, 101
eMarketer, 87
eMarketing Digest, 45
Emtage, Alan, 18
Encryption, 195. *See also* Security concerns
   data encryption standard, 195

Encryption—*Cont.*
   digital object identifier, 201
   header-based systems, 201
Encyclopedia.com, 40
ENews, 42
eNotes, 35
Environmental intelligence. *See also*
    Environmental scanning
   discussed, 11–12
   environmental analysis, 52
   in general, 51–52
Environmental scanning, 11
   discussed, 52–53
   Internet and, 53–54
      styles, 53tb
   macro-environmental websites
      economic environment, 58–61
      in general, 54
      integrated/global information
         resource websites, 54–56
      physical environment, 67–68
      politico-legal environment, 57–58
      sociocultural environment, 61–65
      technological environment, 65–67
ePublicEye, 80
ESRI Business Information Systems, 76
European Society for Opinion and
    Marketing Research, 7
Eurostat, 60
EVEolution, 80
eWatch, 42
Excite, 42
Experimental research, 4. *See also*
    Marketing research
Experts. *See also* Newsgroups
   soliciting advice of, 8, 153, 156–158
Eyestrain, 118

F

Facts and figures, search engine choices for,
   23–24
FastCompany Magazine, 99
FedStats, 54, 55
File
   downloading, 18
      browser plug-ins, 33, 34tb
File transfer protocol (FTP), 18
Filo, David, 18
Financial Data Finder, 190
FIND/SVP, 27
FindArticles.com, 40
FindLaw, 58
555–1212.com, 24
Flaming, 123
Focus groups. *See also* Newsgroups
   discussed, 13
   in general, 167–168
      chat room, 172, 177

Focus groups—*Cont.*
  online focus groups
    advantages, 170, 171tb
    appropriateness, 172–173
    conducting, 173–174
    disadvantages, 170–172
    in general, 11, 168–170
    Google volunteer focus groups,
      175–176tb
    metadexes of market research firms,
      178–179
    organizations that conduct focus
      groups, 176–178
    other resources, 179–180
    participating in, 174–176
FocusChat, 176
Forrester Research, 79, 196
Forum Modalis, 175
Fraud. *See also* Security
  Top 10 Frauds, 196tb
Friedman, Marc, 99
FTP. *See* File transfer protocol
Fuld, Leonard, 92, 99, 100, 101, 103, 104

G

Galaxy, 18, 23
Gallup, 65
Gallup, George, 6
Gartner, 88
Geneva Phonogram Convention, 200
Geo-demographic segmentation tools,
  76–78
Global Environment Business, 67
Global Trends 2015, 54, 55
globalEDGE, 54
GlobalTestMarket, 175
Google, 45
  newsgroups, 137–138, 144, 152,
    156–157, 160–161
  searching with, 26
  volunteer focus groups, 175–176tb
.gov extension, 185
Graphics, Visualization, and Usability
  Center (GVU), 8, 87
Gray, Matthew, 18
GreenBook, 178, 179
Greenfield Online, 86, 175, 176
Greenlee School of Journalism and
  Communication, 74
Greenpeace, 67
Greg Notes, 21
Griffith, Melanie, 101
Guerrilla Marketing Online, 44
Guide to Available Math Software, 127
Gunn, Chris, 153, 154, 157
Guttman's scaling, 6
GVU. *See* Graphic, Visualization, and
  Usability Center

H

Harris InfoSource, 98
Harris Poll Online, 175
Header-based systems, 201
Hemmingway Scott, 98
Hofacker, Dr. Charles, 47
Hotbar, 39
HotLinks, 38
HotWired, 44
html, 6
html text, 123

I

IAHC. *See* International Ad Hoc Committee
iCameo, 175
Iconocast, 44
Iconoculture, 62
IDGs. *See* Internet discussion groups
IFCC. *See* Internet Fraud Complaint Center
Imagitrends, 62
IMRO. *See* Interactive Marketing Research
  Organization
Incentives, 120
Index. *See also* Metadex
  multiple indexes, 22
Individual.com, Personal News Page, 42
Info Select, 35–36
Infomine, 20
InfoNation, 73
Infopoll, 128
Information. *See also* Information gathering
  company information, 96–98
  displaying, 35, 36tb
  exchanging, 33–35
  filtering, 35, 36tb
  finding, 32–33
  managing, 35–36, 38tb
  meta-information, 188–190
  real-time access, 8
Information age, 31
Information gathering
  e-business, 43–44
  e-marketing, 44–45
  e-zines, 43
  personalized retrieval services, 42–43
  portals, 41–42
  resources, 45–48
Information overload, 8
Information Quality WWW Virtual Library,
  187
Information Resources, Inc. (IRI), 83
Inside 1to1, 44
Inside.com, 45
Institute for Research in Social Science
  (IRSS), 63
IntelBrief, 42, 102
Intellectual property, copyright law, 197–202

Intelliquest, 86
Interactive Marketing Research
  Organization (IMRO), 127
Interactive Rewards, 176
Intern, 86
International Ad Hoc Committee (IAHC),
  204
Internet. *See also* Marketing research
  access to, 9
  competitive intelligence and, 94
    conducting, 94–106
  consumer intelligence and, 72
  environmental scanning and, 53–54
  marketing research and
    focus groups, 13
    in general, 8–9, 9–11, 12–13
    Internet surveys, 13
    marketing research revolution, 8
    New Generation Internet, 9
    newsgroups, 13
    other critical concerns, 13–14
  marketing research applications
    competitive intelligence, 12
    consumer intelligence, 12
    environmental intelligence, 11–12
    in general, 11
    personal intelligence, 11
Internet discussion groups (IDGs), 135. *See
  also* Newsgroups
Internet Explorer, enhancements, 35
Internet Explorer Personalizer, 39
Internet Fraud Complaint Center
  (IFCC), 197
Internet Fraud Watch, 196
Internet Law Library, 58
Internet Marketing Center, 44
Internet Protocol (IP), 117
Internet Public Library (IPL), 23, 188
Internet service provider (ISP), 140, 199, 201
Internet survey. *See also* Survey; Survey
  research
  advantages
    completion, 113–115
    design, 112–113
    distribution, 113
    in general, 112
    return, 115
  designing
    aesthetic considerations, 117–118
    in general, 117
    psychological considerations,
      118–120
  disadvantages, 115–117
    user demography, 116
    user psychology, 116–117
  distribution options
    e-mail survey, 122–123
    in general, 121–122
    newsgroups and mailing lists,
      123–124

Internet survey—*Cont.*
  distribution options—*Cont.*
    on-site intercept survey, 123
  do-it-yourself, 126–127
  in general, 111–112
    eyestrain, 118
    incentives, 120
  Internet population samples, 121tb
  online surveying software and support, 127–130
  outsourcing
    in general, 124–125
    online directories of firms and services, 125
    selection criteria, 125–126
  sampling methodologies, 120–121
Internet telephony, 11
Internet2, 9
Internets, 19
Interview, compared to Internet survey, 112
Intranet, 10
InvisibleWeb, 19
iOpinion, 175
IP. *See* Internet Protocol
IPL. *See* Internet Public Library
iRemember, 34
IRI. *See* Information Resources, Inc.
IRSS. *See* Institute for Research in Social Science
ISP. *See* Internet service provider

J

J GUIDE, 54, 56
Job sites, 99–100
JumpStation, 18

K

Kathy Schrock's Guide for Educators, 188
Katiesoft, 36
Kellogg Company, 6
Kelly's personal construct theory, 6
KNOTs, 176
Knowbots, 11
Knowledge Cart, 35
Koster, Martin, 18

L

LANIC, 54, 56
Larry Chase's Web Digest, 44
Law and Politics Internet Guide, 57
Learning, market-focused learning, 10–11
Legal issues, 14. *See also* Consumer protection; Security
  defamation, 204–205
  in general, 193, 194

Legal issues—*Cont.*
  intellectual property and copyright law, 197–202
  obscenity, 205–207
  politico-legal environment, 57–58
  trademarks, 202–204
Lexis-Nexis, 58
Libel, 204
Librarians' Index to the Internet, 20
List-Universe.com, 124
Lycos, 42

M

McCann, John M., 66
McDonalds, 202
Mailing lists. *See also* Newsgroups
  researching, 100
  selecting, 139
  for surveys, 123–124
Market Guard 24/7, 42, 102
Market Opinion and Research International (MORI), 83
Market Research Roundtable, 48
Market Research Society, 6
Marketing, one-to-one marketing, 71, 72
Marketing research
  defined, 2
  evolution
    1905–1918, 6
    1919–1930, 6
    1930–1950, 6
    1950–1975, 6
    1975–1995, 6
    1995–present, 6–7
    pre–1905, 5
  in general, 1–2
    qualitative research, 167
    quantitative research, 167
  information and resources, 45–48
  Internet and
    emerging functions, 9–10
    focus groups, 13
    in general, 8–9, 9–11, 12–13
    information overload, 8
    Internet surveys, 13
    market-focused learning, 10–11
    newsgroups, 13
    other critical concerns, 13–14
  Internet applications
    competitive intelligence, 12
    consumer intelligence, 12
    environmental intelligence, 11–12
    in general, 11
    personal intelligence, 11
  methods
    experimental research, 4
    observational research, 4
    survey research, 4

Marketing research—*Cont.*
  process
    collect and input data, 5
    define the question, 3–4
    follow up, 5
    interpretation, 5
    master plan creation, 4
    reports, 5
    research methods, 4
    samples, 4–5
  research tools, 38–41
  types of, 3
    descriptive research, 3
    diagnostic research, 3
    predictive research, 3
Marketing Tool/Lexis-Nexis, 7
MasterCard-TDS Shopper Clusters, 77–78
MBS Internet Research Center, 175
Media Metrix, 86
Mediamark Research, 85
Meta-information. *See also* Information
  discussed, 188–190
Metadex, 11, 22. *See also* Index
Mind-it, 37
Moderator. *See also* Newsgroups
  focus groups, 168, 169
  newsgroups, 136
Monitoring, 10
Monster Board, 100
Montague Institute, 106
Morgan Polls, 62–63
MORI. *See* Market Opinion and Research International
MouseTracks, 47
MSNBC, 42
MTV, 202
Multivariate analysis, 6
mySimon, 100

N

National Consumers League, 197
National Network of State Polls (NNSP), 63
NEAR (Boolean operator), 24
  example, 26
NeoPlanet, 39
Net Nanny, 207
Netiquette, 14
  for newsgroups, 139–140
Netscape, 42
Netscape Inbox Direct, 34
NetSonic, 34
netXtract, 38
New Competitor Intelligence, 104
New Generation Internet, 9. *See also* Internet
News Online, 43
news.announce.newusers, 147

Newsgroups, 11. *See also* Focus groups; Mailing lists; Newsgroups research methods
  applications, 136–137
  article writing rules, 144–146
  commercial posts, 141–142
  for competitive intelligence gathering, 100
  copyright issues, 142
  creating, 153, 161–165
  discussed, 13
    virtual communities, 13
  expert consultation, 8, 153, 156–158
  FAQs, 124, 140, 152–153
  in general, 135–136
    lurkers, 136
    moderated groups, 136
    moderator, 136
    unmoderated groups, 136
  hierarchy
    Big Ten, 137–138
    in general, 137
    other hierarchies, 138
    regional categories, 139
  netiquette, 139–140, 143–144
  other useful links, 146–147
  posting to, 135, 155–156, 158–160
    cancelling a post, 160–161
  quality of messages, 141, 155
  selecting, 139
  signatures, 142–143
  spam and, 143
  for surveys, 123–124, 146, 153
Newsgroups research methods. *See also* Newsgroups
  in general, 151–152
    main research methods, 152
  step-by-step guide
    advanced methods, 153–154
    in general, 152–153
NewsLink, 101
news.newusers.questions, 146
NFO Interactive, 175
NFO WorldGroup, 84
NNSP. *See* National Network of State Polls
Nonparametric statistics, 6
NOT (Boolean operator), 24
  example, 25
NPDFoodworld, 84
NUA, 88

O

Obscene Publications Act 1959 (UK), 206
Obscenity. *See also* Legal issues
  discussed, 205–207
Observational research, 4. *See also* Marketing research
Octopus, 38

One-to-one marketing, 71, 72
1Jump, 107–108
Onesight, 175
OneSource Information Services, 97
"Online Focus Groups," 179
Online Intelligence Project, 55
Online Success for Internet Business, 137
OnlineNewspapers.com, 101
Opinion Surveys UK, 176
OR (Boolean operator), 24
  example, 25
orcFOCUS, 180
Organization, relation to environment, 51–52
Osgood's semantic differential procedures, 6
Outsourcing
  competitive intelligence function, 102–105
  Internet survey
    in general, 124–125
    online directories of firms and services, 125
    selection criteria, 125–126
Overview of the Environmental Movement in Europe, 67

P

Paid2Survey.Com, 176
Palia, Aspy P., 45, 85
ParaChat, 173
Passwords, 117
People & The Planet, 67
Peppers and Rogers Group Consulting, 95
Personal intelligence
  bookmark management, 36–37, 38tb
  browser personalization and customization, 37–38, 39tb
  discussed, 11
    agents, 11
    knowbots, 11
  displaying information, 35, 36tb
  exchanging information, 33–35
  filtering information, 35, 36tb
  finding information, 32–33
  in general, 31–32
  information gathering
    e-business, 43–44
    e-marketing, 44–45
    e-zines, 43
    personalized retrieval services, 42–43
    portals, 41–42
  managing information, 35–36, 38tb
  marketing research information and resources, 45–48
  research tools, 38–41
Personalized retrieval services, discussed, 42–43
PGP. *See* Pretty Good Privacy

Physical environment, discussed, 67–68
PICS. *See* Platform Internet Content Selection
Planet Feedback, 81
Platform Internet Content Selection (PICS), 207
Plug-ins, browser, 33
Political issues, politico-legal environment, 57–58
Pop-up ads, 35
Pop-up survey, 177. *See also* Survey
Pop-up windows, 172
Popcorn, Faith, 80
Popcorn Report, 80
Population Reference Bureau, 64
Portals. *See also* Information
  discussed, 41–42
Post
  newsgroups, 135, 155–156, 158–160
    canceling a post, 160–161
PR Newswire, 101
Predictive research, 3. *See also* Marketing research
Pretty Good Privacy (PGP), 195
Privacy Amendment (Australia), 119
Privacy concerns, 9, 118, 119. *See also* Security concerns
  cookies, 35, 117, 130
  Pretty Good Privacy, 195
Privacy Issues in Telecommunications, 207
PRIZM, 76–77
Proactivity, 8
Productscan, 105
P$YCLE, 76

Q

Qualitative research, 167
Quantitative research, 167
Quirk's Marketing Research Review, 125, 179

R

RBSE. *See* Repository-Based Software Engineering
Refdesk, 39
Registration, Web site, 33–34, 35tb
Regulation, politico-legal environment, 57–58
Report Gallery, 97
Repository-Based Software Engineering (RBSE), 18
Research-It!, 39
Research tools, discussed, 38–41
Researcher SourceBook, 125
ResearchInfo.com, 48
Rezabek, Roger J., 179

Risk assessment, 10
RoboShopper, 100
Robots, search engines and, 18
Rome Convention, 200
Roper Center, 63, 65
Roper Starch Worldwide, 65
Roy Morgan Research, 63, 83

S

Sample
  defined, 4
  selecting, 4–5
    nonprobability sample, 5
    probability sample, 5
Sampling theory, multivariate analysis, 6
Scambusters.com, 197
Scanning. *See also* Environmental scanning
  in general, 10
Scholarly topic, search engine choice, 20–21
Science, Technology, and Innovation
    Systems Policy Information Map
    (STIMAP), 66
Science and Technical Information Network
    (STN Easy), 66
SCIP. *See* Society of Competitive
    Intelligence Professionals
Scope, environmental scanning, 53
Scott, Tracey, 99, 100, 101
Search. *See also* Search engines; Search
    techniques
  outsourcing, 27–28
  personalizing, 102
Search Engine Watch, 19–20
Search engines, 11. *See also* Search
    techniques
  choosing
    for general facts and figures, 23–24
    for general scholarly information, 21
    for scholarly topic, 20–21
    for simple topic, 22–23
  evolution, 18
  robots, 18
  in general, 18, 105–106
  software, metasearch utility, 22
  today, 18–20
Search Engines Worldwide, 19
Search techniques
  Boolean operators, 24–26
  in general, 24
  improving, 26–27
  spelling concerns, 26
  stop words, 26
  word stems and wildcards, 26
SearchAbility, 18–19
Secondary data, 10
Security concerns, 169. *See also* Legal
    issues; Privacy concerns
  in general, 194–196

Security concerns—*Cont.*
  in general—*Cont.*
    encryption, 195
Server, 136
Service Intelligence, 81
SG-Tech PenOp, 195
Signatures
  Electronic Signatures Act, 195
  newsgroups, 142–143
Simmons Market Research, 86
Slander, 204
Society of Competitive Intelligence
    Professionals (SCIP), 106, 107
Sociocultural environment
  in general, 61–62
  Websites, 62–65
Software
  intelligent software, 9
  metasearch utility, 22
  online surveying software and support,
    127–130
Spain, Scott, 117, 129
Spam, newsgroups and, 143
Speed Download, 34
Spell checking, 145
Sputnik Digest, 88
SRI Consulting Business Intelligence Values
    and Lifestyles, 78
Statistics, nonparametric statistics, 6
STIMAP. *See* Science, Technology, and
    Innovation Systems Policy
    Information Map
STN Easy. *See* Science and Technical
    Information Network
Stop words, 26. *See also* Search techniques
Stoplist, 26. *See also* Search techniques
Streetlink, 98
Style, environmental scanning, 53
Sun Tzu, 93
SurfSaver, 38
SurfSecret, 36
Survey. *See also* Internet survey
  comparative attributes, 112tb
  e-mail survey, 114–115, 122–123
  interviewer bias, 114
  with newsgroups, 123–124, 146
  pop-up survey, 177
Survey-Net, 88
Survey Payday, 176
Survey research, 4
SurveyGuy.Com, 175
SurveySavvy, 175
SurveySite, 175, 177

T

Target market, identifying, 100
Tech Ed, 180

Technographics, 79
Technological environment, discussed, 65–67
Technology Review, 65–66
Technology Review, Inc., 65
TechWeb, 44
Tell Me Now, 27
Testing, product and copy testing, 13
TheStandard.com, 44
Tilburg University, 47
Tile.net, 152
Top99sites.com, 190
Topica, 24
Trade associations, researching, 99
Trade Marks Act of 1994 (UK), 203
*Trademark Registration of Internet Domain
    Names,* 203
Trademarks. *See also* Copyright issues;
    Legal issues
  discussed, 202–204
Trend leaders, 113
TrendPaks, 62
Trendsetters, 176
TRUSTe, 209
Truthfulness, 116–117

U

UCLA College Library, 188
UCmore, 34
UNESCO, 54
United Nations Global Statistics, 73
United Nations Global Trends, 64, 73
United Nations Social Indicators, 64, 74
United States, Internet access, 116
U.S. Census Bureau, 64, 75
U.S. Constitution, 207
U.S. Department of Commerce, 6
U.S. Federal Trade Commission, 197
U.S. House of Representatives, Internet Law
    Library, 58
U.S. Information Infrastructure Task Force,
    119
University of Nevada System Computing
    Services, 18
URL, 117
URL Manager Pro, 38
USA Data, 75
Usenet groups, 136. *See also* Newsgroups

V

Vendor, relation to customer, 8, 72
Verisign, 202
Veronica, 18, 24
Virginia Tech University Library, 187
Virtual communities, 13
Virtual Library, 57
Volition.com, 46, 125, 179

W

Walt Disney Internet Group (WDIG), 42
Wandex, 18
WDIG. *See* Walt Disney Internet Group
Web Marketing Today, 44
Web TV, 11
Web Wombat, 42
WebCascader, 36
WebCopier, 38
WebCrawler, 20
WebFerret, 22–23
WebFree, 36
Website
    defined, 1
    in general, 183–184
    meta-information, 188–190
    registration, 33–34, 35tb
    search tools, 34tb
    source and data evaluation paradigms,
        184–187
    websites about, 187–188

WebSurveyor, 127
WebWasher, 36
Weir, Malcolm, 124
Where to Do Research, 39, 58
Wildcards, searching with, 26
WIPO. *See* World Intellectual Property
    Organization
Working Girl, 101
World Factbook, 54, 55, 74
World Intellectual Property Organization
    (WIPO), 204
World Lecture Hall, 40
World Opinion, 45
World War II, 93
World Wide Web (WWW), introduction, 6
World Wide Web Virtual Law Library, 57
World Wide Web Wanderer, 18
World Wide Web Worm, 18
WWW. *See* World Wide Web
WWW Virtual Library, 20

X

Xerox, 94

Y

Yahoo!, 18, 20, 42, 55, 99
Yahoo! Groups, 161–162
Yang, Jerry, 18
Yankelovitch, 65
Yardeni, Dr. Ed., 60

Z

Zarden Market Research Direct-A-Net, 125,
    179
ZDNet, 44
Zeitgeist, 62